Praise for
Electronic Day Trading Made Easy

"At a time when most trading advice is full of hype and theory, Sarkovich cuts to the chase and provides a step-by-step guide to profitable trading, using examples, effective techniques, proven strategies, and insightful wisdom. A must for new traders and seasoned veterans alike."

—Tim Bourquin, founder, DayTradersUSA.com

"A timely, insightful, instructive, and easy to digest review of the core elements any electronic trader should understand to prepare for successful day trading."

—Philip R. Berber, founder and CEO, CyBerCorp

"An interesting and informative introduction to day trading. In particular, the author presents a clear analysis of the magnitude of the risks while providing guidelines for minimizing those risks and maximizing the probability of gains."

—Stuart Townsend, president, Townsend Analytics, Ltd.

Electronic Day Trading Made Easy

MISHA T. SARKOVICH, PH.D.

Prima Publishing

PRIMA PUBLISHING and colophon are registered trademarks of Prima Communications, Inc. Prima-daytrading.com is a trademark of Prima Communications, Inc. Unauthorized use is strictly prohibited.

Library of Congress Cataloging-in-Publication Data
Sarkovich, Misha T.
      Electronic day trading made easy: become a successful trader by learning how to
   1. Evaluate level II screens. 2. Trade strategically. 3. Analyze technical data. 4. Minimize risk.
   5. Execute trades / Misha T. Sarkovich.
         p.   cm.
   Includes index.
   ISBN 0-7615-2134-8
   1. Electronic trading of securities. I. Title.
   HG4515.95.S27   1999
   332.64'0285--dc21   99-39226
                                                                           CIP

99 00 01 02 03 HH 10 9 8 7 6 5 4 3 2 1

Printed in the United States of America

How to Order

Single copies may be ordered from Prima Publishing, P.O. Box 1260BK, Rocklin, CA 95677; telephone (916) 632-4400. Quantity discounts are also available. On your letterhead, include information concerning the intended use of the books and the number of books you wish to purchase.

Visit us online at www.primalifestyles.com

Contents

Acknowledgments

First of all, I dedicate this work to my family, my wife, Kimberly, and our sons, Stefan and Marco, whose continuous love and support made this conceivable.

Sincere thanks must go to my parents-in-law Eleanor and Ned Keech for their proofreading of the manuscript and their valuable comments. The last word of acknowledgment delightfully goes to Prima Publishing editors Susan Silva and David Richardson for their professional assistance and continuous faith in this work.

Disclaimer

Since this book covers the topic of securities day trading, the book naturally begins with disclaimers. The day trading business involves money (sometimes a lot of money), and we live in a litigious society. Disclaimers are an unfortunate part of the securities trading business.

➤ This book is designed as an introduction to day trading. It is intended only to give readers a general idea of how the day trading business works and how to get started if they desire to trade. The book could never be 100% complete, since the day trading business is continuously evolving.

➤ Much of the information provided in this book represents the author's own opinions. The author encourages all readers to do their own research and verify the information presented in the book.

➤ Day trading is an inherently risky business. Day traders should be prepared to lose their trading capital. Since day traders open and trade margin accounts (where a part of the money put into play is borrowed), it is possible to sustain losses that are greater than one's initial trading capital. *Do not* trade money that you cannot afford to lose.

➤ Day traders must be responsible for their own actions. Each day trader is accountable for every completed trade, even if the trader did not intend to make a specific trade. Please, if you are a beginning trader, be careful when executing trades.

➤ The author does not recommend purchase or sale of any particular security. The author does not guarantee that any specific return can be achieved through day trading. Furthermore, the author does not guarantee suitability of any particular trading transaction or trading strategy.

➤ Electronic day trading is on the cutting edge of technology, and day traders must accept all associated risks of computer equipment, network, and software failures.

Introduction

Over the past two decades, technology has revolutionized the way in which our securities market operates. Securities transactions that were once slow and costly, dependent on long paper trails and intensive human labor, have become instantaneous and inexpensive with the advent of computers. Today, with the click of a button, orders can be entered, executed, and confirmed within seconds.

> *Dr. Richard Lindsey*
> *Director of Market Regulation*
> *U.S. Securities and Exchange Commission*
> *May 1997*

THE AMERICAN DIALECT SOCIETY RECENTLY DUBBED *E-* AS ITS 1998 WORD of the Year. This is hardly surprising. It is hard to find parallels to the explosive growth of electronic commerce, including electronic stock trading. Even after taking into account all the hype, the reality of electronic trading is still spectacular. It is a new phenomenon on Wall Street and one of the fastest growing segments of the U.S. securities market. The Electronic Traders Association (ETA) estimated that electronic stock trading accounts in 1999 for about 15% of the National Association of Securities Dealers Automated Quotations (NASDAQ) market daily volume. That is up from a 10% share from 1997. This daily trading volume is generated by approximately 5,000 full-time electronic day traders. More than half of all limit orders—a trade order to buy or sell stock when a price is fixed—submitted to the NASDAQ market come from those day traders.

When the occasional or part-time traders who trade electronically (or dabble in trading) from their homes over the Internet are added into this equation, the NASDAQ total daily volume attributed to electronic traders is closer to 25%. The research firm Gomez Advisors, Inc., which specializes in online financial services, estimates that in 1999 there are more than 7 million online brokerage accounts. In contrast, full service brokers account for 40 million accounts. Online brokers averaged 336,000 daily trades in the last quarter of 1998, up 125% from the previous year. In the last quarter of 1998, there was a sharp increase in the online brokers' market share, to 13.7% of all equity trades—up from 9.2% the same quarter a year earlier.

The purpose of this book is to provide novice and experienced day traders with a complete step-by-step guide to electronic day trading. This book covers all aspects of electronic day trading including:

➤ Basic trading topics such as interpreting the NASDAQ Level II screen;

➤ Intermediate topics such as technical stock analysis using Moving Averages, MACD, Bollinger bands, and various oscillators;

➤ Advanced topics such as locked and crossed markets between the public (NASDAQ) and private (Instinet) markets;

➤ Order executions using SOES, SelectNet, Island, Instinet, and NYSE DOT;

➤ Trading strategies;

➤ Risk management;

➤ Margin accounts;

➤ Trading psychology; and

➤ Trader's tax consequences.

This book systematically organizes and presents information on day trading for those interested in developing the basics skills needed for online stock trading. However, there is no substitute for experience, and only trading experience will result in full knowledge and appreciation of this new profession.

Trading Electronically

Since the advent of stock exchanges, individuals have been engaged in professional stock trading for their own accounts. Individuals who could afford to do so would hold seats on a stock exchange. Working on the exchange floor gave the professional traders substantial trading advantage, such as instantaneous quotes and order executions. In exchange for that privilege, professional traders would pay many thousands of dollars for an exchange seat. However, with advances in computer and networking technology, as well as the new Securities and Exchange Commission (SEC) regulations, the NASDAQ and NYSE are now accessible to amateur traders.

It is now possible for novice and experienced amateur traders to do their own research over the Internet and execute their own trades electronically from their homes. Essentially, they can trade the way professional traders and money managers have been doing for decades. David Whitcomb, a Rutgers University finance professor, stated in a newspaper article that "most day trading firms see themselves as Wall Street's populists, allowing the little guy to bypass brokers and get the direct access to the market. It is the democratization of trading." Main Street has moved closer to Wall Street.

There are two distinct ways to trade stocks electronically. The first is to trade through a discount broker over the Internet. The convenience of trading at home and the low commissions offered by online brokerages have opened up stock trading to the smallest player possible. Gomez Advisors, Inc. (*www.gomez.com*), currently ranks sixty-nine brokerage firms that offer online trading services over the Internet. Some of the firms are well-known names on Wall Street, such as e.Schwab, E*Trade, Ameritrade, Fidelity, DLJ Direct, and American Express. Those brokerage firms sell more than electronic access to equities' traders. They also sell options, IRAs, mutual funds, and asset and cash management services.

In the early days of Internet trading, the trader simply e-mailed his or her order to the discount broker, who in turn forwarded the trade to a wholesaler or NASDAQ market maker. Execution was often slow, and the level of information inadequate. For example, stock quotes were delayed and NASDAQ information on the particular market making activities were not available. Thanks to technological networking advances, Internet trading has been improved. The entire Internet network is increasingly faster and more reliable.

By some estimates for 1999, 275,000 people may trade online at least once a day through Internet brokers. Experts estimate that 15,000 online brokerage accounts are opened every day; this puts tremendous technological strains on Internet brokers. Due to large traffic on the Internet and large trading volumes by online brokers, system performance is sometimes slow. Real-time stock quotes can be delayed. Order confirmations are slow and can leave the Internet day trader in the dark, to wonder if he or she actually owned the stock and if they could sell it yet.

Reliability remains an important concern. Internet day traders depend on the performance of several electronic service vendors: Internet Service Provider (ISP), data-feed providers, and brokerage computer systems. In late 1999, most Internet brokers offer secure socket layer (SSL) Java Script routing of the trade orders through host servers, not through slow and unprotected e-mail servers. In order to protect themselves, serious Internet day traders build their own system redundancies, such as maintaining two trading accounts at different brokerage firms and having two different ISPs for Internet access.

The second method of electronic trading is working through one of the several specialized electronic day trading firms that have branch offices all over the United States. The day trading firms cater to professional day traders who demand instantaneous quotes and executions. These day trading firms specialize in electronic stock trading only. They tend to be small, new firms. Often the day trading branch office is one large room (that is, trading floor) packed with several computers (with 21-inch monitors) connected to the firm's servers, located in a next-door computer room, which are then connected to the NASDAQ and NYSE systems. Day trading firms provide traders with immediate access to the NASDAQ market makers and NYSE specialists and allow them to execute trades themselves without the middleman, the brokerage firm.

The Electronic Traders Association's (ETA) Internet site (*www.electronic-traders.com*) currently lists approximately forty day-trading firms on its registrar. The ETA was formed by day trading firms to promote public access to the NASDAQ market and to promote price competition. Day trading firms allow thousands of individual day traders to trade directly with NASDAQ Market Makers through NASDAQ's Small Order Execution System (SOES), and other day traders through private Electronic Communications Networks (ECN).

The NASDAQ market (*www.nasdaq.com*) was the first electronic stock market exchange. Created in 1971, it allowed for the first time the buying and selling of stocks through a network of computers. Today, it is the third largest stock market, following the New York Stock Exchange (NYSE) and the Japanese stock market. The NASDAQ is not a physical place or an auction-type exchange where stock buyers meet stock sellers with the help of brokers. It is a decentralized and computerized network of market makers, firms that provide a market for the stock (or liquidity) by simultaneously buying and selling that particular stock. NASDAQ market makers are stock merchants who are required by the SEC to post electronically in the entire network both their best buying price *(BID)* and best selling price *(ASK)* for a particular stock. There is a natural fit between the NASDAQ market and electronic day traders. Consequently, the NASDAQ market has evolved into the primary trading exchange for electronic day traders.

Not Without Risk

Day trading is not simply a "Get Rich Click" scheme. It is not for everyone. Many have tried it, and quite a few of those have failed. But for those who have succeeded, day trading is a financially and intellectually rewarding way to make a living. In the financial world, there is a long-held axiom that there is a positive correlation between risk and reward: the higher the risk, the higher the return. This is clearly true for the business of electronic day trading.

There is only anecdotal evidence (media reports) about the profitability of day trading, and no formal study has been completed that authoritatively documents day traders' income. The variance of income distribution for day traders is huge. Several magazine and newspaper articles have mentioned day traders who are making six- or seven-figure incomes. And in fact, a few experienced traders who have access to large trading capital can earn high levels of income. Most day traders will not reach these levels. However, if properly trained, with enough experience and enough trading risk capital, a day trader can earn sufficient income to take this from a part-time endeavor to a full-time profession.

James Lee, president of the ETA, claims that after a six-month learning curve, a third of the players lose money, another third tread water, and the rest do well. Lee also noted that "day trading is trading and not investing, and people need to understand that. And though it is a very successful business long-term, it is very difficult to get started."

Many individuals have opened trading accounts with electronic day trading firms or through Internet brokers without fully understanding the skills needed or the risks involved in being successful.

In summary, following are some caveats from the Electronic Traders Association regarding the risks of day trading:

➤ Day trading requires skill, discipline, and hard work.

➤ Successful traders regard day trading as a career and not a hobby.

➤ National securities markets are extremely efficient and competitive. New traders will compete against professional traders who have been trading for many years.

➤ Financial markets are very dynamic, and competitive conditions change. What may have been a successful trading strategy in the past might not work in the future.

➤ Only risk capital should be used for day trading. Do not trade money that you cannot afford to lose.

➤ The learning curve is steep. Most people who begin day trading sustain losses or produce only marginal profits during the first three to five months of day trading. Do not trade unless you are willing to sustain losses while gaining day trading experience.

➤ Individuals who are not highly disciplined should avoid day trading.

➤ The new trader should limit both the number of trades he or she makes and the size of the trades to limit losses during the learning process.

➤ In addition to the normal *market risk* (that is, price volatility), the day trader is exposed to occasional trading-execution risks. The entire electronic trading platform (the computer network) could fail due to factors beyond anyone's control.

➤ Market orders can be risky, since large price gaps can occur (for example, buying stock at higher price or selling it at a lower price than anticipated). Sometimes limit orders cannot be executed.

The risk of loss in day trading is substantial; at best the day trader can only manage or control the risk. It can never be eliminated completely. Anyone considering day trading should evaluate their suitability and appropriateness in light of their financial resources and circumstances.

In January 1999, SEC Chairman Arthur Levitt stated, "Investing in the stock market, however you do it and however easy it may be, will always entail risk. I would be very concerned if investors allowed the ease with which they can make trades to shortcut or bypass the three golden rules for all investors:

Know what you are buying.

Know the ground rules under which you buy and sell a stock.

Know the level of risk you are undertaking.

Strategies such as day trading can be highly risky, and retail investors engaging in such activities should do so with funds they can afford to lose."

Well said.

I

Introduction to Day Trading

No SINGLE BOOK CAN CREATE A SUCCESSFUL DAY TRADER. READING THIS BOOK is only one step in the right direction. In section I, we start from square one and define, explain, and illustrate the most basic day trading terms and concepts being used in the profession today.

➤ Section I starts with a description of the trading environment facing day traders today. The relative advantages of day trading, such as the speed and control of trading and going home "flat," are identified. Several important distinctions are made: the day trader versus the investor, the day trader versus the gambler, being reactive versus proactive, and using technical analysis versus fundamental analysis.

➤ The relative risks associated with short holding periods for day trading is then described. The importance of continuous oversight and trading discipline is strongly emphasized. Finally, the benefits and drawbacks of paper (or simulation) trading are discussed.

➤ In section I, we also elaborate on the four essential qualities that day traders must possess: (1) knowledge and skill of stock trading, (2) adequate risk capital as well as potential sources of the trading capital, (3) time to day trade, and (4) the ability to manage risk with a disciplined trading style.

➤ Finally, we briefly introduce the trading markets, such as the National Association of Securities Dealers Automated Quotation (NASDAQ) and the New York Stock Exchange (NYSE).

1

What Is Day Trading?

Day trading consists of the direct opening and closing of stock positions with major stock exchanges, either using a computer on the trading floor of a branch office of a day trading firm that has a direct line to the NASDAQ (National Association of Securities Dealers Automated Quotation) and NYSE (New York Stock Exchange) systems, or using one's home or business computer to access an Internet broker (like E*Trade or e.Schwab). The key word in this definition is *direct*. In day trading, a trader has direct electronic access to NASDAQ market makers or NYSE specialists.

The market makers are NASD brokers and dealers who either buy or sell NASDAQ stocks for the accounts of others, or engage in the securities business for their own proprietary accounts. In essence, the market makers are stock merchants. One NASDAQ stock will have many market makers who are continuously trading in that stock and thus making a market for that stock. On the other hand, one NYSE stock will have one assigned NYSE specialist. The role of the NYSE specialist is to maintain a fair and orderly market in that security. The specialist may act either as a broker and execute orders for other securities brokers, or as a dealer in a principal capacity when trading for his or her own account. The specialist will take on the role of a principal infrequently in order to maintain stock marketability and counter temporary imbalances in the supply and demand of that security.

The day trader does not need a stockbroker. The trader is not using a telephone to call a stockbroker, and the broker is not relaying that order to the brokerage firm's order desk. The clerk is not routing that order to the market maker. Day trading firms eliminate all that. Consequently, day trading firms have eliminated time delays and most of the expenses associated with middlemen processing trade orders. The day traders are their own brokers, and their order executions are fast and affordable.

The trader can simply key in the stock symbol on a computer that has specialized trade execution software, press the appropriate function key (or click the mouse), and buy or sell shares of stock on a major exchange. It is that simple. The software used by the day trading firms for order execution is relatively user-friendly and provides an efficient interface between the stock exchanges and the day trader. Because access is direct, order executions and trade confirmations are fast. Because middlemen are not involved, transaction costs are deeply discounted.

The New Trading Environment

Historically, stock trading has been the domain of professional traders. Trading has been in essence a "private club" with restricted access. Because Wall Street firms have had access to better information and trade execution, they have had a clear trading advantage. Day trading has changed that. For the first time, amateur traders have the tools (real-time quotes and order execution) to compete with the professionals. These tools are now available because of:

> ➤ Technological advancements in computer hardware;

> ➤ Technological improvements in networking science;

> ➤ SEC regulations that mandated direct access to the NASDAQ market for small players;

> ➤ Low-cost commission structure; and

> ➤ Increasing intra-day price volatility.

Technological improvements in computer hardware during the past decade have resulted in computers and servers that are extremely fast and have large amounts of memory (RAM). Consequently, these computers are capable of processing a large quantity of real-time data flow reliably. In addition, such computers are increasingly more affordable.

Small day trading firms and their branch offices can order relatively inexpensive and fast T1 or 56K bps communication lines. Computer networking advances in the last several years have made real-time financial data feed and trade order execution feasible and affordable.

Now, small groups of investors can pool their financial resources and open branch offices of day trading firms in small towns across the United States. Day trading firms are bringing Main Street closer to Wall Street. The technologically feasible and financially affordable electronic access to real-time financial information and order execution has leveled the playing field for all participants. For the first time, an amateur day trader has access to the same information and tools that were once used only by professional traders.

The stock market crash of 1987 propelled the *Securities and Exchange Commission* (SEC) to mandate market makers to provide to individual investors better access to trade execution. In October 1987, when stock prices were free-falling, some market makers simply refused to pick up their ringing phones and execute sell orders for panicked sellers. In other words, the market makers refused to buy stock that was continually declining in value. In 1987, the SEC mandated the market maker participation in the NASDAQ Small Order Execution System (SOES). The SOES was implemented to ensure small customers and traders access to the posted market price, and thus to ensure public confidence in the NASDAQ market. The SOES initially became the dominant execution vehicle for day traders. (Today, more and more day traders are using Electronic Communications Networks, or ECNs.)

In May 1975, Wall Street firms ended the practice of charging fixed *commissions*. This deregulation resulted in the emergence of discount brokers. Then, technological advances in the 1990s brought the emergence of Internet brokers and electronic day trading firms. The new competition decreased trading transaction costs even further. This low-cost commission structure makes daily in-and-out stock trading financially feasible. Day traders can make 50 or more trades a day, and their potential profits are not being eaten up by commissions.

Most day trading firms tend to charge deeply discounted commissions that can range from $15 to $25 per trade. Competition among day trading firms in large metropolitan areas can result in even lower commissions. Furthermore, established and profitable day traders are often able to negotiate even lower commission structures. As a general rule,

Internet brokers offer the lowest commissions (from $8 to $20 per trade for market orders). However, Internet brokers provide a different type of trading service with somewhat slower quotes and order execution.

In the 1990s the U.S. stock market has become increasingly more volatile. That is a derivative of the current dynamic, interdependent, and global U.S. economy. Intra-day price volatility is here to stay, and that is exactly what fuels day trading profit opportunities. The objective of an experienced day trader is to trade volatile stocks in large share blocks and profit from their intra-day price movement.

Speed Advantage

The key advantage of this style of trading is its speed. The technology is advanced enough to afford traders the ability to receive and observe real-time price quotes tick by tick and to send electronically an execution order directly to the NASDAQ market maker. The process of day trading is relatively simple. Day traders sit in front of computer monitors, observe real-time financial data that is packaged in advanced format by sophisticated software (for example, custom tickers, technical analysis charts), and attempt to identify a price trend or momentum. Once the trend is recognized (observed), the trader needs only to react and participate in that trend.

Electronic order execution is fast. With the stroke of a key, orders are sent directly to the NASDAQ Market Makers. Confirmations are received in seconds. Exiting trades is as easy and fast as entering the trade positions, although the submitted market orders might not receive the price that the day traders were hoping for. Sometimes the holding period between the buy and sell orders is only several minutes, because a stock price can move up or down $\frac{1}{4}$ or $\frac{1}{2}$ point in only a few minutes. On 1,000 shares, that translates into $250 or $500 potential profit or loss. The speed of the received order execution and financial information gives the day trader a fighting chance to compete with the professional Wall Street players.

Control Advantage

The other key advantage of day trading is the control of trading. Day traders are always in control of their own trading. They are their own brokers. They examine the financial data, ascertain the trends, and make their own decisions to buy or sell. There are no stockbrokers involved to provide "advice" and "recommendation" on what and when to buy or sell. Day traders receive full credit or blame for the success or failure of their trading.

Since traders have access to real-time price quotes and order execution, there is no need to send *stop orders*, which are orders to buy and sell at a price below the current market price. Investors often use stop buy or sell orders to limit loss or to protect unrealized profits. Stop orders are activated if the market price of the stock reaches the specified stop order price. (Some people in the securities industry believe that brokers have the ability to manipulate the short-term market price and thus have the ability to activate the stop orders, if the stop order price is set too close to the current market price. In such a case, the price could go up or down briefly regardless of the overall trend and activate the stop order, so the broker could execute the order and get the commission.)

Day traders monitor their trading positions in real time, and thus can observe price movement and get out of a position quickly if the market is moving against them. Day traders do not need to submit stop orders; that is, they do not need to advertise the price at which they are willing to get out of the trade. Day traders do not have to assume the risk of being "picked up" by the brokers who "are running the stops." In other words, day traders do not need to be irritated that the short-term stock prices were being manipulated by the brokers just to activate their trade orders.

Also, day traders do not have to worry about the price *slippage*. They monitor market prices tick by tick. During trading, at any point of time the trader always knows the stock's best BID and ASK price. If the market is stable at that point of time, the day trader's buy or sell market order will be executed at the best BID or ASK price. The day trader would route or preference the trader's buy or sell market order to the particular NASDAQ market maker who is posting the stock's best BID and ASK price. Thus, the day trader gets the best price at that time. In addition, day traders working in day trading offices can submit and receive an even better price. Those day traders can cut the *spread* between the BID and ASK prices by offering to buy or sell through private Electronic Communication Networks (ECNs) such as Island or Instinet. Investors and day traders trading over the Internet cannot do that.

Investors who are buying or selling stock through a broker over the phone do not have such a luxury. Most likely, such investors would not know what the actual best BID and ASK prices are at that point of time, because the investor does not have access to real-time quotes. If the broker is also a market maker for that stock, investors will receive the price that is advertised by that broker, which may not be the best price. Day traders are assured that they are receiving the best price because they control their own trades.

Going Home "Flat"

At the end of the trading day, day traders close all of their trade positions and go home "flat." At 4:00 P.M. Eastern Time (or 1:00 P.M. Pacific Time), their jobs are done, no worries or stress. Without any open positions, day traders do not carry any overnight risk exposure. They do not need to worry about a *long* or *short* position—because they do not have overnight positions. The entire stock market could collapse overnight (which admittedly is a very unlikely scenario), and day traders would not lose a penny.

The next day is truly a new beginning. It does not matter how the day trader performed the previous day. Yesterday's performance has no impact on today's outcome. Each morning a day trader starts fresh. With each morning the day trader's computerized account manager will start again with a zero profit and loss balance.

Even if a trader has a winning long position at the end of the day and the trend is continuing, my advice would be still to go flat. Day traders' commission structure is low enough so it does not make sense to assume an overnight long position to save on commissions. If the trader were trading in 1,000-share increments, a long overnight position would translate into substantial overnight risk exposure. A price *gap* (or difference between the previous day's stock closing price and today's opening price) of only 1 point would translate into $1,000 potential loss. Why risk $1,000 in order to save $20 on commission?

Many factors could lead into a situation in which the stock is opening with a price gap. Companies usually wait for market close before management announces bad news. The federal government usually announces economic news at 8:00 A.M. Eastern Time, before the market is opened. Large financial institutions continue to trade after the market closes through private market (for example, Instinet), and thus the price at the market open could be dramatically different than at the previous day's close. Many things can happen to a stock price overnight, so price gaps occur frequently. By holding the overnight position, the day traders essentially relinquish the advantage of being in control.

The Stock Market Is Not a Zero-Sum Game

In my opinion, the equities market is not a zero-sum game. The stock market does not have contracts that must have an equal number of winners and losers. Historically, in the long run the overall stock market has had a positive average long-term rate of return; there is a positive long-term bias.

The market for stock *derivatives*, such as stock options and index futures, *is* a zero-sum game. Options and futures trading involve executing contracts that have stipulated expiration dates between the sellers and the buyers. At the time of expiration, there will be an equal dollar amount of winning and losing positions. When the contract expires, either the contract buyers or contract sellers will have made money. Consequently, options and futures trading are extremely competitive and efficient. In my opinion, there is a transfer of wealth from the less experienced and knowledgeable options and futures amateur traders to the more experienced and knowledgeable options and futures professional traders.

The equities market, on the other hand, has many diverse and heterogeneous market participants. Investors, traders, mutual and pension fund managers, and institutional holders have diverse objectives and holding periods that range from the extreme short-term period (day traders) to the extreme long-term (pension funds). Subsequently, different participants in the equities market will have different price targets and time frames for their decisions. It is quite feasible for a day trader to sell to an investor a stock at a price that is overvalued at that point in time (and thus the day trader would make money on the trade) and for that long-term investor to make money on the stock in the long run. That is possible because there are no equities contracts that have expiration periods. Short-term traders can make money in the short run, and long-term investors can make money in the long run. It is my opinion, because of this, that trading equities is easier than trading options and futures.

2

Day Traders

THE DAY TRADER'S ULTIMATE OBJECTIVE IS TO TRADE EXPENSIVE AND volatile stocks on the NASDAQ and NYSE markets in increments of 1,000 shares or more, and profit from the small intra-day price movement. The trader may make many trades in a single day (sometimes 50 to 100 trades a day), holding onto stocks for only a few minutes (or hours), and almost never overnight. Most day trading is confined to the NASDAQ market, which is better equipped for computerized trading and is laden with expensive and volatile high technology and Internet stocks. Day traders are short-term price speculators. They are not investors, and they are not gamblers.

Day Trader Versus Investor

Day trading is not investing. The day trader's time frame of analysis is rather short: one day. Their only intent is to exploit the stocks' intra-day price swings or daily price volatility. Unlike stock investors, day traders do not seek long-term value appreciation. If the stock value is going up at that point in time, day traders will take a long position (that is, purchase the stock). The day trader would purchase the stock at a low price and (he or she hopes) sell it a few minutes (or hours) later at a higher price.

If the stock value is going down, day traders will take a short position (that is, sell the stock first after borrowing it from the brokerage firm). At that time the day trader would sell short a stock at the high price and buy it a few minutes (or hours) later at a lower price. If the stock values are stable, the day trader will sit on a sideline and simply not trade. Good day traders can play both short and long positions and thus not care whether the market is moving up or down, as long it is not going sideways (demonstrating stable prices).

Stock volatility is generally a rule of the market rather than an exception. Most stock prices move up or down in any given day due to a variety of external factors. Even if the market is relatively calm, there are always stocks that are volatile. Day traders seek to identify a stock that has a trend (either up or down) and then go with that trend. "Trend is a friend" is a common motto among day traders. Day traders seek to pick up a relatively small stock movement, $\frac{1}{8}$ or more on that stock. If day traders are trading a large block of shares (that is, 1,000 shares per trade), then day traders will profit \$125 from a $\frac{1}{8}$ price movement. Conversely, if a day trader acquired 1,000 shares and the trader was wrong (if the stock price goes in the opposite direction), which also happens, then the day trader will lose \$125 from a $\frac{1}{8}$ price movement. Volatility is a double-edged sword.

For expensive stocks that trade for \$100 or more, a $\frac{1}{8}$ or 12.5 cents movement is such a small relative price change that it happens all the time. Consequently, there are plenty of day trading opportunities. It is not uncommon to see a day trader executing many, sometimes as many as 100, trades in a single day. On the other hand, an investor's time frame is much longer. Investors seek a much larger price movement than $\frac{1}{8}$ (they look for 2, 3 points, or higher) to earn the desired rate of return. That takes time. In short, day traders seek to extract an income from intra-day price volatility by trading the stock frequently, while the investors seek a long-term capital appreciation.

Day Trader's Objective Versus Investor's Objective

There is a clear divergence of objectives between the investor and day trader. The objective of an investor is to earn a long-term capital appreciation or long-term return on the investment with a limited risk. Consequently, investors are not concerned with the short-term market price fluctuations, since they are in the stock market for a long haul. They do not care if their trade orders are executed in ten seconds or ten minutes.

They do not mind if the received price for the purchased stock is 12.5 cents or 25 cents higher than anticipated. $\frac{1}{8}$ or $\frac{1}{4}$ point in the stock price will not make a difference in the long run when the objective is to wait for capital appreciation of several points. The expectations are much more modest. At best the investors hope to double their investments in five years.

On the other hand, day traders seek to double their trading capital every few months. Consequently, the objective is not the long-term return on the investment but earning the short-term income. In order to earn that substantial short-term income, and thus possibly double the trading capital every few months, the day traders are willing to absorb inordinate amount of risk. Not surprisingly, the high income is associated with high risk. The day traders are willing to place $20,000 or $50,000 at risk and lose it all in order to double that same amount in a few months of trading. Consequently, day trading is extremely risky.

Since the day traders are affected by the short-term market volatility, they do care whether their trade orders are executed in ten seconds or ten minutes. Even a ten seconds wait for a trade confirmation seems to be a long time for many day traders. Since the day traders are exploiting the small and short-term price fluctuations, the traders demand from the brokerage firms almost instantaneous trade executions. They do notice if the received price for the purchased stock is only 6 cents higher than anticipated, since $\frac{1}{16}$ of a point in the price could make a difference between breaking even or losing money on a trade.

Day Trader's Risk Versus Investor's Risk Tolerance

It is unrealistic and unfair to compare investor's risk with the trader's risk. The risk associated with the potential to earn 20% annual rate of return on investment is substantially smaller than the risk that corresponds with the 200% increase in trading capital after six months of day trading. This trade-off between the financial risk and return is well documented in the financial literature. Since the day traders are pursuing high short-term income from the trading, they automatically and willingly accept that high risk. Unfortunately, the high risk translates automatically into the high rate of failures. The majority of day traders will simply fail and lose some if not all of their trading capital. It is a fact of life for many novice day traders. The potential to earn high income equates automatically to high probability to lose money. If you do not want to lose your money, do not trade stocks—invest your money. Day trading is not investing.

Second, investors are risk averse individuals, while day traders are clearly the risk takers. The day trader's tolerance for the financial risk is substantially higher than the investor's risk tolerance. It is redundant to remind the day traders that they could lose their money day trading. If the day traders seek financial safety and security they could simply purchase Treasury bonds and earn 5% annual rate of return. However, the day trader's objective is on the other side of the financial risk/return spectrum—unsafe and insecure financial environment that provides a potential to earn 500% annual rate of return.

Proactive Versus Reactive

To become a proficient trader, day traders need not anticipate the future price movement for a particular stock. They do not need to be proactive. They need only to be reactive. Their objective is to identify the existing price momentum and go with that trend. In my opinion, it is much easier to observe the present short-term movement than to read and anticipate long-term future prices.

Day traders do not need the knowledge of *fundamental analysis* that investors do. They do not need to know the story behind the stock, or reasons why the stock has been increasing in value. In fact, traders do not need to know anything about the company, or the price history, or the future price targets, or whether the stock is overvalued or undervalued compared to some industry standards. Before making a single day trading–style trade, there is no reason to research any of the stock's fundamentals.

All the day traders need to do is to identify a trend or price momentum. All they need to know is that the stock is moving. The underlying cause of that price movement is irrelevant to the day traders. Also, the day trader does not need to enter the trade at the bottom of that price trend or exit the trade at the top of the swing. It is impossible to ascertain the price turning points exactly. Day traders do not anticipate the price movement; they only react to the observable price trend.

Fundamental Analysis Versus Technical Analysis

On the other hand, investors must anticipate the long-term price trend. They have to research stock fundamentals to determine whether, over the long haul, the stock will go up in price. Therefore, investors need to understand the history of the company, its products, its management, and competitors. Investors will pay close attention to the fundamental analysis indicators that measure the company's overall performance, such as the company's *price/earnings ratio*, its *earning per share, dividends* per share, market capitalization, and yield. None of these fundamental analysis indicators apply to day traders, who focus on the short-term price movement and rely strictly on technical analysis.

By contrast, most day traders extensively use technical analysis. The majority of trading software packages offers a large number of technical analysis indicators that provide valuable insights about stock prices. The focus of technical analysis is almost always a price of a stock. The technical indicators utilize information on the stock price at that point in time, the daily closing or opening stock prices and the highest or lowest price in the selected time period. Furthermore, a technical analyst will also evaluate and incorporate the stock trading volume into the analysis.

In addition, investors using the fundamental analysis indicators need to develop their own well-defined investment strategies. They need to decide if they want to own small capitalization stocks with a high three-month price gain or a large capitalization stock with a high dividend yield and a low price/earnings ratio. This is one of many investment strategies available to investors. Each investment strategy has different risk factors and different return potential. Which investment strategy would the investor follow? Financial literature is crowded with investment advice, and informed investors spend hours reading and researching the fundamentals of a company prior to actually purchasing a stock.

Holding Periods and Risk

The level of *risk* for day traders and investors is dramatically different. An investor's stock-holding period is much longer than a trader's holding period. If the investor makes a wrong investment decision and the position is losing money, the investor can simply hold onto the position and sell the stock when the stock recovers. Time is on the investor's side.

Day traders do not have the luxury of waiting for long-term equity appreciation. They cannot afford to tie up their limited capital in a losing position and wait it out. A good day trader will most likely close losing positions at a loss and seek other trading opportunities. Time is not the trader's ally, and consequently day trading has far more risk than does investing.

The day trader's most important resources are acquired trading knowledge, trading capital, and the time to trade during the market hours. If the day trader ties up his or her limited capital in a long-term position that is a losing trade, then the day trader will be unable to utilize his or her resources effectively.

Oversight and Discipline

Also, the level of oversight between day trading and investors is dramatically different. Since investors seek long-term capital appreciation, they are not as much concerned with daily stock market gyrations. Investors can afford to enter a stock position and walk away from any kind of monitoring, particularly real-time monitoring. On the other hand, day trading is work.

Undisciplined day traders often become investors by mistake. They take a long stock position, anticipating that the price increase will continue. Unfortunately for the day trader, the market could suddenly reverse the trend. A disciplined (or good) trader would get out of that position immediately, and thus minimize the loss. However, some traders would refuse to take a loss, even if it is initially a small loss. Undisciplined traders will hold a position, and hope that the stock will turn around and go up. If that does not happen that day, the trader will hold the position overnight, and then become an investor. If the declining trend continues the next day, the day trader might become a long-term investor. With each passing day, a small loss becomes a larger loss. If the trader has limited trading capital, then all of that capital might be tied up in that long (losing) position.

The following table summarizes the differences between the stock day trader and investor:

Table 2.1 *Electronic Traders Are Not Investors*

Investor	Electronic Trader
Risk averse individual	Risk tolerant individual
Proactive stand, anticipates trends	Reactive stand, observes trends
Performs fundamental analysis	Performs technical analysis
Long-term holding period	Short-term holding period
Few buy and sell activities in a week	Many buy and sell orders in one day
Seeks long-term capital appreciation	Seeks short-term ordinary income
Delayed price quotes acceptable	Real-time price quote system is a must
Real-time order execution is unimportant	Real-time order execution is a must
Passive stock performance oversight	Active stock performance monitoring

Day Trader Versus Gambler

The North American Securities Administration Association (NASAA) executive director was in the spotlight recently for comparing day trading to gambling and suggesting, "If you want to gamble, go to Las Vegas, the food is better." Electronic stock trading is not gambling. Day trading is not a game of chance. It is an emerging profession.

There are many successful day traders who treat day trading as a full-time career. First, the professional day traders are in front of their computer monitors from the market opening to the closing bell. They would be first to tell you that day trading is work, and not entertainment. Second, day traders must know how to trade in order to prosper. Day traders cannot be lucky all the time.

The only commonality between day trading and gambling is the chance or probability of loss. Unlike gamblers, traders have the opportunity to manage their risk. First, day traders have a wealth of real-time financial information at their fingertips. Traders are able see on their large-screen monitors more financial information than the great majority of participants in the stock market. Consequently, traders are able to take educated and calculated risks. Second, traders can execute their orders quickly, and they can get out quickly when they need to. In other words, the day traders have the necessary tools to manage the risk.

It is not realistic to expect that traders will be correct 100% of the time. Even if they are correct 50% of the time, which would be equivalent to a game of chance, traders can still be profitable if they minimize losses when they are wrong (get out quickly at a minimal loss) and allow profits to rise when they are right. This is an important point. To be successful in the long run, day traders must minimize their losses and maximize their profits. Given the quantity and sophistication of the financial information presented to the traders in real time, the probability of being right should be higher than 50%. With the acquired trading experience (that is, at least six months of live trading), that probability should increase.

It is true that many day traders have a gambling mentality. They enjoy the rush of adrenaline when they make the right trade. When they are right, they can see on the screen how much money they are making each second. Sometimes, day traders enter trade positions without receiving a clear buy or sell signal. Then, traders are gambling or betting that the stock will go their way. Sometimes they are right and they make money, and other times they are wrong and they lose money. However, good traders do not gamble. A good trader will enter a position only when he or she receives a clear trading signal. A trading signal can be a technical analysis signal, such as the crossover between the fast and slow Moving Average lines, or it could be a movement in the NASDAQ Level II screen. (Trading signals are discussed in chapter 9.)

My point is that good day traders follow the signals from the trading system they use, and they do not gamble. Bad traders, or soon to be ex-traders, do not have a trading system; they gamble.

3

Do You Want to Be a Day Trader?

Day trading is a new trading style, so it is not surprising that most day traders are young. They tend to be male, computer-literate, and well-educated individuals. In short, day traders are savvy stock market participants who are accustomed to taking risks. Before becoming traders, they usually have already opened accounts with discount brokers or Internet brokers. They are attracted to day trading because of its potential for high returns.

To be a successful day trader, a person needs four essential requirements:

1. Knowledge and skill of stock trading;
2. Adequate risk capital;
3. Time to trade; and
4. Ability to manage risk with a disciplined trading style.

Requirement 1: Knowledge and Skill of Stock Trading

The first and foremost characteristic that day traders need is trading knowledge and skill. Knowledge is power! Anyone trading stocks should read as much as possible about stock trading in general. (Listed at the back of this book are some general resources.) As a new day trader, one competes against experienced professionals, such as the NASDAQ market makers, NYSE specialists, and other day traders. New day traders must have knowledge of the NASDAQ and NYSE securities market and their trading rules to be able to survive. Acquiring those skills is time-consuming and often expensive, and yet they do not guarantee to make anyone a good trader.

If your town has a day trading firm, visit the office and see what kinds of trading education they have to offer. Day trading firms often have free seminars and classes. Sometimes firms charge a training fee, which can be nominal or substantial. Ask if you can talk with others who have taken the training class. Find out who is presenting it and if the training is well organized. Talk to the other traders. Ask them how they trade. Ask them if they are profitable. Pay close attention to the actions (executions) of the profitable traders. Dedicate a few weeks to paper trading.

Paper Trading

Day trading firms use sophisticated financial software for order execution and display of real-time financial data. The software will most likely have a training module (demo or simulation mode) that will provide real-time data flow and somewhat realistic simulated execution. New traders can sit in front of the computer monitor during market hours, view real-time quotes and charts, and "paper trade." *Paper trading* means that buy and sell orders are not actually executed, but only processed and confirmed by the traders' computers. The computer will keep track of trading activities and update trading statistics. Any losses are only paper losses. Paper trading is an easy and comfortable way to become familiar with the trading software and the NASDAQ and NYSE markets. New traders should practice paper trading for several weeks before beginning to trade live.

Before a new trader graduates from paper trading to live trading, he or she should consistently make, day after day, at least a thousand dollars in paper trading profit every day for several weeks. Consistency is crucial. The new trader should then discount the paper trading profit by at least one-half. We suggest this because live trading is dramatically different from paper trading. All paper trading market or *limit orders* (orders to buy or sell at a specified price or at a better price) are filled automatically at the requested limit price or posted market price. In reality, that does not happen very often. Traders will learn quickly that live market orders are not filled at the expected price, and often limit orders are not filled at all.

For example, if a trader is watching real-time quotes on the screen, and there is one market maker with the best posted selling price (ASK), and the trader submits a buy market order for a NASDAQ stock, that order goes into a computerized queue. A *market order* is defined as an order to buy or sell security at the most advantageous price obtainable at that moment of time. If the trader is first in line, the order will be executed; however, it is rare that a trader is the first in line. One of two things could then happen. The trader's order could be executed at the same price if the market maker elects at his or her discretion to refresh the same selling ASK price. However, if the price is moving up fast, then the market maker will not refresh the same ASK price, but will back away and post a higher ASK price. The trader's market order would then get executed at a price higher than expected. If market is moving up very fast, the trader might end up with a substantially higher price than anticipated.

Similarly, when a trader electronically submits a buy limit order for a NASDAQ stock, this order might never get executed at the specified price. If the price trend is up, the market maker will increase the ASK price. That would mean the limit order would never get executed at the lower price. In other words, the stock price may be moving too quickly and could simply pass over the limit order before it is executed. (More information on this topic of order executions will be provided in section IV.)

Finally, paper trading does not involve real money, and thus there is no real risk. Without the genuine risk of losing money, the trader's emotions are not involved. Fear, greed, panic, and hope do not interfere with trading judgments, so it is easier to be a disciplined trader. However, there is no substitute for real-life experience. Simulated or paper trading is not a realistic predictor of future trading results.

The most expensive and reckless trading education is to start live trading without undertaking an adequate and sufficiently long training program. New traders will make mistakes. Some mistakes will simply be the wrong trades (that is, buying a stock when market is going down). Some of those mistakes will be execution errors (that is, pressing the wrong key). Trading software used by day trading firms is sophisticated and complex, and it takes time to master it. It takes time to learn about the NASDAQ and NYSE markets and their trading rules. That is simply part of the learning curve. However, new traders are better off making mistakes in a demo mode than in a live mode. Mistakes committed in a demo mode are much cheaper!

Requirement 2: Adequate Risk Capital

Day traders must have access to adequate trading capital, which will clearly always be at risk. Day traders should be able to sustain losing that capital (although that is not a trading objective). They should never trade money that they cannot afford to lose. I do not advocate obtaining a second mortgage to raise risk capital or using retirement funds or credit card advances.

Most day trading firms generally require a minimum capital of $20,000, although several established day trading firms require at least $50,000 to open an account. All of these accounts are margin accounts. *Margin account* means that the NASD broker is extending credit to customers who are purchasing stocks on "margin." Margin is a credit extended by a NASD broker or dealer to a customer—in essence, a credit issued to finance securities transactions. Under the Federal Reserve Board regulation (Regulation T) that governs the amount of credit that can be extended, the maximum amount that brokers can advance is 50%. That means that a trader's deposit of $20,000 will result in an additional $20,000 credit (advance or loan) from the broker, and the trader will have $40,000 purchasing power. Every brokerage firm has a Margin Department that provides oversight and supervision of the extension of credit. Internet brokers cater to investors who might purchase stocks in increments of 100 shares and thus their minimum account is dramatically less than the minimum of $20,000 needed to open a trading account and trade stocks in increments of 1,000 shares.

Adequacy of Trading Capital

If a trader does not have adequate capital to purchase 1,000 shares of expensive and volatile technology stocks, then the trader is already somewhat handicapped. If a trader opens a margin account with the minimum requirement of $20,000, then the trader can afford to purchase only 400 shares of expensive stock (that is, stock priced at $100 or more per share) for $40,000. If a trader makes a correct buy and a stock goes up $\frac{1}{8}$ point, then he or she would earn $50, which would only cover the trader's buy and sell orders commission costs. Commission cost is commonly $15 or $20 per ticket and thus the trader's round trip commission cost will range from $30 to $40.

With a minimum margin account of $20,000, purchasing power is restricted to $40,000. With $40,000 purchasing power, traders have two options: (1) trade stocks listed for $40 or less in increments of 1,000 shares, or (2) trade the expensive stocks in increments substantially fewer than 500 shares. Both strategies have drawbacks.

Consider the first option. If the day trader were trading a less expensive stock (that is, $40 or less per share) in increments of 1,000 shares (with $40,000 purchasing power), then the stock would need to increase in value 1 point for the trader to earn $1,000. But stocks do not usually go up 2.5% that easily, especially within a single day. Something must drive that stock up 2.5%, such as positive news (for example, higher than estimated earnings, a merger, a projected stock split), and that does not happen very often. Traders need to be patient and spend time monitoring the inexpensive stocks for a 2.5% price movement that earns $1,000. If a trader wants to earn only $125 on a trade, the stock needs to move $\frac{1}{8}$. But that is $\frac{1}{3}$ of a 1% increase in value for a stock that is priced at $40. Again, it takes time for this to happen.

Consider the second option. If a day trader (with $40,000 purchasing power) is trading expensive ($100) stock in increments of 400 shares, then the stock would need to increase in value 2.5 points for the trader to earn $1,000. Again, this does not happen very often. If a trader wants to earn only $125 on a trade, the stock needs to move $\frac{5}{16}$. This may not happen quickly.

Either way, the trader is handicapped. The best long-term scenario is to trade expensive and volatile stocks in increments of 1,000 shares and profit from the small (1% or less) price movement. This happens frequently. But to do that one needs an adequate amount of trading capital.

Please, do not misunderstand this point: New day traders should not begin by trading expensive, volatile stocks in increments of 1,000 shares. That is the domain of an experienced day trader. Even if adequate trading capital is available, the novice trader should start slowly by trading inexpensive stocks that do not move very fast. As a rule of thumb, he or she should start trading with 100 shares and increase the size of the shares traded with gained experience, increasing the trading block by 100 shares every week until he or she reaches the block of 1,000 shares. It is unrealistic to expect that new traders will start making money immediately. Trading is a skill that takes time to develop.

Sources of Trading Capital

The best source of funds for new day traders is the traders' own capital. However, day trading tends to attract young individuals who often do not have access to large sums of money. Often they try to raise money for their trading account by putting up a limited risk capital ($10,000 or less) and then borrowing additional money ($40,000 or less) from their friends, relatives, or other day traders. This would give a trader a sizable deposit of $50,000. With a margin account, the purchasing power is $100,000. Now the day trader has a sufficient trading account to trade expensive and volatile NASDAQ stocks in increments of 1,000 shares and profit from small price movements.

Hypothetically, the loan money is never at risk. All of the trading losses would come from the trader's own initial risk capital. Friends, relatives, or other day traders who provide that loan would monitor the risk by asking for and receiving the trader's daily trading statements. This is an arrangement between private individuals, and requires daily monitoring and trust. If the risk capital is depleted, then the loan will probably be called immediately. What happens if the new day trader loses more than his or her own $10,000? Day trading firms do not want to become involved in such situations.

The other method for securing trading funds is to create a partnership account with a private investor who believes in the trader's future trading potential and who is willing to assume a significant risk of loss. Again, that private investor is most likely to be a friend, relative, or other day trader. This is workable if the new day trader has the experience, track record, or potential to succeed but lacks the funds. The partnership agreement would specify how the profits, if any, are split between the trader and investor (usually it is a 50–50 split). Again, this is an arrangement between private individuals, and most brokerage firms would not want to have any part in it.

Requirement 3: Time to Trade

The third element that future day traders must have is time. Stock exchanges open at 9:30 A.M. Eastern Time (or 6:30 A.M. Pacific Time), and at that time serious day traders are at their trading stations waiting for the market to open. This is the most active and volatile time of day on the stock exchange. There are many different market participants who are placing buy and sell orders: the amateurs (individual investors) and the professionals (mutual and pension funds managers, institutional investors, and other traders). Day traders monitor the activity and try to ascertain trends. If the day trader sees momentum, he will jump in and go with the trend.

Once a day trader takes a position, he or she is glued to the monitor, watching the stock performance tick by tick. With an open position traders are even reluctant to go to the bathroom. In the few minutes the trader might be gone, a profitable trading position can turn into a loss, or a small loss can turn into a much larger loss. The bottom line is that day trading is a job and requires time and effort. The market closes at 4:00 P.M. Eastern Time (or 1:00 P.M. Pacific Time). A serious day trader will be in front of the monitor from the opening to the closing bell.

It is, however, possible to be a part-time day trader, particularly if one lives on the west coast. It is possible to trade from 6:30 to 8:30 A.M. Pacific Time, when the stock market is most active and volatile. After closing all of the trading positions, traders often go to their "day jobs." Some part-time traders return to trade for the market closing, which is the second most active and volatile trading period. And on the west coast it conveniently coincides with the lunch hour. Thus it is possible to engage in day trading and keep one's "day job."

Requirement 4: Ability to Manage Risk with a Disciplined Trading Style

Last but not least, day traders must have the skill to manage risk using a disciplined trading style. Since winning trades take care of themselves, the focus of risk management is on managing the losing trades. The trader must be disciplined to accept the fact that his or her trading decisions can be wrong, to recognize this quickly, and to get out with a minimal loss. This is not as easy as it seems, and discipline becomes crucial.

Traders are often reluctant to admit they've made an error and are unwilling to take a small loss and move on to other trading opportunities. Instead, undisciplined traders start hoping that their losing stock position will reverse its trend. That is when small losses turn into large losses. A $\frac{1}{8}$ or $\frac{1}{4}$ point loss could quickly turn into a $\frac{1}{2}$ to 1 point loss. Instead of losing $125 on 1,000 shares, traders wait too long, and the trade results in a much larger loss.

Day traders have a motto: "Do not fight the tape." The stock market is always right. If the trader has a long position and the price of the stock is declining with each tick, then the market is giving the trader a clear signal: "Get out of that trade." Disciplined traders will get that message quickly and will get out. Further, the disciplined day trader waits patiently for a clear trading signal to buy or sell a stock. Without that signal, the trader will not enter the trade. (Otherwise trading becomes gambling.) A good trader will enter a position only when he or she receives a trading signal to buy or sell short. Finally, a good day trader would not let a winning trade turn into a losing trade. A day trader would take profits regardless of how small they might be. Day traders do not go broke taking profits.

C H A P T E R
4

Trading Places

THE U.S. CONGRESS PASSED THE MALONEY ACT OF 1938 IN ORDER TO protect the public from unfair trading practices and to ensure continued public confidence in the securities business. Rather than enlarge the Securities and Exchange Commission (SEC), the U.S. Congress determined that these objectives could be better met by means of industry self-regulation. In 1939, a proposal was submitted to the SEC for registration of a national securities association to regulate the over-the-counter market. The SEC approved the registration statement, and the *National Association of Securities Dealers* (NASD) was formed.

NASD membership consists of securities brokers and dealers who are authorized by NASD to transact securities business in the United States. A NASD *broker* is defined as any individual, corporation, partnership, association, or other legal entity engaged in transacting securities business for the account of others. A NASD *dealer* is any individual, corporation, partnership, association, or other legal entity engaged in the business of buying and selling securities for its own account.

NASDAQ

The National Association of Securities Dealers Automated Quotation (NASDAQ) system was created in 1971 as a true electronic securities exchange. The NASDAQ, sometimes called the over-the-counter (OTC), market is a negotiated and decentralized marketplace. There is no centralized meeting place or trading floor. Transactions are conducted through a computer network that connects NASD brokers and dealers, rather than through face-to-face meetings on an exchange floor. The NASD regulates the NASDAQ market.

A trading transaction in OTC securities is initiated when a trader places an order with a NASD broker. The NASD broker completes an order ticket, and the order ticket is then routed electronically to the NASD dealer who carries that security in its inventory. The NASD dealer is required to provide continuous bids (BID is the price at which the NASD dealer is willing to buy the security) and offers (ASK is the price at which the NASD dealer is willing to sell the security). Subsequently, the NASD dealer is said to "make a market" in that security. The NASD dealer is called a *market maker*.

To be a market maker in the NASDAQ system, a NASD dealer must meet specific capital requirements and must be registered with the NASD. In essence, a registered market maker who enters BID and ASK prices in the NASDAQ system must be prepared to buy or sell that security from its securities trading portfolio (inventory) at the quoted BID and ASK prices. All market makers buy and sell securities for their own profit, at their own risk. Unlike the centralized securities exchange market (that is, the New York Stock Exchange), where there is only one market maker per security (called a *specialist*), there must be at least two market makers for any OTC security. In most cases there are many market makers competing against each other for the purchase or sale of the NASDAQ securities. All posted BID and ASK quotes are considered to be firm quotes.

The NASDAQ system is an electronic method of communication among NASD brokers and dealers that provides quotes on OTC securities. All NASD member firms subscribe to the NASDAQ system and have terminals that allow them to obtain real-time BID and ASK prices for OTC securities. There are three levels of information in the NASDAQ system. The Level I screen provides subscribers with the inside market of the highest BID and the lowest ASK for a security in which there are at least two market makers. This information is typically available to any NASD branch office of the NASD member firms, as well as to the CNBC and Internet stock quote providers. Information on the market makers who have the highest BID and the lowest ASK prices for the security is not listed on the Level I screen. In essence, the Level I screen posts only the current best BID and ASK prices.

The Level II screen provides all BID and ASK prices, as well as the quotation sizes for all market makers who are making market for that security. The Level III screen allows a market maker in the NASDAQ system to update the relative BID and ASK prices for those securities for which the market maker is authorized to enter quotes. These updated quotations appear on the NASDAQ Level II screen immediately.

All OTC securities traded on NASDAQ must be properly registered and must meet specific criteria regarding issuer assets, the number of shareholders, and the number of outstanding shares. However, the NAS-DAQ market is laden with new technology companies that have smaller capitalization than do the NYSE listed companies. The focus of the NAS-DAQ-listed companies is on growth rather than on income (dividends), and thus there is much more price volatility. Also, it is easier to get listed on the NASDAQ, and thus most young companies go public with a NAS-DAQ listing. There is a natural fit between the NASDAQ market and day trading. The NASDAQ market is an electronic exchange laden with volatile high tech stocks. And that is exactly what day traders are looking for: direct electronic trading access and high intra-day price volatility.

SOES

NASDAQ's *Small Order Execution System* (SOES) is an electronic order execution system that was created in 1985 to facilitate direct public access to NASDAQ market makers. The system was fully implemented in 1987 after the stock market crash left many small investors unable to communicate their sell orders to NASD brokers or dealers. SOES provided for the first time a method for entering and executing trade orders in an automated electronic environment. Most NASDAQ national market securities are eligible for execution via SOES.

The most important component of the SOES system is the fact that SOES is mandatory for the market makers. All market makers who have the best BID and ASK prices are obligated to execute the trade orders for the purchase or sale of a SOES security at the NASDAQ inside BID and ASK prices. This gives the day trader a degree of certainty about the executed prices and the share size. The mandatory nature of the SOES has forced NASD dealers to honor the advertised and posted BID and ASK prices. Many market makers do not like that obligation: they do not like being "SOESed" by the day traders.

The SOES system has opened a window of opportunity for small traders to compete on equal footing with professional traders. SOES was designed for the benefit of the small individual traders and investors, to ensure that the public had direct access and liquidity. Nevertheless, SOES has several restrictions. Day traders can trade up to 1,000 shares for most NASDAQ stocks. For NASDAQ stocks that have small trading volume, the maximum number can be as little as 200 shares per execution. NASD registered representatives and NASD brokers and dealers cannot use SOES for their own accounts.

SelectNet

For NASDAQ stocks, NASD also provides the *SelectNet*, which is also an electronic order execution system. SelectNet was introduced in 1990 and was designed so that market makers could communicate and execute trades electronically among themselves. SelectNet orders are broadcast to NASDAQ market makers only. (SelectNet orders among the market makers are not displayed on Level II screens.) In essence, SelectNet electronic communication system has to a great extent replaced telephone calls among the market makers.

SelectNet has provided the day trader with a tool to electronically submit orders directly to the market makers at a better price than the posted best BID and ASK prices. Unlike SOES, SelectNet is not a mandatory system for the market makers. Market makers have the option to accept or to ignore that offer; a SelectNet order is filled only if the market maker chooses to execute that order. Nevertheless, SelectNet offered a possibility to buy and sell securities between the BID and ASK spread.

Also, SelectNet has provided the day trader with a tool to preference a particular market maker at the quoted BID and ASK price. When the day trader preferences a market maker through the SelectNet, the day trader is stating to the market maker, "You are posting a price to sell and I am willing to pay that price to buy."

ECNs

Electronic Communication Networks (ECNs) are NASDAQ's newest market participants. ECNs provide market makers, institutional investors, and day traders with an anonymous way to enter orders for

NASDAQ stocks at the better price. ECNs allow market makers and any traders to post and display their BID and ASK prices on a national system, so that others can fill these orders. Most often the ECN buy or sell orders would become the best buy and sell prices for the security. Those orders would then show automatically at the top of the BID and ASK book on the Level II screen. Therefore, ECN orders frequently drive the inside market (by creating the best BID and ASK prices).

ECNs were incorporated into the NASDAQ system structure in January 1997 with the SEC Order Handling Rule, which required that all NASD brokers and dealers post the customers' limit orders. The rule was designed to provide limit order protection to the customers. NASD brokers and dealers must post all limit orders entered by the customers, and thus the public buy and sell limit orders are subsequently forwarded automatically and electronically in the NASDAQ as an ECN quote.

All ECNs are proprietary systems. They must be registered with the NASDAQ and NASD in order to participate in the marketplace. As of the end of 1998, there were eight ECNs on the NASDAQ system, each ECN with its own four-letter market participant identification code. The following are the SEC-certified ECNs: Instinet Corporation (INCA), Island ECN (ISLD), Archipelago (ARCA), Bloomberg Tradebook (BTRD), Spear Leeds & Kellogg (REDI), Attain (ATTN), BRASS Utility (BRUT), and Strike Technologies (STRK).

ECNs represent NASDAQ at its best. ECNs foster competition among the market makers and enhance market liquidity. It is a win-win situation. Small investors and day traders can efficiently and inexpensively establish BID and ASK prices for a particular stock to be displayed automatically on Level II screens worldwide. And in essence, small investors and traders have become the market makers in that NASDAQ stock, competing against the NASD registered market makers.

Small investors and day traders now have the ability to access the NASDAQ market in the same fashion as the NASD brokers and dealers, but at a fraction of the cost. Unlike the brokers and dealers, the small investors and traders do not have to incur the cost of the NASD registration and capital requirements. The ECNs have granted to the small investors and day traders an additional direct access to better prices and liquidity. And that access is better than that provided by SOES. It is not surprising that ECNs have surpassed SOES as the day traders' favorite trading platform.

The commonly used ECNs (that is, those with the most liquidity) are the Instinet (INCA) and the Island (ISLD). All ECNs together account for approximately 25% of the NASDAQ volume. Most of that volume comes from the Instinet. Instinet was established in 1969 to serve large institutional investors. Instinet offers to the participating institutions the ability to trade NASDAQ and NYSE stocks among themselves twenty hours a day. In essence, Instinet is a private market with better prices. It is not generally accessible to small investors and traders; only a few day trading firms provide direct Instinet access.

The 1997 SEC Order Handling Rule requires NASD brokers and dealers to post all customers' buy and sell limit orders through ECNs. Those orders are displayed on Level II screens automatically. However, large institutional investors are not required to post their buy and sell limit orders through INCA. In addition, large block orders of 10,000 shares or trades worth more than $250,000 are not required to be displayed through Instinet.

In contrast, Island is much more open and is available to anyone. Anyone can use Island: the market makers, large institutional investors, small investors, and traders. Island was established in 1996, and it is the fastest growing ECN. It is an increasingly more popular trading platform among day traders because the Island is fast, reliable, and relatively inexpensive. It costs a little more in commission to execute an Island order than to execute an SOES order, but it is worth it. It is fun to watch your order show up electronically on the Level II screen next to the quote of a large Wall Street establishment firm. Island epitomizes the democratization of the stock trading process: everyone has equal access.

NYSE

The *New York Stock Exchange* (NYSE), also called "The Big Board" or "The Exchange," was founded in 1792 to promote the orderly trading of listed securities. A board of directors made up of individuals representing the public and exchange members operates the NYSE. The NYSE acts as a model for the other regional exchanges such as the American, Pacific, Boston, Philadelphia, and Chicago stock exchanges.

In order for a company to be listed on the NYSE, that company must have the following:

➤ At least 1,100,000 shares publicly held, with a market value of at least $18,000,000;

➤ Minimum of 2,000 round lot shareholders or a total of 2,200 shareholders;

➤ Average monthly trading volume of at least 100,000 shares for the most recent six months; and

➤ Minimum pre-tax earnings of $2,500,000 for the latest fiscal year.

Consequently, large and well-capitalized companies tend to be listed on the NYSE. Those companies tend to be more established companies in mature industries. NYSE companies are typically more income-oriented than growth-oriented. In other words, they are more interested in generating dividends for their shareholders than growing the companies. Subsequently, NYSE stocks tend to be less volatile than NASDAQ stocks, and are thus less attractive for day traders.

Membership on the NYSE is currently limited to 1,366 seats. A member is an individual who owns a seat on the exchange. A member firm is one that employs an individual (usually an officer or partner) who owns a seat on the exchange. Only a member of the NYSE may transact business on the floor of the exchange. Each NYSE security is assigned a trading post, where the security is bid for and offered; any member wishing to buy or sell a security must do so at the trading post. Those members who are bidding or offering the security are called the "trading crowd."

Every stock that trades on the NYSE floor is assigned a specialist. A specialist may handle more than one stock traded at the same trading post. Specialists maintain a fair and orderly market in their securities. The specialist may act in a principal capacity (that is, as a dealer) when trading for his or her own accounts. He or she will take on the role of the principal in order to maintain marketability and counter temporary imbalances in the supply and demand of a security. The specialist may act in an agent capacity (as a broker) when executing orders for NYSE commission house brokers.

The specialist must maintain a continuous market by standing ready to buy when there are no bidders (buyers) or sell when there are no offerers (sellers) at the trading post. By doing so, the specialist is said to maintain a market in the security. When entering the trading crowd, a broker may ask the specialist for the "size of the markets." This will tell the broker the current prices for the highest buyer and the lowest seller. For example, the market is 40 40¼, 500 by 300. There are buyers for 500 shares at 40 and sellers for 300 shares at 40¼.

The specialist will enter all buy and sell orders in a "specialist's book." The specialist would then match buyers with sellers and thus maintain fair and orderly market in that specific stock. The specialist may never compete with the public orders. He or she can bid higher or offer lower in order to reduce the spread between the bid and offer price. However, there is no Level II screen information available. Day traders who do not have a seat on the exchange would not know the "depth of the market" at any point of time. That information is available only to the specialist on the exchange floor. Hence, day traders on the NYSE deal with a more limited set of stock information than is currently available in real time from the NASDAQ market (on the Level II screens).

All trades of listed securities are reported and shown on *ticker tape*. All listed securities are assigned a letter *symbol*. Also, trades identify the exchange market on which the trade took place. If no symbol appears, the trade occurred on the New York Stock Exchange. Each stock symbol is printed on the top line of the tape, with the price and volume printed below. Certain information about a specific security will also be indicated, such as RTS for rights, WT for warrants, Pr for preferred stock, and WI for when issued. Transactions involving one round lot of 100 shares require no volume representation, and only the stock symbol and price are reported.

Each exchange has an automated system for efficiently executing trade orders. The New York Stock Exchange uses a system called "Designated Order Turnaround" (DOT and Super DOT). The system can be used for market and limit orders and covers both round-lot and odd-lot orders. The DOT system allows orders to be entered on the branch level, directly into the computer execution system. The order bypasses the floor broker and goes directly to the specialist for execution.

To protect investors, the NYSE has imposed restrictions on trading if certain key market *indexes* rise or fall by a significant amount. Program trading and index arbitrage strategies are restricted if the *Dow Jones Industrial Average* changes by 50 points or more from the closing value the previous day. Certain other restrictions apply if the *Standard*

& Poor's 500 futures contract (traded on the Chicago Mercantile Exchange) declines by 12 or more points from the previous day's close. If the Dow Jones Industrial Average declines by 350 or more points from the previous day, the exchange will halt trading and may not reopen for one half-hour. If, on the same day, the decline reaches 550 or more points, the exchange will halt trading and not reopen for two hours. If this happens within the last two hours of trading, the exchange will not open until the next day.

Introduction to Day Trading Tools

THE OBJECTIVE OF THIS SECTION IS TO ESTABLISH A SOUND FOUNDATION FOR the development of day trading skills and techniques. Before readers can progress to more advanced topics of day trading, they should learn and master the basic concepts and tools.

➤ Although many readers are familiar with Level I screen information, in section II we explain in detail the Level I data, in particular the concepts of the highest BID and lowest ASK prices, the spread between the BID and ASK prices, the BID to ASK ratio, intra-day trading volume, intra-day high and low prices, close and open prices, and change for the day.

➤ In addition, we define and explain the activities of the NASDAQ market makers and describe basic Level II screen information, such as the inside BID and ASK and the outside BID and ASK markets, and the depth of the inside market.

➤ Then, we cover how market forces of supply and demand generate the equilibrium price for a stock and how the Level II screen displays that information, with price increases and decreases.

➤ In section II, we also cover monitoring and alert tools used by day traders, such as the time and sales window, market ticker, top advances and declines window, and 52-week or daily high and low.

➤ Finally, ten basic price increase and decrease signals are summarized and presented.

5

NASDAQ Market Makers and Level I Screen

The market makers are NASD-sanctioned securities brokers and dealers. They have two distinct personalities: they are NASD brokers who transact securities business for the accounts of others, and at the same time, they are NASD dealers who engage in the securities business for their own proprietary accounts. It is important that day traders understand this dual nature of the market making business.

In essence, there are two ways that market makers can make money. The first way is to *earn the spread*. The market maker would buy the stock at the lower BID price and sell it at the higher ASK price. In the example in Figure 5.1, the best BID and ASK prices for DELL are $50\frac{1}{2}$ and $50\frac{9}{16}$, respectively. Market makers are buying low ($50.50) and selling high ($50.56) and earning a spread of $\frac{1}{16}$ or 6.25 cents. In this case, market makers are acting as agents or brokers for the public who desire to buy or sell that particular stock. Market makers will buy and sell the stock from their own portfolio (inventory).

If one market maker buys from the public 1,000 shares at the BID price and sells the same 1,000 shares a few seconds later at the ASK price, then the $\frac{1}{16}$ spread translates into $62.50 profit. If the spread remains on the average 6.25 cents during the day, and if DELL *average daily volume* over the 52 weeks remains at 41.5 million shares, then market makers as a group would earn $2.5 million on that stock alone. NASDAQ trading average daily volume over the 52 weeks is approximately 1 billion shares (ranging from 775 million to 1.2 billion shares).

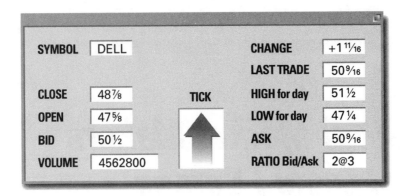

Figure 5.1 *Level I Screen Information*

Collectively, market makers would earn $66 million in one day. Clearly, market making is big business.

The second way that market makers make their money is to trade a stock for their own proprietary accounts. In this case, market makers act as dealers for that stock. The only way to make money trading is to buy low and sell high. All market makers want to accumulate stock shares when the price is low, and then sell the stock from their inventory when the price is higher. When the market maker anticipates that a price will go up, the market maker would buy that stock. When the market maker anticipates that a price will decline, then he or she would sell that stock. In other words, the market maker would start depleting the inventory. The Level II screen tells which market makers are buying and selling that stock.

Not all market makers are created equally. There are approximately 500 market makers providing *liquidity* or market for the more than 5,000 stocks actively traded in the NASDAQ National Market System. Each market maker has a four-letter identification code. Some market makers are large established Wall Street institutional firms. Those firms have access to enormous trading capital, and they employ experienced professional traders whose business is to make money for the firm. Those firms are 800-pound gorillas, such as Goldman Sachs & Co. (GSCO), Morgan Stanley (MSCO), Lehman Brothers (LEHM), and Salomon Brothers (SALB).

The other important market makers are the large full-service retail brokerage firms such as Merrill Lynch & Co. (MLCO), Dean Witter Reynolds (DEAN), Paine Webber (PAIN), Prudential (PRUD), and Smith Barney Shearson (SBSH). In addition, Wall Street has a few wholesalers that do not transact any retail business but represent the securities discount retailers (for example, Charles Schwab) and Internet brokers (such as E*Trade). Those firms are Mayer and Schweitzer (MASH), Hertzog Hein & Geduld (HRZG), Knight (NITE), and Sherwood (SHWD).

These large market makers are capable of stopping the price momentum at any time. Since they have large capital bases, they have huge inventories of stocks, and they can borrow stock from other NASD brokers and dealers. Those market makers are capable of "sitting" at the top of the BID and ASK quote and continuously buying or selling that particular stock at that price level. Within the industry these key market makers are often referred to as the "Ax." It is important to know who the "Ax" is for a particular stock. A list of the fifty most influential market makers is included in appendix 3.

Level I Screen

Most stock market participants are familiar with Level I stock quotes. NASDAQ provides different levels of stock information to its data subscribers. Internet-based brokers usually provide Level I quotes to their customers. A Level I quote displays current "Inside Market" or the best BID and ASK prices for the stock.

The Level I screen is a dynamic window; and during market hours the best BID and ASK information is continuously updated in real time. However, if the trader is using an Internet-based broker, Level I quotes could be delayed several seconds or several minutes. Day trading firms subscribe to real-time data feed service providers who supply real-time stock quotes via satellite dish or dedicated T1 communication lines. However, many Level I stock quotes providers use Java Scripts programs to "refresh" the screen every few seconds, and thus do not display true tick-by-tick data feed. This can sometime lead to inaccurate stock quotes, especially when the stock market is moving quickly.

It is difficult to ascertain a trend based on Level I information alone. Nevertheless, much information can be ascertained from the Level I screen. It is a logical place to begin illustrating the topic of day trading tools.

BID and ASK

The Level I quote features the stock symbol. In Figure 5.1, DELL is used for illustration purposes. A Level I quote states that at that point of time the best BID price for DELL is $50\frac{1}{2}$ or $50.50, and the best ASK price is $50\frac{9}{16}$ or $50.56. This means that the trader or investor can purchase DELL stock from the market makers at $50\frac{9}{16}$ ($50.56) and sell it to them for a lower price of $50\frac{1}{2}$ ($50.50). Therefore, traders and investors are buying stocks at the ASK price and selling them at the BID price. The best ASK price is often called the "inside offer."

On the other hand, market makers who are providing a market (liquidity) for DELL are buying DELL from traders and investors at the BID price of $50\frac{1}{2}$ ($50.50) and selling DELL to traders and investors at the ASK price of $50\frac{9}{16}$ ($50.56). Anyone can see that there is a spread or difference between the BID and ASK prices. Market makers are buying low ($50.50) and selling high ($50.56) and earning the spread. In this case the spread is $\frac{1}{16}$ or 6.25 cents.

Spread

The spread can vary. For well-traded stocks with large daily trading volume, such as DELL, the spread is small—$\frac{1}{16}$ or 6.25 cents—or even smaller at $\frac{1}{32}$ (3.12 cents). Sometimes during trading, the spread can widen to $\frac{1}{8}$ or 12.5 cents or even more. Market forces (that is, supply and demand for DELL) will determine the size of the spread. For thinly (or infrequently) traded stocks the spread is larger.

When the trader purchases stock at the ASK price, he or she is already in the hole (out of money) by $\frac{1}{16}$. The day trader could immediately turn around and sell the stock at the inside BID price and thus lose the spread. If the trader is trading in increments of 1,000 shares, the trader is starting with $62.50 in the hole. DELL will have to go up $\frac{1}{16}$ point just to break even. In other words, both the BID and ASK price for DELL will have to move up $\frac{1}{16}$ point, so the BID price becomes $50\frac{9}{16}$. *Cutting the spread* becomes an important task for the trader. It would be ideal if the trader can purchase DELL at the BID price ($50.50) rather than purchasing at the ASK price. Cutting the spread can be done by trading on the ECNs.

BID to ASK Ratio

The Level I screen also states how many market makers are buying DELL and how many market makers are selling DELL at this point of time. In other words, the Level I screen states how many market makers are on the BID and ASK sides. In Figure 5.1, the ratio of BID to ASK is 2 @ 3 (see lower right corner of the Level I screen). It means that there are two buyers and three sellers. This ratio can be expressed in terms of BID and ASK volume as well. The bullish sign would be a BID to ASK ratio of 5 @ 1, which means that five market makers are buying and only one market maker is selling.

The ratio does not really show the depth of the market because it does not show how many shares each market maker is selling or buying. The ratio is simply stating that there are more buyers than sellers. If the single selling market maker is a large established Wall Street firm that is selling a large block of shares for an institutional investor, then a 5 @ 1 ratio may lead a new trader to think that the market is moving up, when in fact, one seller can "freeze" the ASK price.

Volume

In Figure 5.1, the trading *volume* at that point of time for DELL is over 4.5 million shares. This snapshot is most likely "taken" early in the morning of the trading day. DELL is a well-traded stock. The trader must trade liquid stocks; daily trading volume must be at least 500,000 shares. Liquidity is crucial in order to assure that there will be a seller to close the long position at the end of the trading. It is very risky to accumulate a large share block of thinly traded stocks. Imagine holding 10,000 shares of a stock trading in the $10 range with the daily volume of 100,000 shares. If the price starts to decline, it would be difficult to unload (sell) 10% of the daily volume quickly without driving the price further down.

High and Low

The Level I screen also displays the *high and low prices for the day*. In this example, the high ASK price for the day was $51\frac{1}{2}$, and the low ASK price for the day was $47\frac{1}{4}$. That means that DELL had substantial intra-day price volatility. In this example, it is $4\frac{1}{4}$ points. This range is good. It provides ample opportunity to day trade this stock. Day traders should focus on and trade stocks that have at least 2 points intra-day price movement.

A quick way to ascertain intra-day price volatility is to look for the difference between the high and low prices for the day. If that price differential is small, then the stock is not moving in either direction. That differential between the daily high and low prices is the proxy measure for the intra-day price volatility. There is no point to day trade a stock that is not moving.

To be a successful day trader, the trader needs to trade stocks that are more volatile relative to the overall Standard & Poor's 500 (S&P 500) price index average. The day trader should search for the stocks that have high daily trading volume and relatively high *Beta* value. The Beta coefficient for a particular stock will provide a measure of the market *volatility* associated with that security. The Beta coefficient is a common part of fundamental analysis and can be found in many financial search engines on the Internet (*Yahoo.com, dailystocks.com*). Beta is a statistical measure of the price volatility of a particular stock in relation to the entire stock market's (that is, the S&P 500's) volatility. The S&P 500 index is a composite price index consisting of 500 of the largest companies in the United States.

If the stock has a Beta value greater than 1, then that stock is more volatile relative to the entire stock market. A Beta of 2 would mean that stock went up (or down) on average 10% while the overall market went up (or down) 5% during a certain period of time (for example, 52 weeks). Appendix 2 of this book contains a list of the 100 NASDAQ and NYSE stocks with the highest Beta values (Beta greater than 1.5) and an average daily trading volume greater than 500,000 shares. My recommendation to day traders is to trade stocks that are volatile and liquid.

Close and Open

Another piece of information that is provided on the Level I screen is the *close* price from yesterday and the *open* price for today. In Figure 5.1,

DELL closed yesterday on $48\frac{7}{8}$ and opened today at $47\frac{5}{8}$, or with the gap down $1\frac{1}{4}$ point. There are many reasons why stocks open with the gap up or down (mostly down). For example, companies will wait for the market to close before announcing any news (for example, earnings or dividends). Institutional investors continue to trade after the market hours through Instinet. Market forces (and thus prices) do not stop at the close of the market.

In the example shown in Figure 5.1, DELL opened with a large gap down. If the day trader had 1,000 shares of DELL in the overnight long position, then the trader would start that day with a $1,250 loss. This $\frac{1}{4}$ gap down is seemingly a large gap for a $50 stock. But, the gap could be a lot worse. Something could happen overnight in Asia (or anywhere else in the world) seemingly unrelated to DELL that could cause DELL to open several points lower. Then the loss would be several thousand dollars. The experienced day trader will seldom if ever carry an overnight position; that is simply a good risk management tool. Seeing the price differential between close and open prices on Level I screens has reinforced my belief that day traders should go "flat" at the end of the trading day.

Change

Change on the day is the last information that is available on the Level I screen. In this example DELL went up $1\frac{11}{16}$ from yesterday's closing price. Most trading software packages also have a symbol for the last price tick. In this case the symbol for the last price change is the arrow. And it is an up-tick. Other software packages have "+" or "–" symbols. Some software packages use green or red color-coded BID and ASK prices. A red BID would mean that the last BID was a down-tick. The last tick symbol is a very useful visual tool.

Scanning the Level I Information

A quick glance of the Level I screen at market close would reveal whether that stock is a good day trading stock or not. Figure 5.2 depicts a recent snapshot of Objective System Integrators, Inc. (OSSI).

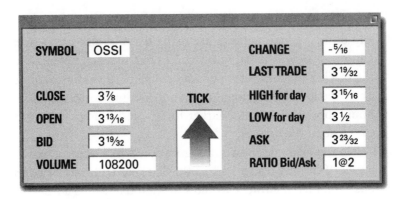

Figure 5.2 *Example of a Poor Day Trading Stock*

OSSI is not a good day trading stock. BID and ASK prices are $3^{19}/_{32}$ and $3^{23}/_{32}$. The spread is small, which is good. However, the trading volume for that day is 100,772 shares. Furthermore, OSSI average daily trading volume for the last 52 weeks is only 108,200 shares. Day traders should trade stocks that have at least 500,000 shares daily trading volume, so OSSI does not have the liquidity to be suitable for day trading. Also, OSSI does not have daily price volatility. The day's price range is $3^{1}/_{2}$ and $3^{15}/_{16}$, which relates to a price changes of 43 cents. This 43 cents might be a high relative price change (11%) for an inexpensive stock such as OSSI, but 43 cents is a small absolute change. It would be difficult to make money day trading OSSI stock if the maximum profit potential is only 43 cents per share.

6

NASDAQ Level II Information

In the past, NASDAQ Level II information was available only to NASD members. Recently in the late 1990s Level II screen information has become available to the general public through several data feed providers. The Level II screen is one of the most effective trading tools for the day trader. Figure 6.1 displays Level I and II screens together.

Inside and Outside Markets

In addition to posting the inside market's BID and ASK price quotations for all market makers, the Level II screen posts in real time BID and ASK prices that are outside the market. *Inside market* is the best (the highest) BID price at which the stock can be sold in the market and the best (the lowest) ASK price at which the stock can be bought in the market at a given point of time. In the hypothetical example in Figure 6.1, DELL has five market makers on the inside BID and ASK prices; thus the current ratio of BID to ASK is 5 @ 5 as displayed by the Level I screen. But this time we see also which market makers are buying and selling, as well as the *share size* of their activities.

In this example, J. P. Morgan Securities (JPMS), Lehman Brothers (LEHM), Mayer & Schweitzer (MASH), Montgomery Securities (MONT), and Herzog Heine Geduld (HRZG) are selling 1,000 shares of DELL each at $50\frac{9}{16}$. In other words, the public (traders and investors) are buying DELL at the quoted ASK price of $50\frac{9}{16}$ (or $50.56 per share)

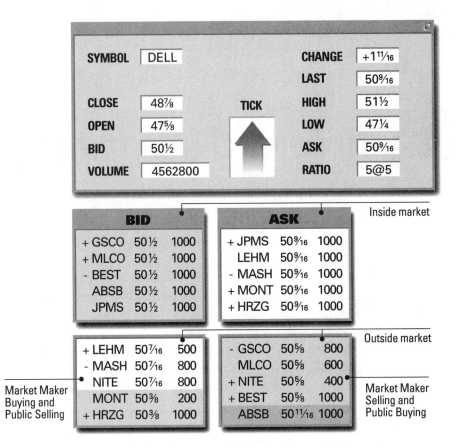

Figure 6.1 *Level I and II Screen Information*

from the five market makers. $50\%_{16}$ is clearly the lowest buying price. A trader could buy 1,000 shares of DELL from Merrill Lynch & Co. (MLCO) at $50\frac{5}{8}$ (or $50.62 per share), but that clearly is more expensive than the best ASK price of $50\%_{16}$. Subsequently, MLCO is away from the market or in the *outside market*. In short, MLCO is not a seller of the stock.

Conversely, Goldman Sachs & Co. (GSCO), Merrill Lynch & Co. (MLCO), Bear Stearns & Co. (BEST), Alex Brown & Sons (ABSB) and J. P. Morgan Securities (JPMS) are buying 1,000 shares of DELL each at $50\frac{1}{2}$. On the other hand, public traders and investors are selling DELL at the quoted BID price of $50\frac{1}{2}$ (or $50.50 per share) from the five market makers. $50\frac{1}{2}$ is clearly the highest selling price. The trader could sell 1,000 shares of DELL to Montgomery Securities (MONT) at $50\frac{3}{8}$ (or $50.37 per share), but that is clearly less than the best BID price of $50\frac{1}{2}$ ($50.50). MONT is away from the market or in the outside market. In essence, MONT is not a buyer of the stock.

Each price level on the Level II screen is a different color for easy reference. In this example, there are five market makers on the BID side who are posting the best selling price, and they are all the same color. On the other hand, there are five market makers on the ASK side who are posting the best buying price; they are also the same color. Both BID and ASK sides have four distinct columns. The first column has "+" and "–" signs that indicate whether the market maker has increased or decreased the BID or ASK price. If there are no "+" or "–" signs, then the market maker has refreshed the same BID or ASK price. The second column is the market maker's four-letter identification code. The third column is the market makers' BID and ASK price. And the last column is the number (size) of shares offered by the market makers at that BID or ASK price.

Figure 6.1 shows only ten market makers represented on the Level II screen. In reality, DELL has many more market makers on both the BID and ASK sides. For a variety of reasons, some market makers may not be active in market making activities, but they are required to post both BID and ASK prices. These market makers would deliberately back away from the best BID and ASK prices. They would post their BID and ASK prices at the bottom of the level II screen.

The Level II screen has two distinct BID and ASK sides. Market makers are required to post simultaneously on both sides. The position of the market maker on the BID and ASK side reveals whether that market maker is a buyer or seller. The market maker's relative position would reveal whether he or she is bullish or bearish on that stock. Figure 6.2 illustrates this point.

Figure 6.2 reveals that MLCO and GSCO are buyers. They are at the top of the BID side, buying the stock at $50\frac{1}{2}$. MLCO and GSCO have joined the BID, and they are in the inside market. Since both MLCO and GSCO are required to be on both sides of the market, GSCO and MLCO have posted a relatively high ASK price of $50\frac{7}{8}$, which is not a competitive price. These two market makers are buyers and not sellers. One could argue that GSCO and MLCO are bullish on that particular stock.

Figure 6.2 *GSCO and MLCO Are Buyers*

GSCO and MLCO are buying stock at the low price $(50\frac{1}{2})$, and antici-pating that stock will go up in value, so they could sell it at the higher price $(50\frac{7}{8})$.

Why would a rational investor buy the stock from GSCO and MLCO at $50\frac{7}{8}$ when the lowest posted ASK price is $50\frac{9}{16}$ from JPMS and LEHM? If the investor does not have access to real-time data feed and Level II screen information, the investor would not know what the best ASK price (the lowest buying price) is. For example, an investor who has an account with Merrill Lynch & Co. (MLCO) and who is buy-ing that stock through Merrill Lynch would most likely pay $50\frac{7}{8}$ (or $50.87 per share). However, day traders monitoring the stock would know the difference. One of the advantages of day trading your own account is the ability to view live Level II screen information, so day traders know that they are getting the best price.

Conversely, Figure 6.3 reveals that MLCO and GSCO are sellers. They are at the top of the ASK side, selling the stock at $50\frac{9}{16}$. They have joined the ASK, and they are in the inside market. Since MLCO and GSCO are required to be on both sides of the market simultaneously, GSCO and MLCO have posted relatively low BID price of $50\frac{1}{4}$, which is not a competitive price. GSCO and MLCO are sellers and not buyers. Figure 6.3 reveals that GSCO and MLCO are bearish on that particular

Figure 6.3 *MLCO and GSCO as Sellers*

stock. They are trying to sell that stock and deplete the inventory, anticipating that the stock will go down in value in the future: GSCO and MLCO are selling stock at the best ASK price (50⅑₁₆), and anticipating that the stock will drop in value, so they can buy it at the lower price (50¼).

Again, why would a rational investor sell the stock to GSCO and MLCO at 50¼ when the highest posted BID price is 50½ from WEAT and COWN? The investor who has an account with Merrill Lynch & Co. (MLCO) and who is selling that stock would most likely receive 50¼ (or $50.25 per share), MLCO's buying price. How would the investor know what the best BID price (the highest selling price) is if he or she does not have access to real-time data feed and Level II screen information? A day trader, because of his or her access to live Level II screen information, would know that they are getting the best price.

Stock with No Price Depth

Thinly traded NASDAQ stocks have only a few market makers who provide liquidity. Most likely, if a stock is thinly traded, there would be only a few or one market maker at any price level. Figure 6.4 depicts a stock with no price depth. This would be a stock to avoid trading.

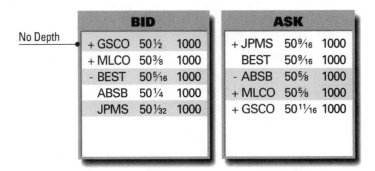

Figure 6.4 *Stock with No Price Depth*

In this example, there are only five market makers providing liquidity for the stock. The trader has an opportunity to buy the stock at $50\frac{9}{16}$ from JPMS and BEST. The spread between BID and ASK is $\frac{1}{16}$, which would mean that price would have to go up $\frac{1}{16}$ just to break even. However, there is only one market maker who is selling the stock at $50\frac{1}{2}$. If GSCO leaves the inside BID, price would drop to $50\frac{3}{8}$. Then the spread between BID and ASK would be $\frac{3}{16}$, which would mean that price would have to go up $\frac{3}{16}$ just to break even. If the market turns quickly in the opposite (lower) direction, MLCO could leave the BID of $50\frac{3}{8}$, and the selling price would become $50\frac{5}{16}$.

It is very risky to trade thinly traded stocks with little depth. A stock should have several market makers on both sides of BID and ASK at one price level. Even actively traded stocks with many market makers could during the trading day end up in the situation depicted in Figure 6.4. Figure 6.4 basically tells the trader that there is very little room for mistakes: the day trader may not be able to liquidate a position at the desired price level when there is very little liquidity. If only one market maker leaves the inside market, the price of the stock will change.

7

Stock Prices

THE FOCUS OF ANALYSIS FOR ANY DAY TRADER IS THE STOCK'S *PRICE*. THE price is the most important and sometimes the only variable. Day traders spend hours glued to their computer screens monitoring short-term stock price fluctuations.

And what determines the price of the stock? Economists would reply in unison, which is a rare event, with two words: supply and demand. The interaction between supply and demand determines the price of anything: goods, services, commodities, and securities. Demand and supply are like a pair of scissors. To cut anything (that is, to establish a price) one needs both halves of the pair of scissors (demand *and* supply).

Supply and Demand

Anyone can be an economist. The two most important words you must learn to say are *supply* and *demand*. In this chapter, we link Level II information with the market forces of supply and demand. The best way to explain the stock pricing mechanism is to define demand and supply and to graphically present the interaction between them. The following information may be tough going at first, but will make more sense after the second reading—so please bear with me.

Demand is a schedule or a line showing the quantity of a good, commodity, or a stock that buyers would purchase at each price level, with other things being equal *(ceteris paribus)*. *Ceteris paribus* is Latin for "everything else being constant." Figure 7.1 displays a negatively sloped demand line. If everything else remains the same, the demand line states that at the high price few people would be willing to purchase that stock, while at the lower price more people would be willing to purchase that stock.

Supply is a schedule or a line showing the quantity of a good, commodity, or a stock that sellers would sell at each price level, with other things being equal. Figure 7.1 displays a positively sloped supply line. If everything else remains the same, the supply line states that at the high price many sellers would be willing to sell that stock, while at the lower price few sellers would be willing to sell that stock.

Equilibrium Price

If the stock price is high at P2 (see Figure 7.1), then Q2 is the quantity of the stock that sellers are willing to sell, and Q3 is the quantity of the stock that buyers are willing to buy at that price. Since the quantity of the stock supplied exceeds the quantity demanded, we have a condition of "surplus." With surplus, there is a natural pressure for prices to drop. As long as there is a surplus, prices will continue to decline.

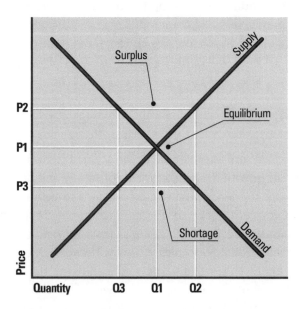

Figure 7.1 *Supply, Demand, and the Equilibrium Price*

Conversely, at a lower price level such as the P3, Q3 is the quantity of the stock that sellers are willing to sell, and Q2 is the quantity of the stock that buyers are willing to purchase. Since the quantity of the stock demanded (Q2) exceeds the quantity supplied (Q3), we have a condition of "shortage." With shortage, there is a natural pressure for prices to increase. As long there is a shortage, prices will continue to increase.

At price level P1, the quantity of the stock that sellers are willing to sell will be equal to the quantity of the stock that buyers are willing to purchase, and we have a condition of *equilibrium*. Equilibrium is a state of balance, so there is no pressure or tendency for the price to change. At the equilibrium price P1, there is no surplus or shortage. The price will remain stable at level P1 as long as there is no change (shift) in demand or supply. As long as "everything else remains equal," the equilibrium price will remain at P1.

The next step is to link the supply and demand market forces to the NASDAQ Level II screen information. Figure 7.2 displays this information. There are five market makers on the BID and ASK side: there are five buyers and five sellers for that stock. The BID side represents the demand schedule, while the ASK side represents the supply schedule for this particular stack at this point in time. The equilibrium price at this time is $50\frac{1}{2}$ and $50\frac{9}{16}$.

Ceteris paribus is the crucial assumption here. Nothing in life remains constant, particularly in the stock market. Thus demand and

Figure 7.2 *Level II and Supply and Demand Forces*

supply lines are always shifting or moving. Whenever something happens in the market (either good news or bad news), it will change stock market participants' perceptions about that stock. If the news is good, more buyers will enter the market and the demand will increase; the demand schedule will shift to the right. If the news is bad, buyers will exit the market and demand for the stock will decrease. In this situation, the demand schedule will shift to the left.

Conversely, if news is good, then more stock sellers will exit the market and the stock supply will decrease; the supply schedule will shift to the left. If the news is bad, then stock sellers will enter the market and the supply will increase; the supply schedule will shift to the right. Since the world of the stock market is dynamic, demand and supply are always moving; there is always an increase or a decrease in demand or supply.

Price Increase

Let us start with the good news. Good news would result in increased demand for the stock from additional investors or traders. Also, good news would restrain the stockholders from selling the stock (because they would anticipate getting a higher price in the future), and thus there would be fewer sellers on the market. Increased demand and reduced supply would result in a new and higher equilibrium price. Figure 7.3 depicts that interplay between reduced supply and increased demand.

Increased demand is depicted with the demand line being shifted to the right. Reduced supply is illustrated with the supply line being shifted to the left. The interplay between the new increased demand and the reduced supply will result in a new equilibrium point (E2) and a new equilibrium price (P2). The level of the price increase (from P1 to P2) and the quantity of the stock exchanged would depend on the magnitude of the shift in the supply and demand. In this example, the volume of stock trading remained the same.

Level II Screen and Price Increase

This basic economics concept of reduced supply and increased demand for a stock can be illustrated on the Level II screen as well. The Level II

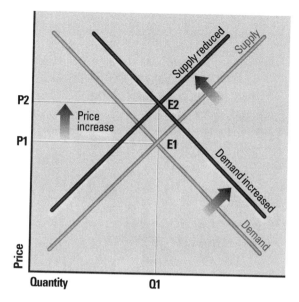

Figure 7.3 *Price Increase*

screen is updated dynamically (continuously). Market makers continuously enter different BID and ASK prices, or join or leave the inside BID and ASK prices. Consequently, Level II screen information is always moving. This is particularly true for fast-trading technology stocks.

It is difficult to link supply and demand market forces to the fast-moving Level II screen. Figure 7.4 attempts to provide that link. The starting point is Figure 7.2. In that example, there were five market makers on the BID and ASK sides: there were five buyers and five sellers for that stock who were bidding and offering the same amount of shares on each side. The equilibrium price at this point in time was $50\frac{1}{2}$ and $50\frac{9}{16}$. Again, suppose that the stock had good news, and there had been a reduction in supply and an increase in demand for that stock. Imagine that we have frozen the Level II screen at that moment. Figure 7.4 will depict that change.

This time there are only two market makers selling the stock on the ASK side; this would translate to reduction in supply of that stock. The color-coded inside ASK side has shrunk from five to two market makers. This is represented in Figure 7.4 by the up arrow on the ASK side, which

Figure 7.4   *Level II Screen Information with Increased Demand and Reduced Supply*

shows that the color of the inside ASK is shrinking and moving up. On the other hand, there are eight market makers buying the stock on the BID side. The color-coded inside BID side has been enlarged from five to eight market makers. This is represented in Figure 7.4 by the down arrow on the BID side, which shows that the color of the inside BID is increasing and moving down.

The best BID and ASK prices are still $50\frac{1}{2}$ and $50\frac{9}{16}$. But this price will not last very long. There is a distinct possibility that the two remaining market makers (JPMS and LEHM) will eventually leave the ASK side. At that time the ASK price will increase to $50\frac{5}{8}$.

On the other hand, there are eight market makers competing to buy that stock. There is a distinct possibility that one of the eight market makers will eventually increase the BID price. At that time the BID price will increase to $50\frac{9}{16}$. This development is depicted in Figure 7.5 by the following "freeze frame" picture of the Level II screen.

The two market makers (JPMS and LEHM) increased their ASK price from $50\frac{9}{16}$ to $50\frac{5}{8}$, and the color representing $50\frac{9}{16}$ "moved up" and disappeared from the ASK side. On the other hand, two market makers (MLCO and GSCO) increased their BID price from $50\frac{1}{2}$ to $50\frac{9}{16}$. The

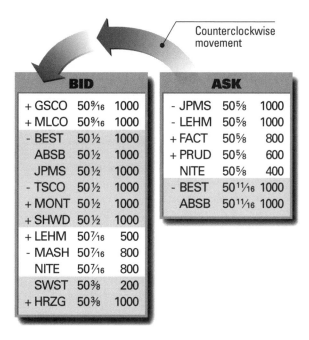

Figure 7.5 *Level II and Price Increase*

color-coded price of $50\frac{9}{16}$ would move in counterclockwise motion from the ASK side to the BID side. The dynamic Level II screen shows this counterclockwise motion whenever there is a price increase.

If the price increase momentum continued, there would be more market makers entering the BID side (that is, buying the stock). At the same time there would be more market makers leaving the ASK side. Figure 7.6 depicts that continued price increase movement. The number of market makers on the inside ASK price has been reduced from five to two. The color-coded price block of $50\frac{5}{8}$ on the inside ASK price has shrunk and "moved up." On the other side, the number of market makers on the inside BID price has increased from two to five. There are now more market makers on the inside BID price. The color-coded price block of $50\frac{9}{16}$ on the inside BID has been enlarged and "moved down." The counterclockwise motion on the Level II screen would thus continue. In short, the color-coded block of the inside BID would increase in size, and conversely the color-coded block of the inside ASK would decrease in size.

Figure 7.6   *Level II Screen and Continued Price Increase Momentum*

For the time being, the best BID and ASK sides have remained the same at $50\frac{9}{16}$ and $50\frac{5}{8}$. The day trader who has access to a live Level II screen would receive a visual confirmation that price increase momentum is there. The day trader in essence has a preview of the future. If the price momentum continues in this counterclockwise motion on the Level II screen, the trader could expect new and higher BID and ASK prices of $50\frac{5}{8}$ and $50\frac{11}{16}$. The counterclockwise motion on the Level II screen would then constitute a BUY signal.

Day traders can observe when the counterclockwise motion on the Level II screen slows down and stops. This would mean that the price increase momentum is losing its steam. (Other investors and traders who do not have the Level II screen could not preview this slowdown in the price increase momentum.) The inflow of money is slowing down; the demand for the stock has ceased to increase. There are no new market makers entering the inside BID, and the stock supply has stabilized and ceased to decrease. The market makers are not leaving the inside ASK price. All of this would tell the day trader that the momentum is shifting. Now would be a good time to exit the long position, or sell the stock. The slowdown in the momentum is a signal to SELL the stock.

It is always easier to sell the stock on the up-tick. When the price momentum changes its direction, the price can quickly drop. If the day trader waits too long, then he or she would be selling on the weakness of the stock. It is always easier to obtain a better price and quicker execution if the day trader sells on the price strength (when prices are still going up).

Price Decrease

Generally, what goes up must come down, and stock prices do not go up continuously. Eventually all price increases will end, and prices will start to decline. There are many reasons that stock prices decline. Some are rational economic reasons, and some involve irrational human behavior. Obviously, bad news can drive stock prices down. So, let us have the bad news.

Bad news results in an increased (higher) supply of the stock from existing shareholders. Shareholders are now willing to "dump" the stock at the current price (anticipating a lower price in the future), and there are more sellers on the market. Also, bad news would restrain investors from buying the stock at the current price (they would anticipate a lower price in the future as well), and there would be fewer buyers on the market.

Increased supply and reduced demand have resulted in a new and lower equilibrium price. Figure 7.7 depicts that interplay between reduced demand and increased supply. The level of the price decrease (from P1 to P3) and the quantity of the stock exchanged would depend on the magnitude of the shift in the supply and demand. Again, in this example the volume of the stock trading remained the same.

This basic economics concept of reduced demand and increased supply for the stock can be illustrated on the Level II screen as well. Figure 7.8 attempts to provide that link. The starting point is again Figure 7.2. In that example, there were five market makers on the BID and ASK side; there were five buyers and five sellers for that stock. The equilibrium price at this point of time was $50\frac{1}{2}$ and $50\frac{9}{16}$.

Suppose that stock had bad news, and there has been a reduction in demand and an increase in supply for that stock. Imagine that we have frozen the Level II screen for that moment. Figure 7.8 depicts that change.

Now there are only two market makers buying the stock on the BID side; this would translate into a reduction in demand for that stock. The

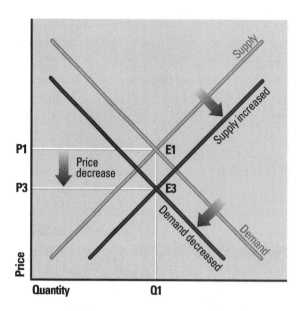

Figure 7.7 *Price Decrease*

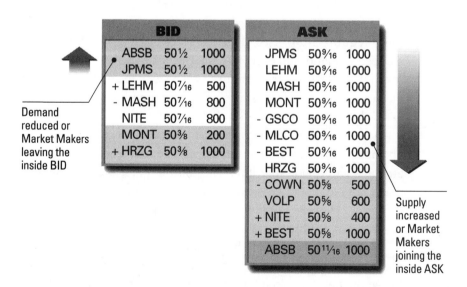

Figure 7.8 *Level II Screen Information with Increased Supply and Reduced Demand*

color-coded inside BID side has shrunk from five to two market makers. This is represented in Figure 7.8 by the up arrow on the BID side, which shows that the color-coded inside BID is shrinking and moving up. On the other hand, there are eight market makers selling the stock on the ASK side. The color-coded inside ASK side has been enlarged from five to eight market makers. This is represented in Figure 7.8 by the down arrow on the ASK side, which indicates that the color-coded inside ASK is increasing and moving down.

The best BID and ASK prices are still $50\frac{1}{2}$ and $50\frac{9}{16}$. But this price will not last very long. There is a distinct possibility that the two remaining market makers (ABSB and JPMS) will eventually leave the inside BID side. At that time the BID price will decrease to $50\frac{7}{16}$.

On the other hand, there are eight market makers competing to sell that stock. Now, there is a distinct possibility that one or more of the eight market makers (or new market makers who are not currently on the inside ASK) will eventually decrease the ASK price. At that time the ASK price will decrease to $50\frac{1}{2}$. This development is depicted in Figure 7.9 by the following "freeze frame" picture of the Level II screen.

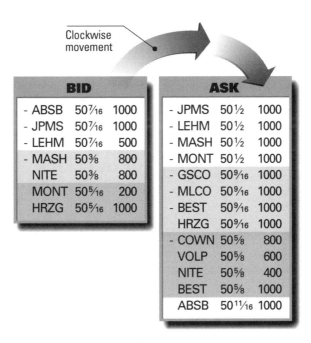

Figure 7.9 *Level II and Price Decrease*

The two market makers (JPMS and LEHM) decreased their BID price from $50\frac{1}{2}$ to $50\frac{7}{16}$. One market maker (LEHM) refreshed the same price of $50\frac{7}{16}$ and thus LEHM joined the inside BID. The color representing $50\frac{1}{2}$ "moved up" and disappeared from the BID side. On the other hand, four market makers (JPMS, LEHM, MASH, and MONT) lowered their ASK price from $50\frac{9}{16}$ to $50\frac{1}{2}$. This is shown as a new color-coded price and will show up on the ASK side. In essence, the color-coded price of $50\frac{1}{2}$ would move in clockwise motion from the BID side to the ASK side. The dynamic Level II screen shows this clockwise motion whenever there is a price decrease.

This price decrease momentum would continue, and more market makers would enter the ASK side (that is, sell the stock) and at the same time leave the BID side. Figure 7.10 depicts that continued price decrease movement. The number of market makers on the inside BID price has been reduced from three to one. However, there are now altogether six market makers on the inside ASK price, and the the color-coded price block of $50\frac{1}{2}$ has "moved down." The clockwise motion on the Level II screen continues. The inside BID color-coded block would decrease in size, and conversely the inside ASK color-coded block would increase in size.

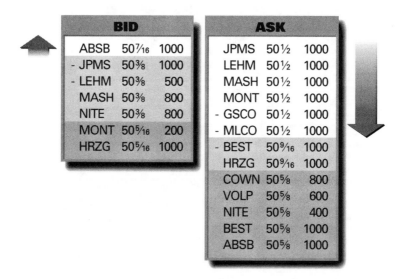

Figure 7.10 *Level II Screen and Continued Price Decrease Momentum*

For the time being, the best BID and ASK side has remained the same at $50\frac{7}{16}$ and $50\frac{1}{2}$. The day trader who has access to a live Level II screen would receive a visual confirmation that the price decrease momentum is there. The day trader has something of a preview of the future, and could expect that the best BID and ASK prices will eventually decrease to $50\frac{3}{8}$ and $50\frac{7}{16}$. If the price decrease momentum continues in this clockwise motion on the Level II screen, the trader would receive a signal to short sell the stock.

Furthermore, day traders can observe when the clockwise motion on the Level II screen slows down and stops. This would mean that price decrease momentum is losing its steam. (Other investors and traders who do not have access to the Level II screen would not be able to "preview" this slowdown in the price decrease momentum.) The outflow of money is slowing down, and the stock supply has ceased to increase. There are no new market makers entering the inside ASK, and some market makers may be refreshing at a higher ASK. The demand for the stock has stabilized, and it is no longer decreasing. Market makers are not leaving the inside BID price; this tells the day trader that the momentum is shifting. Now would probably be a good time to exit the short position. In other words, buy the stock and close the short position.

8

Trading Alerts

Now that we have covered the most important day trading tool, the Level II screen, our attention will shift to other tools that provide trading alerts and signals. There are several trading software products that package trading alerts in different formats. In my opinion, in addition to the NASDAQ Level I and II screens, the three most important trading tools are the Time and Sales window, the Market Ticker, and the Top Advances and Declines window. Day traders use these tools as alerts, reminding them to take a closer view of a particular stock or as a signal that the price momentum is shifting.

Time and Sales Window

One of the most important trading tools is the time and sales window. This window is a standard feature of any trading software package and appears on the traders' computer screens. This tool shows tick by tick what is actually being traded. The Time and Sales window displays "prints" of the actual price and size of the buying and selling activities on a stock, to reveal whether the public is buying or selling the stock. In addition, it reveals the actual size (shares) and the respective prices of all buying and selling transactions. The day traders commonly call the Time and Sales information *prints*.

You cannot see that information on the NASDAQ Level II screen. The Time and Sales window complements the Level II information. It tells traders not only what the market makers are willing to do, but what is actually being executed right now in terms of price and size. Some traders need only a Level II screen with a Time and Sales window in order to trade proficiently.

Figure 8.1 displays the Time and Sales window. In this example, the inside ASK price is $50\%_{16}$, which represents the price at which the public is buying that stock. So all trades that were executed at the ASK price of $50\%_{16}$ represent stock purchases. If the day trader is considering taking a long position, it would be reassuring to see the public buying that stock as well. A preponderance of buying transactions in the Time and Sales window can be translated as a bullish signal.

One way that the stock would go up in value is for the public to continue to buy it. The day trader would like to observe in the Time and Sales window that trades are being executed at the ASK price ($50\%_{16}$). In addition, the day trader needs to pay close attention to the size of the purchase. It would be reassuring to see the public buying that stock in increments of 500 or 1,000 shares. Small lots of 100 or 200 shares do not really move the market.

Figure 8.2 represents a Time and Sales window with a preponderance of sales. A preponderance of selling transactions in the Time and Sales window can be interpreted as a bearish signal. In that example, the inside BID price is $50\frac{1}{2}$, which represents the price at which the public is selling the stock. All trades that were executed at $50\frac{1}{2}$ represent stock

Figure 8.1   *Time and Sales Window with Buying Trades*

Figure 8.2   *Time and Sales Window with Selling Trades*

sales. If the day trader is considering taking a short position (selling the stock first in anticipation of a price decline), it would be a positive sign to see the public selling that stock as well.

Continuous stock selling is one way that the stock would decline in value. In essence, the day trader, who is considering taking a short position, would like to see in the Time and Sales window that trades are being executed at the BID price. Again, the day trader needs to pay close attention to the size of the sales. It would be reassuring to see the public selling the stock in increments of 500 or 1,000 shares, since small lots of 100 shares do not push the price down.

For liquid or actively traded stocks such as DELL, INTC, or MSFT, buy and sell trades are continuously being executed; the executed trades are continuously running on the Time and Sales window. For instance, all trades displayed in the Time and Sales window in Figure 8.1 occurred that moment. However, less liquid stocks need to have a stamped time next to each trade, so that the trader can ascertain a momentum. The day trader should be extremely cautious about trading stocks that show little activity in the Time and Sales window. If the Time and Sales window does not show activity, there is no point in trading that stock.

In addition, the Time and Sales window might display prints of trading activities in which the executed price was between the BID and ASK prices. That indicates that market makers either purchased the stock from the public for a price higher than the posted BID price or sold the stock to the public for a price lower than the posted ASK price. Most likely, these trading transactions were completed through one of the Electronic Communications Networks (ECNs), such as SelectNet. Finally, some displayed prices in the Time and Sales window are simply not accurate at that point in time. They might be old prices that have been submitted late.

Market Ticker

The market ticker is another alert tool. It reports on inside BID and ASK quote changes for any stock. It can be set up to track price changes for the entire universe of NASDAQ or NYSE stocks, or it can be customized to follow only a select group of stocks. Market tickers are often used to track a group of commonly traded large volume volatile stocks and to spot the price momentum. The day trader can individually select particular stocks to be tracked.

For example, the day trader might have a list of ten or twenty stocks that meet his or her trading criteria. The trader would enter the stock symbols of that list into his or her personal ticker. From that point on, the ticker would highlight all changes in the inside BID and ASK prices for those stocks. In the event that the day trader does not have such a personalized list of stocks, the ticker can be programmed to track a universe of all NASDAQ or NYSE stocks that meet certain trading criteria. For example, a trading criteria could be "stocks greater than $20 per share, with the spread less than $\frac{1}{8}$ and daily trading volume over 500,000 shares."

Ticker reports can have two distinctly different formats. The first option is to customize the ticker to report only the actual changes in the inside BID and ASK prices. This type of ticker format reports on change in the Level I price information. If the trader monitors only twenty stocks, this type of ticker would not move very fast. The ticker would report only when the actual price had changed. Therefore it is easy to follow.

Figure 8.3 represents such a Level I ticker. The ticker report is color-coded for easy reference. All stocks with the last up-tick or increase in price are reported in green. Stocks with the last down-tick or decrease in price are reported in red. Since Figure 8.3 here is not colored, all "green" up-ticks are displayed in black, and all "red" down-ticks are shaded. The most recent inside BID and ASK price change is reported at the top of the ticker page.

MARKET TICKER			
DELL	$50\,9/16$	$50\,5/8$	$+1\,1/8$
CIEN	$27\,1/4$	$27\,5/16$	$+1\,1/4$
SUNW	$101\,1/16$	$101\,1/8$	$-\,5/16$
AMZN	$110\,7/8$	$110\,15/16$	$+1\,1/16$
INTC	$130\,3/8$	$110\,7/16$	$+\,7/8$
INWO	$26\,15/16$	27	$-\,5/8$
DELL	$50\,1/2$	$50\,9/16$	$+1\,1/16$
CSCO	$99\,7/8$	$99\,15/16$	$+\,7/8$
WCOM	$83\,15/16$	$83\,7/8$	$+15/16$
YHOO	150	$150\,1/8$	$+2\,1/4$

Figure 8.3 *Market Ticker (Level I Information)*

Usually, the trader would position a ticker report to be prominently visible on the monitoring screen. The trader would notice that DELL was reported twice. Initially the best BID and ASK prices for DELL were $50\frac{1}{2}$ and $50\frac{9}{16}$. The ASK price was increased to $50\frac{9}{16}$ as indicated by the "green" (black) ASK color. The next DELL was also "green." On this occasion both the BID and ASK prices were increased.

This development would alert the trader that DELL is moving up; the ticker report would be used as a stock alert tool. At that time the trader would open the Level I and II screens for DELL, along with the Time and Sales window. Then the trader would open a chart of DELL that contains some technical charting analysis. The technical charting analysis window might be already on the monitoring screen and is loaded with a certain type of technical analysis (two exponential moving averages).

The second format for ticker reports is to customize the ticker to report all the changes within the inside BID and ASK side made by all market makers or ECNs. This is the Level II information limited to the inside BID and ASK quotes. Whenever one market maker enters into the inside BID and ASK quote, this action would be reported by the ticker. The best BID and ASK price has remained the same, but nevertheless, the entrance of that market maker into the inside BID and ASK quote would be shown to the day trader. Since commonly traded large volume volatile stocks have many market makers, this type of ticker reporting tends to be very active and busy. Sometimes this ticker report moves very fast and is difficult to follow.

MARKET TICKER				
DELL	[MONT]	50 9/16	50 5/8	+ 1 1/8
CIEN	[MLCO]	27 1/4	27 5/16	+ 1 1/4
DELL	[TUCK]	50 1/2	50 5/8	+ 1 1/8
AMZN	[GSCO]	110 7/8	110 15/16	+ 1 1/16
DELL	[NEED]	50 1/2	50 5/8	+ 1 1/8
DELL	[HRZG]	50 1/2	50 5/8	+ 1 1/8
DELL	[PRUD]	50 1/2	50 9/16	+ 1 1/16
CSCO	[NAWE]	99 7/8	99 15/16	+ 7/8
DELL	[RAGN]	50 1/2	50 9/16	+ 1 1/16
YHOO	[ABSA]	150	150 1/8	+ 2 1/4

Figure 8.4 *Market Ticker with Market Makers (Level II Information)*

Figure 8.4 displays this type of the market ticker format. The best BID and ASK price for DELL went up only once from $50\frac{1}{2}$ and $50\frac{9}{16}$ to $50\frac{9}{16}$ and $50\frac{5}{8}$. However, DELL showed up six times on that ticker. Consequently, it is not easy to monitor this type of the market ticker.

Top Advances and Declines

The Top Advances and Declines report is another commonly used alert tool. It shows the top ten stocks in terms of volume and largest dollar advance and decline for that point in time that day. Figure 8.5 displays such a report. The report is updated dynamically in real time, and it is always current. Most trading software packages provide this alert feature for the NASDAQ and NYSE stocks.

A day trader would most likely focus on the top ten advances and declines. The volume indicator does not really change much. For the NASDAQ stocks, it is always the same large capitalization technology companies such as Microsoft, Dell, Intel, and Cisco. However, the top ten advances and declines is a different story. Different stocks will populate this window each day. The Top Advances and Declines report is also biased toward the expensive and volatile technology stocks.

Since the report is ranked in absolute dollar terms, usually expensive stocks are listed first. Some expensive Internet stocks with high intra-day

NASDAQ VOLUME		NASDAQ TOP ADVANCES		NASDAQ TOP DECLINES	
MSFT	9,852,700	ASDV	+4 5/16	CPWR	-2 7/8
DELL	8,752,300	NETA	+4 1/4	PSQL	-2 5/8
INTC	5,653,000	SDTI	+3 7/8	MICA	-2 1/4
WCOM	4,823,500	AMZN	+3 3/8	DCTM	-2
CSCO	4,230,200	CIEN	+2 1/4	PLAT	-1 15/16
COMS	3,860,400	SEBL	+2 3/16	AMAT	-1 7/8
ORCL	3,243,100	HYSL	+2 1/8	SYBS	-1 5/8
AMZN	3,105,500	LGTO	+2 1/16	JDEC	-1 7/16
YHOO	3,025,820	CTXS	+2	BMCS	-1 5/16

Figure 8.5   *Top Advances and Declines Alert*

volatility are commonly on the top advances and declines list. For those expensive and volatile stocks, a $10 absolute price change is still a small relative percentage change. At one point in time, Amazon.com (AMZN) and Yahoo (YHOO) were trading at the range of $200 plus per share. A $10 price change would constitute a 5% relative price change, which was quite a common occurrence.

Some NASDAQ stocks that show up in the top advances and declines window are not good stocks to day trade. They tend to be small companies that have a low daily trading volume. It is difficult to get the buy and sell orders filled at the price the day trader wants. Also, they show up suddenly after some specific or particular bad (or good) news. The volatility is then short lived. The stock price would tend to stay at that level. Subsequently, the day traders can not really specialize and follow these stocks.

52-Week or Daily High and Low

The *52-Week* or *Daily High and Low* are two additional alert tools available to day traders. This alert window is available in most trading software packages for the NASDAQ and NYSE stocks. It shows the top ten stocks that hit the new intra-day or 52-week highs and lows prices. Some software packages have a price filter so the day trader can exclude stocks that are inexpensive. The report is updated dynamically in real time. It is always current for that particular point in time that day. Figure 8.6

NASDAQ 52-WEEK HIGH		NASDAQ 52-WEEK LOW	
AMGEN	78	JDEC	13 $^{15}/_{16}$
BMET	44½	BPAO	7 ¾
CHANF	10	ADSC	4
CPWM	28⅞	CDEN	6 $^{1}/_{32}$
CPTL	16½	CMDL	6 ¼
CSTR	17$^{11}/_{16}$	DTLN	18 ⅜
KIDE	38⅞	DYMX	2 ¼
JAKK	18⅞	INPR	3 ¾
WCOM	93¾	LKFNP	10 $^{1}/_{16}$

Figure 8.6   *52-Week High and Low*

displays a 52-Week Highs and Lows report for the NASDAQ stocks. A similar report can be displayed for the NYSE stocks.

The objective of this 52-week high is to focus on the price breakouts. A *breakout* is a movement of a stock price out of an established price trading range. The 52-week high price would be translated as a stock price breakout above the long-term price resistance level. *Resistance* is the upper boundary of the trading range, where selling pressure tends to keep the price below the established range. When a new stock symbol is displayed on the Day Highs report, the day trader could interpret this event as a stock price breakout above the intra-day price resistance level.

If the price breaks out of the 52-week high price, the day trader would expect that stock price momentum to continue. At that time, the day trader would start to monitor the stock in anticipation of continued price increase momentum. In other words, the day trader would pool that stock into the Market Ticker. If the stock keeps showing up in the Market Ticker as a green up-tick, the day trader would open the Level I and II screens and technical analysis charts for that stock. The key is that the day trader was alerted about that stock.

The 52-week low price would be translated as a stock price breakout below the long-term support level. *Support* is the lower boundary of the trading range, where buying pressure tends to keep the price from decreasing below that established range. If a price breaks below the 52-week low price, the day trader would expect the stock price to continue to decline. Again, the key is that the day trader was alerted about the possibility to short that stock. Just as some day traders utilize mostly the Level II screen and the Time and Sales window, others trade profitably day in and day out by simply buying the 52-week high stocks and short selling the 52-week low stocks.

Ten Basic Price Increase Signals

The following is a summary of observable events that characterize price increase or potential for price increase for a particular NASDAQ stock:

1. "Green" or up-tick BID and ASK prices show on the Market Ticker window;

2. Counterclockwise movement on the Level II screen, as more market makers leave inside ASK and join inside BID;

3. The first market maker enters a new high BID (that is, a higher BID than the rest of the market makers);

4. The last market maker leaves the inside ASK (and thus a higher ASK becomes the new inside ASK price);

5. An "ax" or key market maker joins the inside BID on the Level II screen (that is, buying the stock);

6. An "ax" or key market maker refreshes the inside BID price on the Level II screen (after being hit for the trade order the market maker chooses to keep the price at the inside BID or continues to buy);

7. An "ax" or key market maker leaves the inside ASK on the Level II screen (that is, stops selling the stock);

8. An "ax" or key market maker simultaneously leaves the inside ASK and joins the inside BID;

9. Buying trades go off at ASK price on the Time and Sales window (indicating that the public is buying);

10. Buying trades go off at 500 or 1,000 shares volume on the Time and Sales window (indicating that the public is buying a substantial quantity of shares).

Ten Basic Price Decrease Signals

Conversely, the following is a summary of observable events that characterize price decrease or potential for the price decrease of a particular NASDAQ stock:

1. "Red" or down-tick BID and ASK prices show on the Market Ticker window;

2. Clockwise movement on the Level II screen as more market makers leave inside BID and join inside ASK;

3. The first market maker enters a new lower ASK price (that is, a lower ASK than the rest of the market makers);

4. The last market maker leaves the inside BID (thus the lower BID becomes the new inside BID price);

5. An "ax" or key Market Maker joining the inside ASK on the Level II screen (selling the stock);

6. "Ax" or key Market Maker refreshes the Inside ASK price on the Level II screen (that is, after being hit for the trade order the Market Maker chooses to keep the price at the Inside ASK or continues to sell);

7. An "ax" or key Market Maker leaves the inside BID on the Level II screen (stops buying the stock);

8. An "ax" or key Market Maker simultaneously leaves the inside BID and joins the inside ASK;

9. Selling trades go off at BID price on the Time and Sales window (indicating that the public is selling);

10. Selling trades go off at 500 or 1,000 shares volume on the Time and Sales window (indicating that the public is selling a substantial quantity of shares).

It is unrealistic to expect that all ten signal events will occur simultaneously to produce a clear buy or sell signal. It is important, though, that he or she recognize a great majority of the signals listed in order to ascertain the price trend.

III

Introduction to Technical Analysis Tools

SINCE THE CURRENT DYNAMIC FINANCIAL MARKET GENERATES A CONTINUOUS flow of financial information, technical analysis is essential in determining what is relevant in that sea of financial data. Technical analysis tools clarify and present the wealth of financial data in formats that can be easily reviewed and interpreted. These technical analysis tools are effective in reducing a great deal of the "noise" that is always present in the financial markets. In section III, we focus on the basic technical analysis tools and concepts that are often used by professional day traders today.

➤ Section III starts with data formats of technical analysis, which are then followed by clarification of the most common chart types, such as the tick-by-tick price chart, bar, line, and candlestick charts.

➤ After introducing the concepts of the Simple, Weighted, and Exponential Moving Averages, we describe how Fast and Slow Exponential Moving Averages and Moving Average Convergence/Divergence (MACD) tools are being used by day traders to generate buy and sell trading signals.

➤ Oscillator indicators are then presented to show whether a particular stock is overbought or oversold. Fast and slow stochastic oscillators and momentum indicators are used as examples.

➤ The Bollinger bands concept is then introduced as a measure of intra-day price support and resistance.

➤ Finally, in section III we cover how broad market index overlays and On-Balance Volume (OBV) indicator are being used to gauge overall market and trading volume movements.

9

Technical Analysis

O NE PICTURE IS WORTH A THOUSAND WORDS. A QUICK LOOK AT A CHART that's loaded with technical analysis data would immediately reveal the current status of a stock. However, *technical analysis* means different things to different people. Some traders are chartists, who try to identify future price trends by plotting prices and identifying patterns. A chartist would draw a price chart with trend lines, triangles, rectangles, "head and shoulders," double bottoms or tops, or any other patterns. In my opinion, classical charting is an art; it is not known how much science, if any, is behind these descriptive charts. However, day traders seldom use them.

Most day traders use computerized technical analysis tools that provide valuable insights about stock prices. These software packages contain a large variety of technical analysis indicators. The technical indicators utilize information about closing or opening prices, trading volume, and the highest or lowest stock price in a selected time period. In this book, we focus on the technical analysis indicators that use the current price as the basic unit of analysis, since these indicators are the most useful tools for the day trading business.

To be effective, technical analysis should be simple. There is so much financial data coming across the computer screen that it is easy to get bogged down in sophisticated and esoteric technical information. My strong preference is to keep the technical analysis style as simple as possible. In this chapter, we discuss only basic price trend indicators and oscillators.

Technical Analysis Formats

Technical analysis for day trading is a form of stock market analysis that studies demand and supply for securities based primarily on the short-term stock price pattern. It is not surprising that the focus of technical day trading analysis is always the stock price at a particular moment. Since the day trader's objective is to exploit intra-day price volatility, it would be irrelevant to chart and analyze historical stock prices, such as weekly or monthly price averages. It is important to chart and analyze the intra-day prices on a one-minute interval basis. One should keep in mind the long-term price trends, since they provide information on historical price support and resistance, but for the most part, technical analysis of historical data has little import for the short-term day trader.

Technical analysis software packages are very easy to use and modify. Most of them are Microsoft Windows-based products with pull-down menu options. Constructing a technical analysis chart is a simple exercise. A day trader can pack many technical analyses into one chart alone. In addition to displaying the stock price information on the chart, a day trader can overlay several other technical analysis tools on the price data. Each technical analysis line can be color coded for easy reference. After a few days of practice, a day trader can proficiently read, interpret, and understand technical analysis tools.

Most sophisticated stock trading software packages contain a technical analysis library that includes many of the most commonly used technical indicators. Those technical analysis indicators can be modified to suit any trading preference by changing the format of the input values. A day trader can display and analyze different components of the intra-day price. If the unit of time is a one-minute interval, then the day trader can use for the technical analysis any of the following price data for that one-minute period: open BID, close BID; open ASK, close ASK; high BID, low BID; high ASK, and low ASK. To modify the format of the technical analysis input values, one can plot ASK prices rather than BID prices, or use open ASK prices rather than close ASK prices. My own preference is to leave the default price of the close ASK price as the input format price for the analysis.

Furthermore, the time periods in the technical analysis are based on "price data compression." Stock price information can be compressed into intra-day, daily, weekly, or monthly price periods, or left as tick-by-tick prices. The intra-day price period can be modified into any time format, such as one-minute, three-minute, five-minute, or fifteen-minute. Day traders would most likely use the one-minute data compression to stay current with the price movements.

Tick-by-Tick Price Chart

Thanks to computer technology advances, it is now possible to plot stock prices tick by tick in real time. A graphic presentation of the tick-by-tick price chart is shown in Figure 9.1. However, it is extremely difficult to perform technical analysis and to evaluate patterns based on tick-by-tick prices. It is better to use tick-by-tick charts to follow the stock after the trade position has been taken. One can then confirm the trade executions and visually monitor the next price movement.

The tick-by-tick price chart in Figure 9.1 displays a zigzag pattern line chart. The current BID price is at the bottom of the zigzag pattern and the ASK price at the top. The spread is the difference or the distance between the top and bottom. Usually, the spread is constant (for example, $\frac{1}{16}$) and the distance is the same. Sometimes, the spread narrows and the gap between the top and bottom becomes smaller.

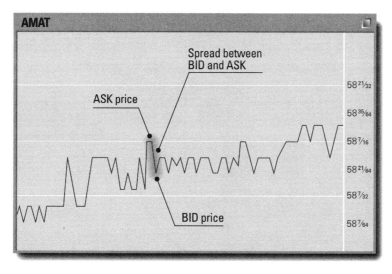

Figure 9.1 *Tick-by-Tick Price Chart*

Stock price information can be expressed visually as a bar, line, or candlestick chart. *Bar charts* are expressed as vertical lines, with left and right handles that represent the opening and closing stock prices for the selected period. *Line charts* show the same type of price information over time. For example, the day trader can select to plot in a line chart format the close ASK price on a one-minute interval basis. In essence, opening BID, closing BID, open ASK, high and low BID, and ASK data would be ignored. This would provide one clean price line—a line connecting the one-minute interval close ASK price observations.

Candlestick Chart

Candlestick charts (see Figure 9.2) are plotted as vertical rectangular boxes that connect opening and closing prices for that time period. Vertical lines called "wicks" extend from the rectangles to encompass the extreme high and low prices for the time period. If the closing price for

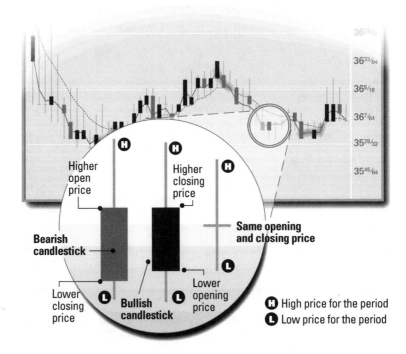

Figure 9.2 *Candlestick Chart*

that time period ends above the opening price, then the rectangular box would be "painted" in a particular color.

For easier visual identification, we have selected the color black to identify when the closing price ends above the opening price (called a "price up-tick"). When the closing price for the time period finishes below the opening price (called a "price down-tick"), then the rectangular box is gray. When the opening and closing prices remained the same, then there would be no rectangular boxes.

Moving Average

The most common technical analysis indicator is the Moving Average (MA). The *Moving Average* is commonly the starting point of any technical analysis study. There are many reasons that Moving Average analysis is the most frequently used technical analysis tool for day trading. MA is a simple mathematical concept, and most people find it easy to relate to this tool. MA tends to eliminate some of the market *noise*. It filters out tick-by-tick price quotes and points to a trend. In other words, the MA line smoothes out the price gyrations and fluctuations that can confuse interpretation of a price movement. The MA line would emphasize the direction of a trend, and confirm trend reversal.

The *Moving Average crossover,* between the fast and slow MA lines, also provides a clear buy and sell signal that is easy to spot. Either the buy or the sell signal is displayed, and nothing in between. A day trader who follows the MA crossover signal will always be in the market. However, the MA system does not work very well for a "choppy" market that does not show a clear short-term trend. The MA system does work well for a trending market where prices are clearly going up or down.

The most serious drawback to the Moving Average is that it is a lagging indicator: there is a time *lag* between the actual price line and the MA line, because the MA line trails the actual price.

The Moving Average is the sum of a selected number of previous price values divided by the total number of those values. In other words, a three-minute MA would be the sum of the prices of the previous three minutes divided by 3. However, the three minutes are not considered equal: the last or the most recent minute is more important than the previous minute or the first minute. Thus the technical analysis differentiates between the Simple Moving Average, the Weighted Moving

Average, and the Exponential Moving Average by assigning different weights to different minutes.

Simple, Weighted, and Exponential Moving Averages

The *Simple Moving Average* (SMA) is a basic concept. Every minute has equal weight: the last or the most recent minute has $\frac{1}{3}$ weight, the second minute has $\frac{1}{3}$ weight, and the first minute has $\frac{1}{3}$ weight. This, however, is too simplistic. Instead let us assign a weight to each minute interval, and create a *Weighted Moving Average* (WMA). The last or the most recent minute is the most important one, so we will assign 50% weight to that price value. The second minute would have 30% weight, and the first minute would have 20% weight. Altogether, the three minutes of price values would account for 100% of the SMA value.

These assigned weights are purely arbitrary. Most technical analysts strictly use the *Exponential Moving Average* (EMA), which uses a mathematical method that automatically provides the greater weight to most recent price actions. In this book, we will use the EMA exclusively.

Fast and Slow Exponential Moving Averages

Figure 9.3 presents two EMA lines. The first line is the Fast EMA of three periods of one-minute intervals. This EMA is called the Fast EMA, because it will follow or "hug" the actual price movement very closely. There will be very little time lag between the three-minute Fast EMA and the actual price change. The Fast EMA will smooth out the actual price fluctuations to some degree, so it would be easy to spot a trend almost in real time. In essence, the Fast EMA eliminates some of the market "noise" or brief gyrations.

The second line in Figure 9.3 is the Slow EMA of nine periods of one-minute intervals. A rule of thumb is that the period of the Slow EMA should be three times greater than the period of the Fast EMA. The day trader could select any two periods of one-minute data intervals that has the 3–1 ratio—three-minute and nine-minute bars or five-minute and fifteen-minute bars. If the day trader wants to reduce more

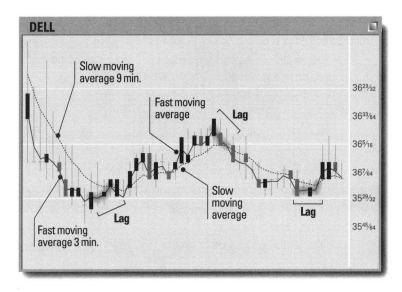

Figure 9.3 *Fast and Slow Exponential Moving Average Lines*

of the market noise and obtain fewer trading signals, the trader would select longer time periods for the Fast and Slow EMA—nine-minute and twenty-seven-minute bars.

This EMA is called the Slow EMA because it will follow the actual price movement very loosely. There will be a substantial time lag between the nine-minute Slow EMA and the actual price change. The reason for that is simple. The nine-minute Slow EMA incorporates the stock price of 9 minutes ago, and thus lags the current price. That lag can be very visible when there is a sharp change or movement in prices. Figure 9.3 demonstrates graphically this Slow EMA lag. The Slow EMA will smooth out greatly the actual price fluctuations, and makes it easy to spot the longer price trend.

When Fast and Slow EMA lines are plotted together, we obtain a crossover or a trading *signal*. When the Fast EMA (three-minute) line is greater than or above the Slow EMA (nine-minute) line, stock prices are going up. This is true by definition. The Fast EMA line must be greater than the Slow EMA line in order to pull the slower EMA line to a higher price value.

Conversely, when the Fast EMA line is smaller than or below the Slow EMA line, then stock prices are going down. Again, this is a mathematical truism. The Fast EMA line must be smaller than the Slow EMA line to pull the slower EMA line to a lower price value. Figure 9.3 illustrates this point.

There are three trading signals or crossovers in Figure 9.4. The first signal occurs when the Fast EMA line crosses over and goes above the Slow EMA line. It is a signal that stock prices are going up, and thus it is a signal to open a long position on that stock (that is, purchase the stock). Note that prices were already moving up when the crossover occurred. Again, that shows the time lag. A day trader following the EMA crossover signals would never pick the stock price at the bottom and sell at the peak. However, since the day trader is plotting the EMA of the three periods of one-minute interval price observations in real time, the time lag is minor.

The second signal occurs when the Fast EMA (three-minute) line crosses and goes below the Slow EMA (nine-minute) line. It is a signal that stock prices are going down, and thus it is a signal to close that long position on the stock (that is, sell the stock). That would close the first trade. Prices were already moving down when the crossover occurred. Again, that is the time lag.

After closing the long position, a day trader would enter immediately into a second trade. He or she would sell short that particular stock. In other words, the day trader would sell the borrowed stock at

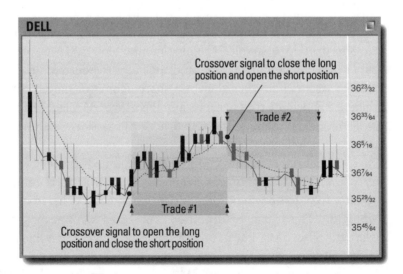

Figure 9.4 *Fast and Slow Exponential Moving Average Lines Crossover*

the higher price, wait for the price decrease, and then purchase the stock at the lower price and cover the short sale. The short position would be closed when the Fast EMA crossed over and above the Slow EMA. That would be the signal to buy the stock and cover the short sale. At the same time, it would be a trading signal to open the long position.

Note that the day trader is always in the market. There is always a signal to open a long or short position. There is a clear and distinct possibility that the day trader will overplay the market. If the market is not trending (that is, exhibiting small price gyrations), the day trader would, for example, enter the long position and quickly discover that prices had reverted back. A day trader would be *whipsawed* by the market price gyrations. The stock prices might go up only $\frac{1}{8}$ of a point and then decline, so the day trader would quickly sell that stock to cover that long position.

To avoid being whipsawed by the market noise, the day trader needs to pay attention to the movements on the Level II screen and the Time and Sales window to ascertain if there is a true price movement. In addition, the day trader could increase the number of time intervals in the Slow EMA line from nine to twelve. That would make the Slow EMA slower; it would avoid many crossover buy or sell trading signals, and thus would reduce many "whiplash" trading signals. However, the slower EMA line would result in an increased lag time.

The day trader can utilize other technical analysis tools that point to the strength of the upward or downward price movement. One of those technical analysis tools measures the extent of the divergence and convergence between the Fast and Slow EMA lines. If the *divergence* or distance between the Fast and Slow EMA lines is increasing, then the price movement is gaining strength. If the distance between the Fast and Slow EMA lines is decreasing or *converging*, then the price movement is losing strength. This concept is elaborated in the Moving Average Convergence/Divergence analysis.

Moving Average Convergence/Divergence

Moving Average Convergence/Divergence (MACD) analysis was developed by Gerald Appel in 1985. MACD is a derivative of two EMA lines. MACD is an excellent price trending indicator. Also, MACD is considered to be somewhat of an oscillator tool. An *oscillator* is a line that indicates whether a stock is *overbought* or *oversold*. In other words, an oscillator would indicate whether prices moved too far or too fast in either direction and thus are vulnerable to reaction or reversal. The best way to explain MACD is to construct MACD from scratch.

The MACD is constructed by subtracting the Fast EMA (three-minute) line from the Slow EMA (nine-minute). When stock prices are increasing, the Fast EMA line is greater than the Slow EMA, and thus the MACD line is positive. If stock prices continue to increase at the faster rate, then the gap between the Fast EMA line and the Slow EMA will continue to increase also, and thus the MACD line will be positive and will continue to grow as well. Figure 9.5 illustrates this point.

Conversely, when stock prices are decreasing, the Fast EMA line is below the Slow EMA, and thus the MACD line is negative. If stock prices continue to decline at a faster rate, then the gap between the Fast EMA line and the Slow EMA will also continue to increase; the MACD line will be negative and will continue to grow as well. The MACD line will quickly tell the trader if the price trend is up or down and whether that positive or negative price trend is increasing or decreasing.

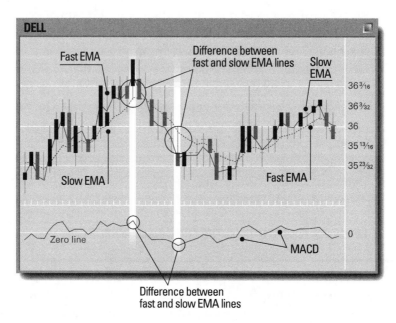

Figure 9.5 *Moving Average Convergence/Divergence (MACD)*

If the MACD is positive or above the zero line and if there is a divergence (that is, increase in the spread) between the MACD and zero line, then the day trader would interpret that as a bullish sign. If MACD is still positive, but there is a convergence (that is, decrease in the spread) between the MACD and the zero line, the day trader would interpret that as a sign that bulls in the market are losing steam. The day trader would then expect a price reversal. In essence, the day trader would receive a warning sign that stock prices will probably stop increasing and will begin to decline.

On the other hand, if the MACD is negative and below the zero line, and if there is a divergence between the MACD and the zero line, the day trader would interpret that as a bearish sign. If MACD is still negative, but there is a convergence between the MACD and the zero line, then the day trader would interpret it as a sign that bears in the market are losing steam; that is, that stock prices will most likely stop decreasing and begin to increase. The day trader would then expect a price reversal.

The crossover between the Fast and Slow EMA lines corresponds to the crossover between the MACD and zero line. In essence, the MACD line is a derivative of the two EMA lines. The MACD conveys the same information as the Fast and Slow EMA lines. However, the information on the direction and strength of the price movement is easily visualized with the MACD line.

The next step is to create a MACD signal line. The MACD *signal line* is the exponential moving average of the calculated MACD. For example, the MACD signal is the EMA of the nine periods of MACD values. The signal MACD line will smooth out the actual MACD fluctuations. In essence, MACD is a "fast line" and signal MACD is a "slow line."

The signal MACD line is needed to get the clear buy or sell signals that are the crossovers between the MACD and Signal MACD lines. These crossovers between the MACD and signal MACD lines are often used as buy or sell signals. In essence, the MACD is the fast line and the signal MACD is the slow line. When the MACD crosses over and above the signal MACD line, that would indicate a bullish signal to buy. When MACD crosses below the signal MACD line, that would constitute a bearish signal to sell the stock.

The final step is to plot the MACD histogram. The bar in the MACD histogram is displayed as the difference between the MACD and signal MACD lines. The size and the pattern of the MACD histogram bars would act as an oscillator indicator. When the MACD crosses over and above the signal MACD line, then the MACD histogram would have positive values. A positive MACD histogram would indicate a bullish signal to buy.

Also, the MACD histogram helps to visualize the level of price divergence or convergence between the MACD and MACD signal lines. The absolute price differential between the MACD and signal MACD values is small, but the computer program will automatically resize that small value. The key is to visualize whether there is convergence or divergence between the MACD and signal MACD lines. If the MACD histogram is increasing in value, then the bullish sign has been intensified. If the MACD histogram is decreasing in values, then bulls are running out of steam.

When the MACD crosses below the signal MACD line, then the MACD histogram would have negative values. A negative MACD histogram would constitute a sell signal. The key is to focus and visualize whether there is convergence or divergence between the MACD and signal MACD lines. If the MACD histogram is negative and decreasing in value, then the bearish sign has been intensified. If the MACD histogram is negative and decreasing at a diminishing rate, then the bears are running out of steam.

10

Oscillator Indicators

WE LEARNED IN CHAPTER 9 THAT THE MACD LINE IS A DERIVATIVE OF the Fast and Slow EMA, and that it acts as an oscillator indicator. There are other technical analysis tools that have been specifically designed to be oscillator indicators. These technical tools tell the day trader where the current closing price of a stock is relative to the most recent price range of the market. In this book, we focus on the most relevant and popular oscillator tools used in the day trading business.

An *oscillator* is a line that indicates whether a stock is overbought (prices have risen too steeply, too fast) or oversold (prices have fallen too steeply, too fast) and thus are vulnerable to reaction or reversal. The *Bollinger bands* indicator is one of several oscillator indicators commonly used by day traders and is available on trading software packages.

Bollinger Bands

John Bollinger developed the Bollinger bands indicator. Using this technical tool is an excellent way to determine intra-day price support and resistance. Price *resistance* is a price level at which prices have stopped rising and have either moved sideways or reversed direction. Price resistance indicates an overbought market. Price *support* is a price level at which prices have stopped falling and have either moved sideways or reversed direction. The price support level indicates an oversold market.

The Bollinger bands indicator is an improvement from standard fixed percentage bands that have commonly been used by professional traders. Traders have used two fixed percentage bands around the current price, such as plus 10% and minus 10%, as the support and resistance levels. A plus 10% from the current price would become the price resistance band. A minus 10% from the current price would become the price support band. Fixed percentage bands were not very flexible. They created two parallel lines that did not change with increased or decreased intra-day price volatility.

The Bollinger bands indicator uses *standard deviations* for the two bands instead of fixed percentage lines. As the intra-day price volatility increases for a particular stock, the price variance increases as well. A higher variance from the average price would automatically increase the standard deviation. The standard deviations automatically adjust for the increased or decreased intra-day stock price volatility. If the Bollinger bands increase (that is, widen), that would automatically indicate a higher intra-day price volatility. If the Bollinger bands decrease (that is, become narrower), that would indicate a lower intra-day price volatility, or more stable prices.

As a starting point, assume that stock price observations have normal distribution around the average: that prices deviate equally on the plus and minus side of the existing Moving Average price. Statistical theory tells us that 65% of all price observations would reside on plus 1 standard deviation (+1 St.D.) and minus 1 standard deviation (–1 St.D.) from the mean. Furthermore, 95% of all price observations would reside on plus 2 standard deviation (+2 St.D.) and minus 2 standard deviation (–2 St.D.) from the mean.

If we select +1.85 St.D. and –1.85 St.D. for the upper and lower Bollinger band lines, we could assume that there is an approximately 80% probability that all prices will fall within the upper and lower bands. The upper band of +1.85 St.D. above the Moving Average point constitutes the intra-day price resistance level at that point of time. The lower band of –1.85 St.D. below the Moving Average point constitutes the intra-day price support level at that point of time. In other words, there is only 20% probability that actual prices would move above or below the two Bollinger band lines.

A day trader should always try to stay within the Bollinger bands trading range. After all, there is an approximately 80% probability that

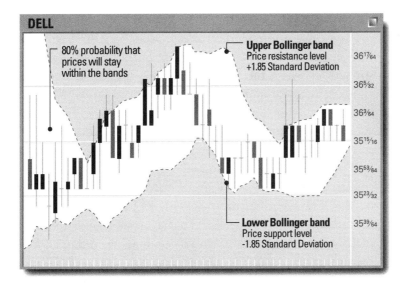

Figure 10.1 *Bollinger Bands*

the price will remain in this range. Would you bet your money on a 20% probability? It would not be a good idea to open a long position (buy the stock) when the price has reached the intra-day price resistance level (the upper Bollinger band). When the stock prices approach the upper Bollinger band, the stock is overbought.

Conversely, it would not be a good idea to open the short position (sell short the stock) when the price has reached the intra-day price support level (the lower Bollinger band). When the stock prices approach the lower Bollinger band, many day traders recognize that the stock is oversold. Bollinger bands are an excellent tool for identifying the price *extremes* in the intra-day market (See Figure 10.1).

Momentum

The *momentum indicator* (MOM) is another technical analysis tool that can be useful in the day trading business. The momentum indicator is an oscillator-type indicator used to ascertain whether there is an upward or downward price *momentum* and to determine overbought or oversold markets. In this chapter, the momentum indicator is plotted as a line in a separate diagram that is attached to the main chart. (In other software packages, momentum indicator is plotted as a histogram that is, in bars). The momentum indicator helps to visually determine the pace or strength at which the stock prices are going up or down: It ascertains whether the price momentum (positive or negative) is gaining or losing its steam or strength.

The momentum indicator (MOM) is calculated by subtracting the current closing price from the closing price of several periods ago. The past period can be any period selected by the day trader. It is my preference to use the same period that is used for the Slow EMA. In this chapter, the Slow EMA has been constructed by using the stock closing price of nine one-minute intervals. That means that the current momentum indicator value is calculated by subtracting the current closing price from the closing price nine minutes ago: $MOM = P(t) - P(t - 9)$. Figure 10.2 displays the momentum indicator.

If the current closing price were higher than the closing price nine minutes ago, the MOM value would be positive. Conversely, if the current closing price were lower than the closing price nine minutes ago, the MOM value would be negative. If the current closing price is the same as the closing price nine minutes ago, the MOM value would be zero.

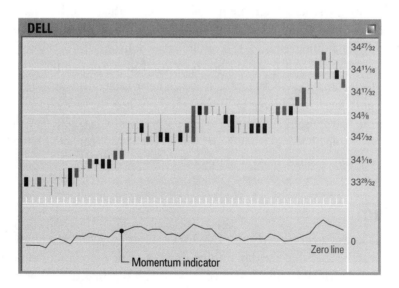

Figure 10.2   *Momentum Indicator*

Therefore, the MOM indicator would oscillate or fluctuate above or below the zero line.

If the MOM values were positive and increasing, that would constitute a bullish sign. Conversely, if the MOM values were negative and decreasing, that would be a bearish sign. If MOM systematically fluctuates around the zero line between the positive and negative values, that would point to choppy markets. It is difficult to day trade stocks that have extremely choppy MOMs.

If the MOM values rise too far above the zero line, that could indicate an overbought market. If the MOM values were positive but the MOM reverses its direction and starts to move down toward the zero line, that would be an early sign that the positive (upward) price momentum is losing its steam. Conversely, if the MOM values fall too far from the zero line, that could indicate an oversold market. Also, if the MOM values were negative but the MOM reverses its direction and starts to move up toward the zero line, that would be an early sign that the downward price momentum is losing its steam.

Stochastic Oscillator

George Lane developed the *stochastic oscillator* indicator in the 1970s. The indicator was designed to show when a stock becomes overbought or oversold within a certain trading range. It is one of the most popular *overbought/oversold indicators* available. Most trading software products today feature stochastic analysis.

The stochastic indicator generates readings between zero and 100. It is commonly accepted that readings higher than 75 constitute an overbought market. The term *overbought* means that the stock prices went up too fast and too far because of a high influx of buyers. Relatively high prices might have attracted sellers who would enter the market, sell the stock, and make the profit. In that case, the price movement would reverse its trend. It would be a signal or warning to day traders not to purchase the stock—not to open a long position. In essence, the overbought stochastic market line at 75 would constitute an arbitrary price resistance line.

Conversely, it is commonly accepted that readings lower than 25 constitute an oversold market. An oversold market is a situation in which stock prices have declined rapidly due to a large influx of sellers. At that time, the relatively low prices would have attracted buyers who would enter the market to pick up the stock at the perceived bargain price. In that case, price movement might reverse its trend. It would be a signal or warning not to sell short the stock. Consequently, it can be a signal to day traders to look for the possibility of opening a long position. The oversold stochastic market line at 25 would constitute an arbitrary price support line. Figure 10.3 depicts the stochastic oscillator.

The stochastic oscillator fluctuates between the two market extremes. When plotted on the chart, the stochastic indicator shows very jagged peaks and troughs. Anything between 25 and 75 oscillator readings would indicate the normal trading range. Again, the indicator refers to the location of the current price in relation to its price range over a specified period of time. Since we have been using nine one-minute intervals throughout the technical analysis material, Figure 10.3 uses a stochastic oscillator that is based on nine one-minute intervals as well. The time period most commonly used by the trading software products, as a default feature, is fourteen bars or fourteen one-minute intervals.

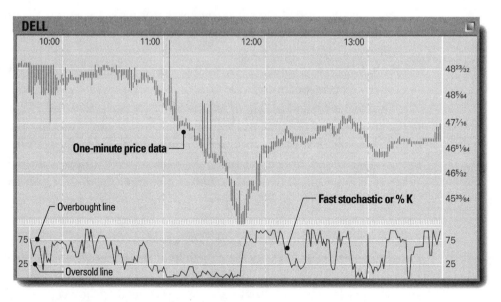

Figure 10.3   *Stochastic Oscillator Indicator*

Fast and Slow Stochastic

The stochastic oscillator or the "fast stochastic" is often labeled in technical analysis literature as the %K. The fast stochastic (%K) is defined as the difference between the current stock price and the lowest stock price in the last nine minutes, which is then divided by the difference between the highest and lowest prices in the last nine periods.

The chart of the stochastic indicator appears to have very jagged peaks and troughs. Many traders prefer to use the "slow stochastic" (or %D), which is the slower or smoothed-out stochastic oscillator. The slow stochastic is basically a moving average of the fast stochastic. Therefore, the moving average stochastic line (%D) will result in a *smoothing* out of some of the jagged peaks and troughs of the fast stochastic line.

Some technical analysts plot the fast stochastic line next to the slow stochastic line. The two lines (%K and %D) would generate many crossovers. The crossovers can be interpreted as buy and sell signals. For example, if the fast stochastic crosses over and goes above the slow stochastic, that would constitute a buy signal. If the fast stochastic crosses and goes under the slow stochastic, that would constitute a sell signal. My personal preference is to treat and use the stochastic oscillator indicators strictly as overbought and oversold indicators and not as trading buy and sell signals.

CHAPTER 11

Broad Market Measures and Trading Volume

It is always a good idea to monitor the broad market. It is my opinion that it is also a good idea to follow the overall market direction. The late Mao Tse-tung once advised that one should not "piss against the wind." If a day trader were to go against the overall market, there is a distinct possibility that the trader would end up "wet."

If overall stock market prices are declining, it would not be a good idea to open a long position. The trader doing so could be right, and the stock could appreciate in value, but the odds are against it. If the trader is opening a long position and the overall advance-to-decline value is negative for that day, the probability of having the winning trade is diminished. The advance-to-decline value is negative if the number of declining stocks is greater than the number of advancing stocks.

One way to monitor the broad market is to monitor Standard and Poor's 500 Index (S&P 500), which is an indicator of the general stock price movement for the 500 largest companies in the United States. Many trading software packages allow the day trader to superimpose or to overlay a stock index such as the S&P 500 Index next to the stock prices being monitored. The S&P 500 Index values are commonly quoted by the stock data feed providers. The software would automatically resize the index next to the prices of a particular stock. It is an easy way to ascertain if the prices of an individual stock are moving in the same direction as the broad market.

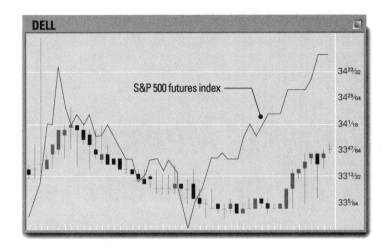

Figure 11.1 *Broad Market Index Overlay*

Figure 11.1 provides an example of a technical analysis chart with a broad market overlay. If your trading software does not have an overlay feature, my recommendation is to open a separate window and monitor at least one broad market index. In the example shown in Figure 11.1, the stock price of DELL was highly correlated at that moment of analysis with the broad stock market as measured by the S&P 500 Futures.

There are approximately 35 NASDAQ-listed companies in the S&P 500 Index. For day traders, the S&P 500 Index may be too broad a measure of the overall market. Some day traders who trade mostly NASDAQ stocks pay closer attention to the more narrow market indexes such as the NASDAQ 100. Some day traders who specialize in a few technology stocks closely monitor certain sector industries indexes such as the Internet Index (INX), Technology Index (TXX), and Software Index (CWX) on the Chicago Board Options Exchange (CBOE) or Semiconductor Index (SOX) on the Philadelphia Exchange.

Many day traders pay very close attention to the S&P 500 Futures trendline. The S&P 500 Futures is a portfolio of the same stocks that are part of the S&P 500 Index. The S&P 500 Futures is a standardized futures contract with an expiration date that is actively traded on the Chicago Mercantile Exchange. In essence, the S&P 500 Futures is a financial derivative. The value of the S&P 500 Futures contract is tied directly to the underlying cash value of the S&P 500 Index. In fact, the delivery of the contract is the cash settlement of the difference between the original transaction price and the final price of the index at the termination of the contract. The price of the index futures will be highly correlated with the value of the corresponding index. The activity of the index arbitrageurs assures that the deviations between the price of the index futures and the value of the underlying cash index are relatively minor.

Many day traders believe that the S&P 500 Futures is the leading market indicator. A cash index, such as the S&P 500 Index or the Dow Jones Industrial Average index, is a lagging indicator. It reflects the actual or historical price or cash changes of the underlying stocks that comprise that cash index. Someone first must compile and input the changes in the price of the underlying stocks that comprise the S&P 500 Index and then the Index value will change, and thus the S&P 500 Index is considered to be a lagging indicator.

On the other hand, the S&P 500 Futures contract is a financial derivative or a financial instrument that is traded on the Chicago Mercantile Exchange. The value of this derivative instrument is highly correlated with the underlying cash value of the S&P 500 Index. The futures index reflects to a great extent anticipation by market professionals and speculators about the future of the broad market. In essence, the broad market sentiment is quickly and efficiently reflected in the price of the S&P 500 Futures contract. Because the S&P 500 Futures contract is actively traded and the price of the contract is immediately transparent, the day trader can plot and overlay the price value of the futures contract against the stock price. There is no time lag due to compiling of the price changes of the underlying S&P 500 Index stocks. That makes the S&P Futures contract a leading indicator. Instead of plotting the value of the S&P 500 Index (that is, the lagging indicator), the day trader can plot the price of the S&P 500 Futures Index (that is, the leading indicator).

Trading Volume

The stock price movement is clearly the most important dimension of technical analysis. However, trading *volume* is the fuel that generates that price change. For many technical analysts, the volume is a proxy variable (that is, a substitute variable) of the money flow.

First of all, the Time and Sales window already provides the actual and exact size and direction of the money flow. A day trader can quickly and clearly ascertain in real terms whether the public is buying or selling. For instance, the Time and Sales window prints the actual share size associated with the BID and ASK prices. If 10,000 shares were traded at the ASK price and only 1,000 shares were cleared at the BID price, the public bought 10,000 and sold only 1,000 shares at that point in time. This information alone indicates the potential for a price increase—quantity demanded exceeds the quantity supplied.

On the other hand, plotting the raw trading volume in real terms on the chart would reveal the combined buying and selling size of the trading but not the direction of the trading (whether it is buying or selling). In other words, all of the public buying and selling volume is presented as one single volume statistic.

Second, most stocks that are commonly traded by day traders always have substantial *daily volume*. Thus technical analysis focuses on the deviation from normal trading activities. Increasing volume is often accompanied by higher prices. Conversely, declining volume is an advance warning of a possible price *correction*. Most traders use trading volume statistics to confirm the existing price movement. However, volume statistics are always subject to brief distortions. For instance, option expirations and program trading can clearly affect intra-day volume without providing any underlying cause for the price increase or decrease. In addition, *spikes* in the trading volume without any gradual increase over several hours may be the result of news leaks or certain stock analyst comments.

One of the simplest volume indicators is the *On-Balance Volume* (OBV) indicator. Joseph Granville developed the OBV indicator in the 1960s. On-Balance Volume is plotted as a line representing the cumulative total of the trading volume. When the closing price for a one-minute trading interval is higher than the closing price for the previous one-minute trading interval, then that trading volume is assigned a plus sign. If the closing price ends on the up-tick, the OBV indicator assumes that the stock is under acquisition or *accumulation*. If the closing price for the one-minute trading interval is lower than the closing price for the previous one-minute trading interval, then that trading volume is assigned a negative sign. In other words, if the closing price ends up on the down-tick, then the OBV indicator assumes that the stock is under *distribution,* or subject to selling. The OBV is a simple running cumulative total of the plus and minus (that is, upside and downside) trading volume.

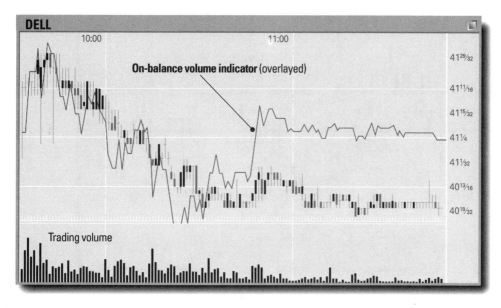

Figure 11.2 *On-Balance Volume Indicator and Trading Volume*

The OBV indicator can be overlaid on the price data or plotted in a separate subgraph. The OBV illustrates trading volume flow to determine whether there is buying or selling pressure. Figure 11.2 illustrates the On-Balance Volume (OBV) indicator for the intra-day one-minute interval prices and volume of DELL.

A day trader would like to observe the price and the OBV indicator moving in the same direction. If both the price and OBV are moving up, the trend is considered strong. If the price is going up but the running cumulative OBV line is declining, divergence exists, and there is a distinct possibility of a price reversal. Conversely, if both the stock price and the OBV indicator are moving down, a downward trend is considered strong. If the stock price is going down but the running cumulative OBV line is increasing, there is a distinct possibility of a price reversal.

Technical Analysis Chart with Combined Indicators

Finally, day traders can combine several technical analysis indicators into one single chart. Figure 11.3 is an example of such a combined

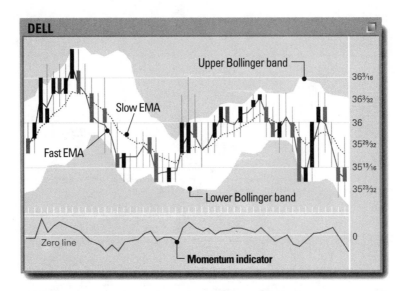

Figure 11.3 *Combined Technical Analysis Indicators*

effort. The graph is crowded with several technical analysis indicators, such as the Fast and Slow EMA lines, Bollinger bands, and momentum indicator. Sometimes it is difficult to differentiate among different lines on a small chart, although the lines could be color coded for easier reference. The day trader can pack a lot of analysis in a small chart. It is my opinion that more is preferred to less information. However, novice day traders usually start with a few technical analysis indicators, and then with the experience, add additional indicators. Often too much analysis tends to cause confusion or even lead to trading paralysis.

Introduction to Order Executions

In SECTION IV, WE DEFINE, EXPLAIN, AND GRAPHICALLY ILLUSTRATE THE mechanics of day trading. In essence, in this trade management section we describe how professional day traders execute their trades efficiently and precisely. The NASDAQ, NYSE, and ECN order execution platforms are described in great detail.

➤ Different types of trade orders, such as market, limit, stop, and stop-limit orders are explained. Then order qualifiers such as the day order, good until canceled, all or none, and others are described. Clarification on using limit versus market orders and priority of orders is presented. Trading terminology such as "bidding, buying, offering, and selling" is explained.

➤ NASDAQ's Small Order Execution System (SOES) and SelectNet "broadcast" versus SelectNet "preference" orders are explained in detail, along with an explanation of the SelectNet "preference" buy and sell order trading strategies.

➤ Island (ISLD) as an Electronic Communications Network (ECN) is then introduced. We then explain the concepts of bidding the high BID versus bidding the BID through Island, and offering the low ASK versus offering the ASK through Island. In addition, Island order mechanics and Island book, which displays every Island buy and sell order, are clarified.

➤ Then Instinet (INCA), the largest ECN is covered, followed by discussion on private versus public financial markets. At that time, concepts of locked-up markets versus crossed-up markets and locked-down markets versus crossed-down markets are introduced. Subsequently, trading strategies using Instinet are discussed. In particular, the author explains what constitutes a bullish or bearish signal.

➤ Finally, the New York Stock Exchange (NYSE), its specialists, and Super DOT are defined and explained. We discuss trading strategies on the NYSE as well as utilizing limit orders on the NYSE.

➤ Since short selling is much different than common buying and selling of stocks, we explain in detail the concept of short selling and its order mechanics.

12

Trade Orders and NASDAQ SOES

Traders or investors can enter a number of different types of orders on the NASDAQ and NYSE. The type of order used is determined mostly by a trader's or investor's individual objectives. Following is a list of trade execution orders. Figure 12.1 provides additional illustration.

1. Market order: The most common type of trade order is the *market order*. It does not specify a price but instead is executed at whatever price is available when the order reaches the floor of the exchange. A market order will always be executed, but traders or investors cannot be sure of the execution price.

2. Limit order: When customers wish to buy or sell a security at a specific price, they enter a *limit order*. A limit order can only be executed at

Figure 12.1 *Types of Execution Orders*

the specified price or better. A buy limit could be executed at the limit price or lower, and a sell limit could be executed at the limit price or higher. A buy limit order is placed below the current market price of the security (ASK price), while a sell limit order is placed above the current market (BID price). Since a limit order is entered away from the market, it is unlikely that the order would be executed immediately. Therefore, a limit order is usually given to a broker to hold until it can be executed. It is possible that the order may never be executed, because the limit price is not reached or there are other orders at the same price with higher priority.

3. Stop order: A *stop order* becomes a market order to buy or sell securities once a specified price is attained or penetrated. The specific price indicated by the investor is called the *stop price*. Once the order is activated, the investor is guaranteed execution, but there is no guarantee of the execution price. A sell stop order is always placed below the current market price of the security (BID price). It is typically used to limit a loss or protect a profit on a long stock position. A buy stop order is always placed above the current market price (ASK price). It is used to limit a loss or protect a profit on a short sale.

4. Stop-limit order: A *stop-limit order* is similar to a stop order in that a stop price will activate the order. However, once activated, the stop-limit order becomes a buy limit or sell limit order, and it can only be executed at a specified price or better. It is a combination of the stop order and the limit order. A stop-limit order eliminates the risk of a stop order when the investor is not guaranteed an execution price, but exposes the investor to the risk that the order may never be filled. A sell stop-limit order is always placed below the current market price of the security (BID price). It is used to limit the loss (or protect a profit) on a long position. Once activated, it becomes a sell limit order. A buy stop-limit order is always placed above the current market price of the security (ASK price). It is used to limit the loss (or protect a profit) on a short position. Again, once activated, it becomes a buy limit order.

Order Qualifiers

In addition to the types of orders that an investor may enter, there are various qualifications that may be used to fill an order. The following is a list of the order qualifiers:

1. Day order: Every order is a day order unless otherwise specified. If not executed, it is automatically canceled at the end of the day.

2. Good 'til canceled (GTC) or open order: This is an order that remains in effect until executed or canceled. The floor broker should periodically update GTC orders.

3. At the opening: This is an order to buy or sell at the opening price. If not executed at the opening, it will be canceled.

4. At the close: This order is to be executed as close to the closing price as possible. There is no guarantee that the price will be the closing price.

5. Not held (NH): This qualification gives the floor broker discretion as to time and price of an order. If the floor broker does not execute or does not obtain the best price, the broker will not be held responsible. An NYSE specialist cannot accept a not held order.

6. All or none (AON): According to this qualification, the entire order must be filled on the same transaction. The order does not have to be filled immediately, but can be executed during the course of the trading day.

7. Immediate or cancel (IOC): This qualifier dictates that as much of the order as possible must be executed immediately. The portion that is not immediately executed is canceled.

8. Fill or kill (FOK): This qualification combines the all or none and immediate or cancel orders. The entire order must be executed immediately or the entire order is canceled.

Limit Versus Market Orders

As a general rule, the day trader should use the buy limit order rather than the buy market order. Specifying the buying price is always a good risk-management practice. If the market is moving very fast and the day trader is using market orders, the trader might overpay for a security. The day trader needs to be in control and buy the stock at the "right" price. If the buy market order is used, the day trader is abdicating somewhat his or her ability to control the price. The day trader is "chasing" the stock.

If the day trader has a long stock position and the price is dropping quickly, the day trader should routinely use the sell market order rather than the sell limit order. If the market is moving down fast and the sell limit order is being used, the order might not get filled, and the day trader would miss the market altogether. The objective is to minimize the risk and get out of the stock quickly. In such circumstances, the sell market order would be a better choice.

Day traders use the market orders sparingly. Sometimes when the market is "tanking" and the day trader is desperate to get out of a stock (if he or she has waited too long), then a market order is appropriate. Conversely, if a stock is appreciating in value and the day trader wants to close a profitable long position—if the day trader is selling with the up-tick price or the green BID bar on the trading screen—the day trader might use the market order.

Priority of Orders

Since a number of orders can arrive at the exchange floor at approximately the same time, a priority of orders has been established to determine which order will be executed first. The priority of trade orders is the following:

1. Price
2. Time
3. Size.

The first priority always is price. The highest BID and lowest ASK will always come first. After price, time is the determining factor. If all bidders or offerers are equal in price, then whoever came into the trading crowd first will come before later bidders or offerers. If the orders are equal in price and time, then the size of the order is the determining factor. Normally, the larger order will receive priority.

This means that market orders do not have any priority over limit orders. Suppose that the best BID and ASK prices are 50 and $50\frac{1}{8}$, and the following is the orders sequence received at the trading post:

1. LMT Buy $50\frac{1}{8}$ 300
2. MKT Buy $50\frac{1}{8}$ 1,000
3. MKT Buy $50\frac{1}{8}$ 2,000.

If this is the order sequence, the limit buy order for 300 shares will be executed before the two market orders. The point of this exercise is to show that limit orders do not have any inherent disadvantage over market orders. Hence, it is better for a day trader to be in control of trading and submit a limit order than a market order.

Trading Terminology

There are four trading terms that probably need differentiation: bidding, buying, offering, and selling securities. The trading terminology definitions are the following:

1. Bidding: *Bidding* is passive buying. The day trader is a price maker: he or she is trying to purchase securities at a better or lower price than the inside ASK price. Most commonly, the day trader will bid to purchase the security at the inside BID price, the lowest possible price that the day trader can buy the stock. If the day trader is less aggressive, the trader could bid the high BID, which is the price higher than the inside BID and lower than the inside ASK. Most commonly the day trader will use one of the ECNs or SelectNet to execute those trades.

Either way (bidding the BID or high BID on Island or SelectNet), the day trader needs a seller. There is no guarantee that the day trader will find that seller, or that the trade will be executed at that price level. The day trader's objective is to cut the spread between the BID and ASK prices and buy the stock at the lower price. This is a difficult task if the market is moving up. If the price of the stock has a clear upside momentum, why would anyone sell the stock at the lower price?

2. Buying: *Buying* is aggressive purchasing. The day trader is a price taker: he or she is sending an order to purchase a stock at the posted or advertised inside ASK price. The day trader is aggressive; he or she wants this stock badly and quickly because of the upside price momentum. The day trader is willing to sacrifice the spread. The day trader is taking the stock from someone offering the stock for sale at the inside ASK price through the SOES or ECNs: either a market maker posting the best inside ASK price within the SOES, or another day trader offering to sell the shares at the best inside ASK price through the Island. Since the purchasing price is the inside ASK price, there is a very good probability that the order will get filled.

3. Offering: *Offering* is passive selling. The day trader is a price maker; he or she is trying to sell securities at a better or higher price than the inside BID price. Most commonly, the day trader will offer to sell the security at the inside ASK price, the highest possible price at which the day trader can sell that stock. If the day trader is less aggressive, the trader could offer the low ASK, which is the price higher than the inside BID and lower than the inside ASK. Again, the day trader would use one of the ECNs or SelectNet to execute those trades.

Either way (offering the ASK or low ASK on Island or SelectNet), the day trader needs to find a buyer. There is no guarantee that the day trader will find that buyer, and no guarantee that the trade will be executed at that price level. The day trader's objective is to cut the spread between the BID and ASK prices and sell the stock at the higher price. This is a difficult task if the market is moving down. If the price of the stock has a clear downside momentum, the buyer has an incentive to wait for the price to move further down before buying the stock.

4. Selling: *Selling* is aggressive selling. The day trader is a price taker: he or she is sending an order to sell a stock at the posted or advertised inside BID price. The day trader is an aggressive seller. He or she wants badly to dump the stock, and quickly because of a downside price momentum. The day trader is willing to sacrifice the spread between the inside BID and ASK prices. The day trader is giving that stock to someone who is bidding the stock for purchase at the inside BID price through the SOES or ECNs: either a market maker posting the best inside BID price within the SOES, or another day trader bidding to buy the shares at the inside BID price through the Island. Since the selling price is the inside BID price, there is a very good probability that the order will get filled.

Figure 12.2 helps to illustrate this point.

NASDAQ SOES Orders

The NASD's Small Order Execution System (SOES) was designed specifically for the benefit of small investors or traders. Day traders or

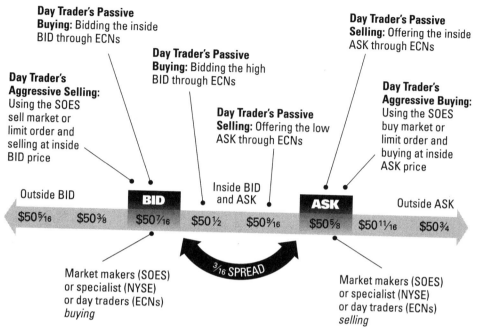

Figure 12.2   *Bidding, Buying, Offering, and Selling*

investors always buy the stock at the posted low ASK price or sell the stock at the posted high BID price from the market makers through the SOES system. The execution order is routed directly to the NASDAQ market makers. SOES orders are executed on a first-come, first-served basis, in price order. This assures that the day traders or investors receive the best posted price.

The second key feature of the SOES is its mandatory nature. The NASD requires that all market makers post their BID and ASK prices and subsequently honor those trades. Since SOES orders are mandatory for the market makers and are executed automatically, the SOES system is a very powerful trading execution tool. When stock prices are moving up fast, the SOES buy order is an excellent tool for getting into the market quickly at a guaranteed price. Conversely, if stock prices are declining quickly, the SOES sell order is an excellent tool for getting out of the market quickly at a guaranteed price.

The speed of the SOES order execution depends on how many market makers are at the inside BID and ASK market and how many other day trading SOES orders are in the computerized queue. The unanswerable question is how many and how quickly the market makers are refreshing the inside BID and ASK quotes. The market makers are only required to post the minimum required size (1,000 shares for the most actively traded stocks) on the Level II screen, and that is exactly what they do. Thus the posted 1,000 shares on the Level II screen may not be the actual trading size. The market makers do not like to open their trading hands and disclose to the public the true size or interest of their buying or selling intentions. The "Ax" market maker can continue to refresh 1,000 after 1,000 shares of any particular stock at the lowest ASK price (that is, continue to sell), and thus effectively stop any price momentum.

Getting in the market with the SOES is one of the most common execution methods of day trading. Once day traders ascertain an upward price movement, they quickly jump into the market through the SOES limit order. They buy the stock at the posted inside ASK price rather than trying to bid into the stock at the inside BID price or higher BID price. The SOES grants them quick execution at the guaranteed best ASK price at that time. The key is to get into the market quickly to pick up that price momentum.

After a day trader takes a long position in a stock and after the stock appreciates in value, the day trader then commonly tries to get out of that position through an ECN (for example, Island). If the BID and ASK prices are 50 and $50\frac{1}{8}$, the day traders have three options for selling the stock:

1. An SOES sell limit order at the inside BID price of 50; or
2. An offer to sell the stock at the current inside ASK price through the ECN at $50\frac{1}{8}$; or
3. An offer to sell the stock at a lower price than the current inside ASK price through the ECN at $50\frac{1}{16}$.

The probability is high that the day traders would use one of the last two options to get a better selling price for the stock. Most likely, the day traders would try to cut the spread, sell the stock at $50\frac{1}{16}$, and earn an additional $\frac{1}{16}$. The additional $\frac{1}{16}$ on a 1,000-share increment block translates into a $62.50 gain.

The SOES treats limit orders priced at the current inside BID and ASK market as market orders that are immediately executed. The SOES orders are unpreferenced orders, which are executed against the market makers in rotation. The SOES does not execute an unpreferenced order against a single market maker more than once every 15 seconds. That means the market makers can be "SOESed" by the day trader, and the market makers have the option to refresh the same price or back away to the outside BID and ASK market.

SOES Mechanics

All NASDAQ stocks have an SOES limit. Most day trading stocks have a 1,000-share limit. Most trading software automatically displays the tier limit under the share amount allowed under SOES. The day trader cannot send out through SOES an execution order for more than the tier limit. If the market makers are not available at the inside BID or ASK market, the SOES order will be canceled automatically. If the only party available at the inside BID or ASK market is an ECN, such as the Island, the SOES order will be rejected. Certain small capitalization stocks may display a few market makers on the Level II screen, but the stock may not be traded through the SOES. In that case, the trading software would generate a message: "No SOES market maker available."

From the day trader's perspective, the maximum SOES order size for a security is either 1,000, 500, or 200 shares, depending on the price and trading volume of that security. Only public customers' orders that are not larger than the maximum order size may be entered by the SOES order entry firm (the day trading firm or NASD broker or dealer) into SOES for execution against the SOES market maker. Orders in excess of the maximum order size may not be divided into smaller parts for purposes of meeting the size requirements for orders entered into SOES.

The SOES previously had a five-minute rule that was repealed in the summer of 1998. That rule stated that if an order was filled through SOES, the day trader could not trade that same stock in the same direction within 5 minutes. In other words, the day trader could not buy 1,000 shares of Dell and then buy another 1,000 or any other amount of Dell within 5 minutes of buying the original 1,000 shares. Again, that rule has been rescinded.

Several orders that are based on a single investment decision and that are entered for accounts under the control of associated persons will be deemed to constitute a single order. The size of those orders will be aggregated for determining the compliance with the SOES order size limits. An associated person will be deemed to control an account if he or she exercises discretion over the account or has been granted a power of attorney to execute transactions in the account, or if the account belongs to a member of his "immediate family." In other words, NASD does not want to have a single day trader ordering "Buy Dell" to ten associates or assistants who would simultaneously input that buy order for 1,000 shares each through the SOES. As the name implies, SOES is designed for the benefit of small traders and investors.

Placing an SOES order is a simple task. The day trader would select the stock by typing in the stock symbol on the keyboard. Then he or she would press the default function key for the action to enter the SOES order. Users can choose between limit and market SOES orders by pressing different function keys.

Canceling a live SOES order is a simple task as well. The day trader would load the stock by typing in the stock symbol. Then the day trader would hold down the Shift key while pressing the C key to cancel the order. If the day trader does not manually send the cancel order and the order is still alive (that is, not executed), then the order will be canceled automatically after the user-defined preset time (60 seconds). The day trader will receive confirmation on the computer screen that the order has been canceled.

13

NASDAQ's SelectNet Orders

SELECTNET IS AN EXECUTION ORDER SERVICE OWNED AND OPERATED BY NASDAQ. While the SOES execution service is mandatory for market makers, use of SelectNet is completely voluntary. As the name implies, the day trader would "select" and offer to the market makers a bid to buy or offer to sell shares of a stock. However, the submitted order does not have to be filled by the market makers.

In essence, SelectNet is a completely voluntary and interactive marketplace between the day traders on one side and the market makers and ECN market participants on the other. A SelectNet order will get filled only if the market makers perceive that the day trader's bid or offer is a "good deal." Day traders who are using trading execution software that has the SelectNet feature can either "broadcast" their bids or offers to all market makers, or "preference" a single market maker or ECN market participant.

SelectNet Broadcast Orders

The first option is to "broadcast" the bid and offer. Day traders can broadcast to all market makers their bid to buy a stock at the current inside BID price. They can also broadcast to all market makers their bid to buy a stock at the higher BID price. The day trader's bid would be posted throughout the NASDAQ network to all market makers, but it would not show up on Level II screens. In other words, the offer to buy the stock at the inside BID price or higher BID price will be visible only to marker makers.

Why would a day trader want to use the SelectNet broadcast as an execution vehicle? If the buy order gets filled, the day trader would buy the stock at the inside BID price. At worst, the day trader would buy the stock at the higher BID price. Either way, the day trader will be better off with the SelectNet broadcast than buying the stock through the SOES at the best ASK price. Isn't it always better to buy at the lower price than the higher price? The day trader will always be better off buying the stock at the inside BID or higher BID price than at the lowest ASK price.

However, the key phrase is "if the bid offer gets filled." There is no guarantee that the market makers will fill the order. The day trader only hopes that the order will get filled. He or she might hope that one of the market makers who is currently buying the stock at the inside BID price (that is, the market maker is already on the inside BID side) might fill the order.

SelectNet Preference Orders

The second option is to "preference" a single market maker through SelectNet. When the SelectNet preference order is submitted to the market maker, that order will show up on the market maker's computer screen. The market maker would have 15 seconds either to fill the order or to move off of the posted price. In essence, the day trader is "reminding" the market maker that the posted price needs to be honored. The SelectNet preference bid forces the selected market maker to act by either accepting or rejecting the bid. It is a good practice to refresh SelectNet orders after 15 seconds if the order is not executed by the market maker.

On the other hand, the day trader cannot cancel the SelectNet order for 10 seconds. So if the market starts to move in the opposite direction during that time, the day trader does not have the option to cancel the order. The probability is that the market maker would have filled the order during that time. After 10 seconds, the day trader can manually send a cancel order, or the order will be canceled automatically by the software after a user-defined preset time (15 seconds). At that time, the day trader would receive a confirmation message on the computer screen that the SelectNet order had been canceled.

SelectNet Order Execution Mechanics

Placing a SelectNet order is a relatively simple task. The day trader would type in the stock symbol in the appropriate window and press the Enter key. At that time, the day trader would hold down the Shift key while pressing the default function key for the SelectNet order routing action. Figure 13.1 displays an example of a SelectNet window that would open, along with Level II screen information.

If the asterisk (*)shown in Figure 13.1 is selected, the software will send a SelectNet broadcast order to all market makers. The day trader could send out a SelectNet preference order to a particular market maker with a click of the mouse button. In this example, the day trader can "select" one market maker who is advertising to buy Dell at $64\frac{3}{8}$: The day trader could send his bid to sell Dell at $64\frac{3}{8}$ to Goldman, Sachs & Co. (GSCO), or to Bear Sterns & Co. (BEST), or to Smith Barney, Inc. (SBSH), or to Instinet (INCA) seller.

The day trader can access any market maker through SelectNet preferencing. The trader simply selects a price, and the software will match that price with all the available market makers at the price shown on the Level II screen. In Figure 13.2, as the price arrow in the box is clicked, the market maker window will change, displaying the market makers and ECNs available at that price.

The day trader can use the up and down arrow to the right of the price box to adjust the price. Clicking on these arrow keys or using the

Figure 13.1 *SelectNet Order Execution and Level II Screen*

keyboard arrow keys will increase or decrease the price by $\frac{1}{32}$. When the day trader clicks on the OK button shown in Figure 13.2, the order is sent through the NASDAQ SelectNet network. If the day trader increases the inside BID price by $\frac{1}{32}$ or $\frac{1}{16}$, he or she is broadcasting to all market makers in the universe that he is bidding to buy the stock at the high BID price, which is higher than the current inside BID price.

In essence, day traders who want to buy a stock through the Select-Net have two alternatives. First, they can bid to buy the stock at the inside BID price, or, as the day traders would say, "Bid the BID." Second, they can bid to buy the stock at the price higher than the current inside BID, or, as the day traders would say, "Bid the high BID."

Conversely, day traders who want to sell a stock through SelectNet would also have two options. First, the day traders could offer to sell the stock at the inside ASK price, or "offer the ASK." Second, the day traders could offer to sell the stock at a price lower than the current inside ASK, or, as the day traders would say, "Offer the low ASK."

Unlike with SOES, there is no tier size limit on a SelectNet order. The day trader can bid to buy or offer to sell in increments of 2,000 or more shares. Since SelectNet is a voluntary order execution system, no one is forced to honor any trade. In fact, the market makers have the option to execute partial orders through SelectNet at their discretion.

In addition to the posted market makers, the day trader can also access Instinet (INCA) and other ECNs through the SelectNet order execution system.

SelectNet Preference Buy Order Trading Strategy

One common day trading strategy is to use the SelectNet preference order to get in or out of a stock when the market is moving quickly. The day trader can bid or offer on SelectNet as a way to take advantage of market momentum. Figure 13.2 will help to illustrate this point.

Let us say that the inside market is $50\frac{1}{2}$ to $50^{19}\!/_{32}$ for this stock. Let us also assume that the stock has strong upside momentum. The day trader wants eagerly to buy 1,000 shares of this stock. There is only one market maker on the Level II screen who is posting the lowest ASK price of $50^{19}\!/_{32}$. If the day trader decides to utilize the SOES buy limit order at $50^{19}\!/_{32}$, he or she will probably not be the first trader in the computerized queue, and the SOES buy limit order would probably not get filled.

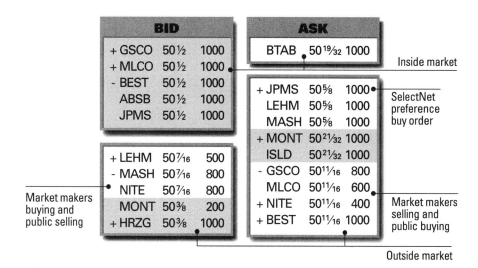

Figure 13.2 *SelectNet Preference Buy Order Routing*

If B. T. Alex Brown, Inc. (BTAB) leaves the inside ASK price, the new lowest ASK would become $50\frac{5}{8}$. At that time, the day trader can submit an SOES buy limit order at $50\frac{5}{8}$. Again, he or she would compete with many other day traders who would attempt to execute the same SOES buy market or limit orders at that price. If the upside price momentum is strong, the day trader might miss the market. There are only three market makers who are posting 1,000 shares for sale. Those market makers could refresh the price and sell more than the posted 3,000 shares. If the market is moving, it is likely that the best ASK price will go up quickly above $50\frac{5}{8}$.

Rather than risking the opportunity altogether to buy a stock that is moving up fast, day traders can elect from the beginning to preference the market makers who are on the outside market at that time. Using our example in Figure 13.2, the astute day trader could immediately submit the SelectNet preference buy order for 1,000 shares to J. P. Morgan Securities, Inc. (JPMS) or Lehman Brothers, Inc. (LEHM) for $50\frac{5}{8}$, although the lowest ASK price at that time is $50\frac{19}{32}$. In essence, the day trader would forgo the best ASK price and pay $\frac{1}{32}$ more. But that would enhance the probability that the day trader would end up owning the stock that is currently moving up in value.

SelectNet Preference Sell Order Trading Strategy

Conversely, let us assume that the stock has strong downside momentum. The inside market is $50^{17}/_{32}$ to $50^{5}/_{8}$ for this stock. The day trader wants eagerly to get out of the long position and sell 1,000 shares of this stock. There is only one market maker on the Level II screen who is posting the highest BID price of $50^{17}/_{32}$. If the day trader decides to utilize the SOES sell limit order at $50^{17}/_{32}$, the day trader will probably not be the first in line in the nation. The probability is that the SOES sell limit order would not get filled.

If Mayer & Schweitzer, Inc. (MASH) leave the inside BID price, the new highest BID would become $50^{1}/_{2}$. At that time, the day trader can submit an SOES sell limit order at $50^{1}/_{2}$. The day trader would compete with many other traders who would attempt to execute the same SOES sell market or limit orders at that price. If the downside price momentum is strong, the day trader might miss that price as well. There are only two market makers who are each posting 1,000 shares for purchase. Those market makers could refresh the price and buy more than the posted 2,000 shares. However, if the market is moving downward the probability is that the best BID price will further decrease quickly.

Rather than risking the opportunity to dump the stock that is moving down fast, day traders can elect from the beginning to preference the market makers who are on the outside market at that time. Figure 13.3

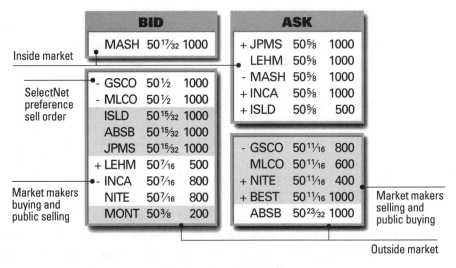

Figure 13.3 *SelectNet Preference Sell Order Routing*

illustrates this point. The astute day trader could immediately submit the SelectNet preference sell order for 1,000 shares to Goldman, Sachs & Co. (GSCO) or Merrill Lynch (MLCO) for $50\frac{1}{2}$. The day trader would forgo the best BID price and sell for $\frac{1}{32}$ less. But that would enhance the probability that the day trader would end up dumping a stock that is declining in value.

C H A P T E R

14

Island Orders

In January 1997, the Securities and Exchange Commission (SEC) made a ruling regarding limit order display. That rule dramatically changed how execution orders are handled when buying and selling securities in U.S. equities markets. The rule has helped individual day traders and investors to become an integral part of the stock trading world. It has ensured that individual day traders and investors have the same access to the most favorable pricing available as their professional and institutional counterparts.

The SEC requires that all stock exchanges must display traders' or investors' limit orders in their quotes when they're priced better than market maker BID and ASK quotes. This means that the trader's best-priced limit orders are displayed on the trading screens of all market participants. Consequently, this allows limit orders to receive much greater visibility and more timely execution.

In addition, the SEC declared a new "Quote Rule" that requires all market makers to publicly display their most competitive quotes. In the past, market makers commonly placed orders on proprietary systems that have been priced more favorably than their public BID and ASK quotes. Private trading systems such as the Instinet would have posted prices that were only available to financial professionals. Now, the market makers are required to post the same most favorable BID and ASK prices regardless of whether the stock is traded in a public market (for example, on NASDAQ) or in a proprietary system (for example, Instinet). This rule assures that market makers do not set dual prices for the same stock.

The NASDAQ market makers or the NYSE specialists have four options they can exercise upon receipt of a limit order. They may elect to:

1. Change the quote and the associated size to reflect the new limit order;
2. Execute the limit order;
3. Deliver the limit order to a different exchange market that complies with the rules;
4. Send the limit order to another market maker who would comply with the rules.

Like any other rules, the SEC rule has exceptions. The first exception applies to any customer limit order that is executed upon receipt of the order. The second exception applies to any limit order that is placed by a customer who expressly requests that the order not be displayed. The third exception applies to odd lot orders, which are not required to be displayed. The fourth exception applies to block size orders of at least 10,000 shares, or for a quantity of stock having a market value of at least $20,000, which need not be displayed unless the customer so requests. The last exception applies to "all or none limit orders," so that the exchanges can avoid operational difficulties regarding partial order executions.

ECNs

The Electronic Communications Network (ECN) is a proprietary electronic execution system that widely disseminates to the public orders entered by day traders, market makers, and specialists, and permits such orders to be executed against in whole or in part (called a "partial fill"). The objective of the ECNs is to broadcast firm prices that are quoted by day traders, market makers, and specialists in securities. The recent SEC analysis of stock trading activities has produced evidence of the existence of a two-tiered securities market. The NASDAQ market makers routinely trade stocks at one price with their retail customers and at better prices with institutional clients through the ECNs. For example, a great majority of all BID and ASK prices displayed through an ECN such as Instinet were posted at better prices than those posted publicly on

NASDAQ. There are several privately owned ECNs in existence today. The most prominent are Island (ISLD), Instinet (INCA), Terranova (TNTO), Attain (ATTN), Bloomberg Tradebook (BTRD), and Spear, Leads, & Kellogg (REDI).

Island

Island is an ECN with the ticker symbol ISLD. It is owned and developed by Datek Securities, and its purpose is to match bids and offers electronically. Orders that are not matched immediately in the Island book will then be displayed on Level II screens if the order is over 100 shares and at the inside BID and ASK. Unlike SOES orders, Island orders do not have tier size limits. All Island orders are left as day orders.

Island automatically rejects all orders that are crossed or locked. A locked up market occurs when the inside BID and ASK prices are the same. A crossed up market occurs when the inside BID price is higher than the current or proposed ASK price. That means the day trader could buy the stock at the lower ASK price and simultaneously sell it at the higher BID price. A crossed market also happens when the inside ASK is lower than the proposed current BID price. Again, that means the day trader could simultaneously buy the stock at the lower price and sell it at the higher price.

When a trade order is entered into Island, the Island system directs the order first to an Island server for order matching and then to the NASDAQ SelectNet system. Day traders can access Island directly or through the SelectNet execution system. Placing Island orders directly to Island, as opposed to preferencing Island via SelectNet, is the faster of the two routes. Most day trading firms have an Island server that routes Island orders directly to the Island system. (It is important that a new day trader verify this before opening an account with any day trading firm.)

Island *fills* are quick and relatively inexpensive. Island trades usually cost $1 more than SOES orders. If the Island system has a better BID or ASK price available than the trader's submitted BID or ASK price, the Island will fill the order at that better price. The day trader should not use "fill or kill" orders through Island, since it is likely that the orders will not get filled. The downside of Island orders is partial fills.

The Island execution system displays the day trader's Island order on the Level II screen only if the day trader has entered the highest BID or the lowest ASK. If several day traders enter multiple Island orders at the same BID or ASK price, the Island system will simply add up the share sizes to reflect all submitted orders. Island orders must be greater than 100 shares to be displayed on the Level II screen.

Using the Island execution system is crucial for a successful day trading business. The Island provides day traders with additional liquidity and opportunity to obtain a better price. Figures 14.1 and 14.2 illustrate this point well. Figure 14.1 represents a starting point. The inside market is $50\frac{1}{2}$ and $50\frac{5}{8}$, which means that the stock has a spread of $\frac{1}{8}$. There are five market makers on each side of the stock demand and supply. The inside BID and ASK prices seem stable.

Let us assume that the day trader wants to take a long position in this stock. The day trader could use the SOES to buy 1,000 shares of this stock from one of the five market makers who posted the lowest ASK price of $50\frac{5}{8}$. Since the spread is $\frac{1}{8}$, the day trader could attempt to cut the spread and buy the stock for a better price. The Island order is an excellent vehicle through which to accomplish this task.

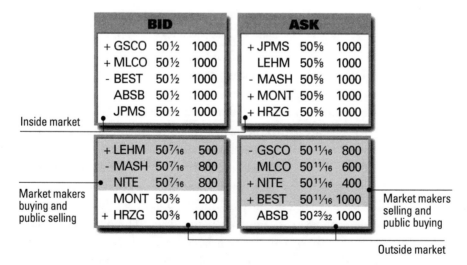

Figure 14.1 *Inside and Outside Market Before the Island Order*

Bidding the High BID

The day trader could bid to buy the stock at the higher BID price than the posted inside BID of $50\frac{1}{2}$. Suppose that the day trader enters his or her Island (ISLD) bid to buy the stock for the higher price of $50\frac{17}{32}$, which is $\frac{1}{32}$ higher than the inside BID shown in Figure 14.1. Figure 14.2 displays the Level II screen after the day trader entered the Island order and bid the high BID price.

The new inside market for the stock is $50\frac{17}{32}$ and $50\frac{5}{8}$. The probability of this Island order being executed is excellent. The day trader is advertising nationally that he or she wants the stock and has submitted to pay the best selling price in the nation for it. Other day traders or market makers with access to the Island system and who are selling the stock at this point of time could accept the trader's bid and sell the stock at $50\frac{17}{32}$. The probability is great that the order would get filled. The shares of that stock would be sold to the day trader at $50\frac{17}{32}$ rather than being sold at the lower price of $50\frac{1}{2}$ to the five listed market makers.

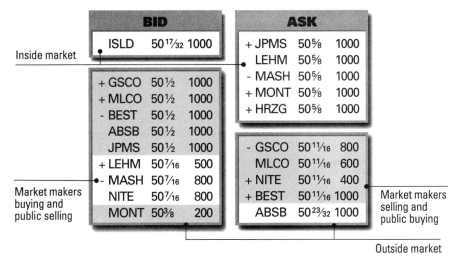

Figure 14.2 *Inside and Outside Markets After Bidding the High BID Through Island*

Someone who has access to the Level II screen and Island execution system would have to enter the sell order for 1,000 shares at $50^{17}/_{32}$. The Island would then automatically match the two orders, and both orders would get filled. After the Island system has matched and executed the buy and sell order for 1,000 shares at $50^{17}/_{32}$, the Island bid will disappear from the Level II screen. The inside market BID and ASK prices will revert back to $50^{1}/_{2}$ and $50^{5}/_{8}$. Assuming that there were no other changes, the Level II screen would look again like Figure 14.1.

Bidding the BID

The day trader has the option to attempt to buy the stock at a price lower than $50^{17}/_{32}$. He or she can simply bid the BID. In other words, the day trader can submit the bid through Island to pay the same price for the stock as the other five market makers. Figure 14.3 shows this. The day trader can bid through Island the same inside BID price of $50^{1}/_{2}$ for the stock. However, the probability is now lower that the order will get filled, because the day trader has the competition of five other market makers who are buying the stock for that price.

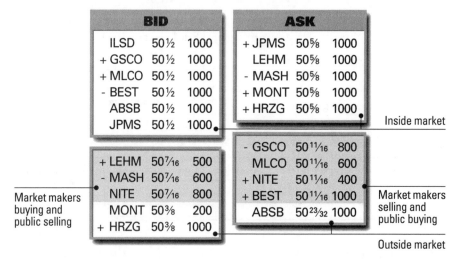

Figure 14.3 *Inside and Outside Market After Bidding the BID Through Island*

Conversely, suppose that the day trader wants to close an existing long position in that stock. The day trader could use SOES to sell 1,000 shares of that stock to one of the five market makers who posted the lowest BID price of $50\frac{1}{2}$, as displayed in Figure 14.1. Again, the spread is $\frac{1}{8}$. The day trader could attempt to cut the spread and sell the stock for a better price. Again, the Island order is an excellent vehicle through which to complete this assignment.

Offering the Low ASK

The day trader could offer to sell the stock at the lower ASK price than the posted inside ASK of $50\frac{5}{8}$. Suppose that the day trader decided to enter the Island offer to sell the stock for the lower price of $50\frac{19}{32}$, which is $\frac{1}{32}$ lower than the inside ASK in Figure 14.1. Figure 14.4 displays the Level II screen after the day trader entered the Island order and offered the low ASK price.

The new inside market for that stock is $50\frac{1}{2}$ and $50\frac{19}{32}$. The probability of this Island sell order being executed is great. The day trader is

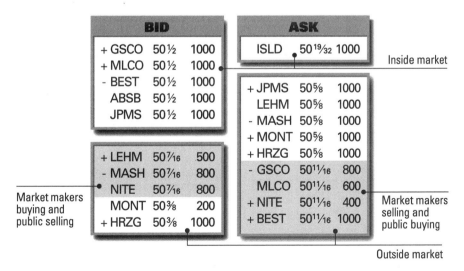

Figure 14.4 *Inside and Outside Market After Offering the Low ASK Through Island*

broadcasting nationally that he or she wants to sell the stock and is willing to accept the lowest selling price in the nation for that stock. Other day traders or market makers with access to the Island system and who are buying this stock at this point of time could accept the offer and buy the stock at $50^{19}\!/_{32}$. Thus, the probability is great that the sell order will get filled.

The mechanics of the Island order are the following: Someone who has access to the Level II screen and Island execution system would enter the buy order for 1,000 shares at $50^{19}\!/_{32}$. The Island would automatically match the two orders, and both orders would get filled. After the Island system has matched and executed the buy and sell order for 1,000 shares at $50^{19}\!/_{32}$, the Island offer will disappear from the Level II screen. The inside Market BID and ASK prices will revert back to $50\,^{1}\!/_{2}$ and $50^{5}\!/_{8}$.

Offering the ASK

The day trader also has the option to attempt to sell the stock at a higher price than the $50^{19}\!/_{32}$. He or she can simply offer the ASK. In other words, the day trader can submit the offer through Island to accept the same selling ASK price for the stock as the other five market makers. Figure 14.5

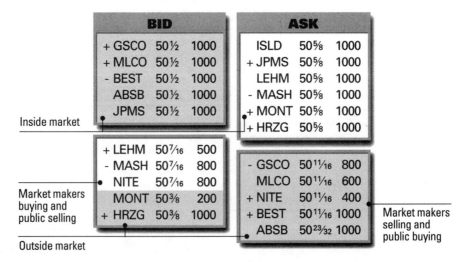

Figure 14.5 *Inside and Outside Markets After Offering the ASK Through Island*

shows this. The day trader can offer through Island the same inside ASK price of $50\frac{5}{8}$ for the stock. However, the probability is now lower that the order would get filled, since the day trader now has competition.

Island Order Mechanics

Placing or entering an Island order is a relatively simple task. The day trader would type in the stock symbol in the appropriate window and hit the Enter key. Then he or she would press the Island function keys for the buy and sell orders. The Island order box will appear on the screen. The day trader can then adjust the price with the arrow keys next to the price box or use the keyboard arrow keys. The day trader can adjust the price up to bid the high BID or down to offer the low ASK. The day trader would click the mouse to move the up and down arrow to the right of the price box to adjust the price by $\frac{1}{32}$. When the trade order is ready, the day trader would click on the OK button to send the order or press the Enter key.

It is also a simple task to cancel an Island order. The day trader would load the stock in the appropriate window and hold down the Shift key while pressing the C key to cancel the order. If the day trader does not manually send the cancel order, the order will be canceled automatically after a predefined and preset time (for example, 10 seconds). At that time the day trader would receive a confirmation message on the computer screen that the Island order has been canceled.

Island Book

The Island book allows the day trader to see every Island buy and sell order for a particular stock. In essence, the Island book displays the "depth" of the Island at different price levels. The Level II screen allows the day trader only to see the Island high BID and low ASK prices or the inside market. The Island book shows all bids and offers at every price level as well as the available quantity of shares. Thus the concept of the Island book is similar to the NASDAQ Level II screen.

However, the fact that the Island book shows actual shares is an important distinction between the Level II screen and the Island book. Market makers are required to post the required minimum stock share sizes (that is, tier limit) offered to sell or purchase on the Level II screen, and that is exactly what is shown on the Level II screen. The market makers do not wish to show their full hands. For instance, a market maker broadcasts that 1,000 shares of Dell are offered for sale. In reality, the same market maker might be selling 100,000 shares of Dell. From the Level II screen, the day traders cannot tell the actual size of the Dell inside or outside market.

On the other hand, the Island book displays the actual size of the inside or outside market for any stock. This is very useful information. Imagine that the day trader can see 100,000 shares of Dell being offered for sale at one price level higher than the inside ASK price. That would indicate that the supply of Dell is being increased dramatically. There is a distinct possibility that the price of Dell will decline in the near future. Figure 14.6 demonstrates this.

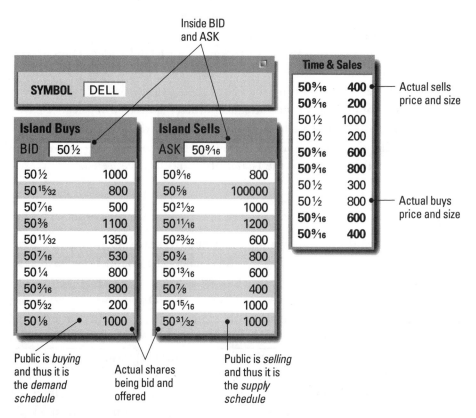

Figure 14.6 *Island Book*

The day trader can simply type in a stock symbol (for example, DELL), and the Island book will display the inside BID and ASK price and the total number of shares available at that level. In this example, there are 1,000 shares at $50\frac{1}{2}$ at the Island buys and 800 shares at $50\frac{9}{16}$ at the Island sells. In addition, the Island book displays all available price levels and share sizes. All actual bids and offers at the same price level are lumped together. For instance, the large 100,000 offer for sale at $50\frac{5}{8}$ could be possible, as it could be comprised of many smaller orders. The Time and Sales Island window displays the price, share amount of all "prints," or actual individual buys and sells. These are commonly color coded on the computer screen (green for buys and red for sells). In our black and white Figure 14.6 display, bold lettering represents red or the Island sells.

All Island orders are based on the FIFO system: First In, First Out. It is important to know what is being traded on Island. The day trader who has access to the Island book can plan an exit strategy. Suppose that the day trader has a long position in Dell. The day trader observes a large 100,000 sell offer at $50\frac{5}{8}$. He or she might submit an offer to sell Dell at $50\frac{19}{32}$. That would ensure that his or her offer is first in line for Island execution. In addition, that offer would place the day trader ahead of the large sell offer of 100,000 at $50\frac{5}{8}$. In essence, the day trader would make sure that he or she gets out before the anticipated price decline that comes with the large sell offer.

Short Selling

Short selling means that the customer is selling a stock that he or she does not own. The seller will borrow and deliver the "shorted" stock to the buyer at the settlement date, which is the standard "$T + 3$" date, or trade plus three business days. Since the seller has sold a stock that he or she does not own, the brokerage firm must lend him or her the stock first. The stock must be on the brokerage firm's "short list" of shortable stocks.

Short selling can exert downward pressure on a stock's price and force the price to drop abruptly and significantly within a single trading day. Because of this, both NASDAQ and the listed exchanges, such as NYSE, have a short sale rule that prohibits short selling on a down-tick. This short sale rule was developed to prevent speculative selling in the

NASDAQ or exchange-listed securities from accelerating a further decline in the price of that security.

Listed exchanges such as the NYSE have a "tick test," which states that the last reported sale price on the consolidated tape must be a plus tick. The SEC short sale rule prohibits short sales of exchange-listed securities if the current price is below the previous reported last sale price (minus tick or zero-minus tick). In other words, the last sale must be a plus tick before the trader can execute the short sale. The rule is simple and enforceable because the trade reports in most exchange-listed securities occur on a single exchange floor by a single specialist, who ensures the sequential trade reporting.

The NASDAQ market is much different. The trade reporting in NASDAQ securities involves different market makers for the same stock who are reporting trades from different locations to the NASD via a computer interface. NASD requires that all trades must be reported within 90 seconds of execution. That means that two sequential trades might not be reported to the NASD at the same time, and thus they may not appear on the NASDAQ tape in sequential order. Consequently, the NASDAQ short sale rule was designed as a "BID test" rather than a "tick test."

The NASD short sale rule prohibits short sales if the BID price is below the current inside BID price for a NASDAQ security. The trading software system calculates automatically if the inside BID is an "up BID" or a "down BID," so that traders will have that information at their fingertips when attempting to execute short sales. The day trader would pay close attention to whether the current BID price tick arrow is up or down and whether the inside BID is green or red. If the inside BID is green or the current BID tick arrow is up, then the short sale is legal. The day trader can then short the stock.

However, the day trader has an alternative. He or she does not need to wait for the up-tick to try to execute the short sale. Even if the stock is declining continuously in value (a continuous down-tick), the day trader can attempt to create his or her own up-tick. In essence, the day traders can use Island order execution and short sell the stock on a down-tick. All that trader would need to do is to offer to sell the stock $\frac{1}{16}$ higher than the current inside BID price. And thus, the day trader would create his own up-tick. The risk to the day trader is that he or she now has that $\frac{1}{16}$ to overcome—the spread is that much larger.

Short Selling Mechanics

Suppose that the day trader decided to enter the Island offer to sell the stock for the lower ASK price of $50\frac{9}{16}$. This is $\frac{1}{16}$ higher than the current inside BID and $\frac{1}{16}$ lower than the previous inside ASK price shown in Figure 14.1. Figure 14.7 displays the Level II screen after the day trader entered the Island order and offered to short sell the stock at the low ASK price and $\frac{1}{16}$ higher than the inside BID.

The new inside market for that stock is $50\frac{1}{2}$ and $50\frac{9}{16}$. From the viewpoint of trade mechanics, the probability of this short sell order being executed is good. The day trader is advertising nationally that he or she wants to sell the stock and is willing to accept the lowest selling price in the nation for that stock. The short selling day trader needs to find one day trader or investor or market maker who has access to the Island execution system and who is willing to buy that stock at this point of time. The buyer would accept that offer and buy the stock at $50\frac{9}{16}$.

The only question is whether the buying traders or investors are willing to buy a stock when the stock is dropping in value. The day trader is short selling the stock because he or she anticipates further price reduction. Other day traders or investors in the market perhaps

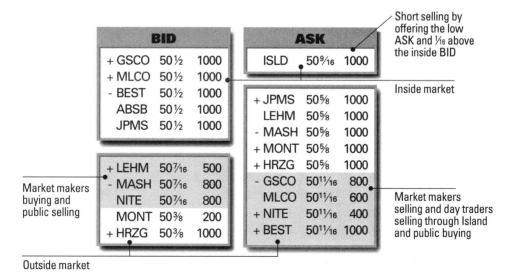

Figure 14.7 *Short Selling by Offering the Low ASK Through Island*

perceive the same downward trend as well. Thus, the probability is uncertain how quickly the short sell order would get filled.

The mechanics of this short sale Island order is the following. Someone who has access to the Level II screen and Island execution system would enter the buy order for 1,000 shares at $50\frac{9}{16}$. The Island would automatically match the two orders, and both orders would get filled. After the Island system has matched and executed the buy and sell order for 1,000 shares at $50\frac{9}{16}$, the Island offer will disappear from the ASK side of the Level II screen. The inside Market BID and ASK prices will revert back to $50\frac{1}{2}$ and $50\frac{5}{8}$.

It is important that day traders are proficient and comfortable with the mechanics of short selling. Short selling is one-half of the day trading equation. Day traders cannot expect to go long on every single trade. There will be days when the overall market is declining, and the day traders will need to go short. It is difficult to make money on long positions when the overall market values are descending.

When the price ascending movement stops and price reverts in value, there is a sudden influx of sellers who are trying to get out of the stock quickly. Sellers rush to close their long positions in order to minimize losses or protect profits. On the other hand, there is little movement on the demand side. Buyers are waiting for a bargain. They are waiting for the price to decline further in value before stepping in and buying the stock. So the price tends to drop quickly.

Short selling is potentially very lucrative. The short sellers can make more money more quickly than traders or investors who specialize in long positions. The prices tend to decline much faster than they appreciate in value. A brief look at any price chart would generally reveal a gradual price increase followed by a sharp decline. The quick drop in value can be attributed to panic selling. Fear of losing money is a powerful motivator.

15

Instinet

INSTINET, WITH ITS INCA TICKET SYMBOL, IS THE LARGEST ELECTRONIC Communications Network (ECN). It is a private corporation, headquartered in New York City and owned by the Reuters Group PLC. Instinet Corporation is registered with the SEC as a NASD broker/dealer; it is a member of all U.S. stock exchanges and other major international stock exchanges. It was created in 1969 to furnish equity transaction services specifically to an international base of institutional investors (that is, fund managers).

As the name implies, Instinet is a trading network of large financial institutions. It does not take the role of a principal: Instinet does not buy or sell securities for its own account. Its only business is to provide 24-hour access to securities brokerage services for the benefit of its institutional customers. As a proprietary ECN, Instinet provides its institutional customers with a vehicle with which to transact their securities trading business among themselves at a lower cost and often at a better price.

The day trader can execute an Instinet order by preferencing INCA through the NASDAQ SelectNet. In addition, many day trading firms have a stand-alone Instinet order execution computer on the trading floor. But Instinet is important not only as a vehicle that executes trade orders. Instinet transactions represent activities of large financial institutions. Day traders must pay attention to Instinet transactions, because those transactions can provide insight into the activities of the Wall Street professionals.

There are a few proprietary software packages that track or filter the trading activities on the Instinet. First, the software keeps track of the volume of shares of a stock that is being bid and offered by the financial institutions through Instinet. Second, the software keeps track of prices that are bid and offered by the financial institutions. Most important, the software will keep a record if and when there is a price differential between the stock prices on the public exchange (that is, NASDAQ) and the private exchange (that is, Instinet). This information can provide insights to the day trader on whether there is the potential for a particular stock price to go up or down.

Locked-Up Markets

Let us suppose that there is a difference in the Dell stock price and share volume that are bid and offered between the public (NASDAQ) and private (Instinet) markets. Suppose that the NASDAQ ASK price is identical to the Instinet BID price. This would constitute a "locked-up market." Since prices in the private market are generally *higher* than prices in the public market, this constitutes a bullish, or buy, sign, because it is assumed that large financial institutions that trade large sums of money on Instinet know more about the financial markets than the individual investors and traders who trade on NASDAQ.

Figure 15.1 displays the following locked-up markets:

Instinet ASK	>	NASDAQ ASK
Instinet BID	>	NASDAQ BID
Instinet BID	=	NASDAQ ASK

The Instinet BID and ASK prices are higher than the NASDAQ BID and ASK prices; this constitutes a buy signal.

The inside BID and ASK prices for Dell are $50\frac{1}{2}$ and $50\frac{5}{8}$. There are three market makers buying on the BID side and two market makers selling Dell shares on the ASK side. It is impossible to ascertain the actual size of buying and selling by the market makers, because market makers are not required to post the size. They are required only to display the minimum shares that they are willing to buy and sell. In reality, the volume flow can be many times larger than the posted minimum. Therefore, the $\frac{3}{2}$ ratio of BID to ASK market makers is the only indication of the volume flow in the public market.

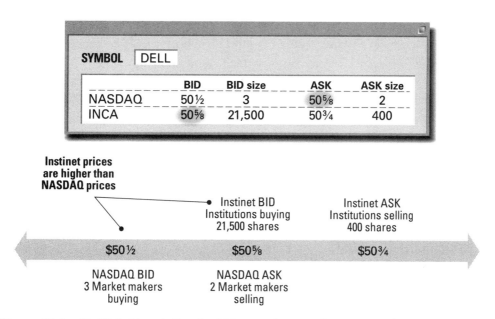

Figure 15.1 *Bullish Signal: Locked-Up Markets with Large Bid Volume*

On the other hand, the private market (Instinet) has a different price and volume structure for this stock. The high BID and the low ASK price for Dell on Instinet is $50\frac{5}{8}$ and $50\frac{3}{4}$. It is simple to ascertain the size of buying and selling by the financial institutions, because the participating Instinet institutions post the sizes of their bids and offers. Together the institutions are bidding to buy 21,500 shares of Dell. On the other hand, the institutions are offering to sell only 400 shares of Dell. Therefore, the ratio of BID to ASK volume is positive $(^{21,500}/_{400})$, and it is an indication of the actual volume flow in the private market.

Figure 15.1 reveals that the NASDAQ and Instinet markets are already locked up: the Instinet BID price and NASDAQ inside ASK prices are the same. Also, look at the buying volume of the Instinet. Once the 400 shares are sold on the Instinet, financial institutions that want to purchase Dell will move to the public market. They would start buying Dell shares in the public market from the two market makers on the ASK side. That would clearly deplete the existing supply of Dell shares that are being offered for sale by the two market makers at $50\frac{5}{8}$. Those market makers would quickly increase the price (due to higher demand), or they would leave the inside ASK price. Later, different market makers would come in with a new higher inside ASK price.

Figure 15.1 also displays the locked-up Instinet and NASDAQ markets with substantial Instinet BID volume. This constitutes a clear buy signal. Sometimes the Instinet and NASDAQ markets can be locked up, with the Instinet volume on the ASK side. Imagine that there are 21,500 shares in the Instinet BID book and 40,000 shares in the Instinet ASK book. That would mean that there are many more Instinet sellers than there are Instinet buyers. The sheer size of the selling volume would act as a suppressing force on any future price increase.

Crossed-Up Markets

Suppose that there is a major difference in the stock price and share volume that are being bid and offered between the public (NASDAQ) and private (Instinet) markets. This time the NASDAQ ASK price is lower than the Instinet BID price. That would constitute a "crossed-up market." The crossed-up market also constitutes a very strong bullish or buy signal. Figure 15.2 displays the crossed-up markets. Since the prices in the private market are much higher than the prices in the public market, this constitutes a very strong bullish sign:

Instinet ASK	>	NASDAQ ASK
Instinet BID	>	NASDAQ BID
Instinet BID	>	NASDAQ ASK

The difference between the locked-up and crossed-up markets is subtle. In the crossed-up markets, the Instinet BID is even higher than the NASDAQ ASK. This alone will create an arbitrage opportunity.

In Figure 15.2, the inside BID and ASK prices for Dell are $50\frac{3}{8}$ and $50\frac{1}{2}$. Again, there are three market makers buying on the BID side and two market makers selling Dell shares on the ASK side. The $\frac{3}{2}$ ratio of the BID to ASK market makers is the only indication of the volume flow in the public market. The private market has a dramatically different price and volume structure for this stock. The high BID and the low ASK price for Dell on Instinet are $50\frac{5}{8}$ and $50\frac{3}{4}$. There is a $\frac{1}{8}$ spread between the Instinet BID and NASDAQ inside ASK prices. The institutions are bidding to buy 21,500 shares of Dell and offering to sell 400 shares of

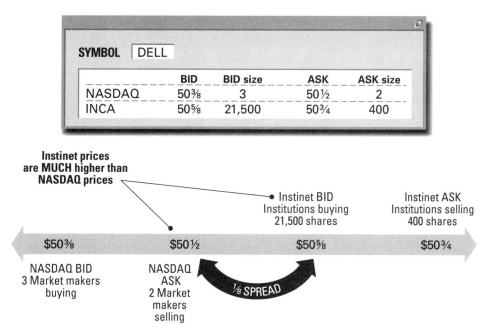

Figure 15.2 *Strong Bullish Signal: Crossed-Up Markets with Large Bid Volume*

Dell. Therefore, the ratio of BID to ASK volume is positive (that is, $^{21,500}/_{400}$); it is an indication of the actual volume flow in the private market.

Since there is a major difference in the buying and selling prices of the two markets (the $\frac{1}{8}$ spread), there is potential for a price *arbitrage*. That means the institutional trader could buy the stock on the NASDAQ at the lower inside ASK price from two market makers, and simultaneously sell it at the higher BID price on the Instinet. This would be a riskless trading transaction. The arbitrage would result in higher demand for Dell shares in the public market and increased supply of Dell shares in the private market. The ultimate result would be increased Dell prices in the public market and lowered Dell prices in the private market. The $\frac{1}{8}$ spread between the Instinet BID and NASDAQ inside ASK prices would gradually disappear, and the markets would cease to be crossed.

Also, the buying volume on the Instinet indicates a strong potential for the price to increase. Once the 400 shares are sold on the Instinet, financial institutions that want to purchase Dell will move to the public market. They would again start buying Dell shares in the public market from the two market makers on the ASK side. That would again deplete the existing supply of Dell shares that are offered for sale by the two market makers at $50\frac{1}{2}$. Those market makers would quickly increase the price (due to higher demand), or they would leave the inside ASK price. Later, different market makers would come in with a new higher inside ASK price. Again, the next inside ASK price would be higher ($50\frac{5}{8}$).

Figure 15.2 displays the crossed-up Instinet and NASDAQ markets with the large Instinet BID volume. That constitutes a strong buy signal. The Instinet and NASDAQ markets can be crossed up, with large Instinet volume on the ASK side. Suppose that there are 21,500 shares in the Instinet BID book and 40,000 shares in the Instinet ASK book. That would mean that there are more Instinet sellers than there are Instinet buyers, and the selling volume would suppress any future price increase.

Locked-Down Markets

Suppose that there is a difference in the Dell stock price and the share volume that are bid and offered between the public and private markets. Imagine that this time the NASDAQ BID price is same as the Instinet ASK price. That situation would constitute a "locked-down market." Figure 15.3 displays the locked-down markets. The prices in the private market (Instinet) are generally lower than the prices in the public market (NASDAQ), so this would constitute a bearish sign:

Instinet ASK	<	NASDAQ ASK
Instinet BID	<	NASDAQ BID
Instinet ASK	=	NASDAQ BID

The Instinet BID and ASK prices are lower than the NASDAQ inside BID and ASK prices; this constitutes a sell signal.

The NASDAQ inside BID and ASK prices for Dell are $50\frac{5}{8}$ and $50\frac{3}{4}$. There are three market makers buying on the BID side and two market makers selling Dell shares on the ASK side. The $\frac{3}{2}$ ratio of the BID to ASK market makers is the only indication of the volume flow in the public market. On the other hand, the private market has a different

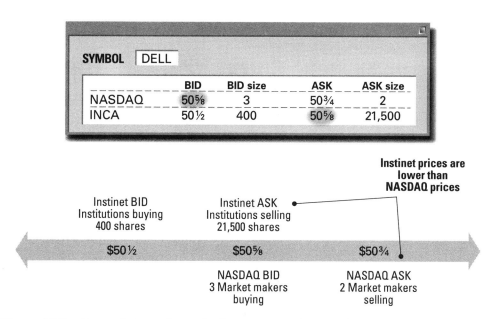

Figure 15.3 *Bearish Signal: Locked-Down Markets with a Large ASK Volume*

price and volume structure for this stock. The high BID and the low ASK price for Dell on Instinet is $50\frac{1}{2}$ and $50\frac{5}{8}$. The institutions are bidding to buy 400 shares of Dell. Furthermore, the institutions are offering to sell only 21,500 shares of Dell. Therefore, the ratio of BID to ASK volume is negative ($\frac{400}{21,500}$); it is an indication of the actual volume flow in the private market.

In Figure 15.3, the selling price on the private market is the same as the buying price on the public market. Also, look at the selling volume on the Instinet. Once the 400 shares are bought on the Instinet, financial institutions that want to sell Dell will move to the public market. They would start dumping the large volume of Dell shares in the NASDAQ market. The three market makers on the BID side would most likely stop buying Dell shares that are being bid for purchase at $50\frac{5}{8}$. Those market makers would quickly lower the price due to the higher supply of Dell coming from the institutional investors. In other words, they would leave the inside BID price, so the prices are coming down.

Figure 15.3 also displays a substantial Instinet ASK volume. The locked-down markets and the large Instinet ASK volume constitute a sell signal. Sometimes it is possible to have the Instinet and NASDAQ markets locked down, and the large Instinet volume on the BID side (that is, buying side). Imagine that there are 40,000 shares in the Instinet BID book and 21,500 shares in the Instinet ASK book. That would mean that there are more Instinet buyers than Instinet sellers, and the buying volume would act as a support to any future price decrease.

Crossed-Down Markets

Again, suppose that there is a major difference between the public (NASDAQ) and private (Instinet) markets in the stock price and share volume that are bid and offered. This time the Instinet ASK price is much lower than the NASDAQ BID price. That situation constitutes a "crossed-down market." The crossed-down market constitutes a strong bearish or sell signal.

Instinet ASK	<	NASDAQ ASK
Instinet BID	<	NASDAQ BID
Instinet ASK	<	NASDAQ BID

The Instinet BID and ASK prices are substantially lower than the NASDAQ inside BID and ASK prices. This constitutes a strong sell signal. There is a subtle difference between the locked-down and crossed-down markets. In the crossed-down markets, the Instinet ASK is even lower than the NASDAQ BID. This alone will create an arbitrage opportunity. Figure 15.4 displays the crossed-down markets.

In Figure 15.4, the NASDAQ inside BID and ASK prices for Dell are $50\frac{5}{8}$ and $50\frac{3}{4}$. Again, there are three market makers buying on the BID side and two market makers selling Dell shares on the ASK side. The $\frac{3}{2}$ ratio of the BID to ASK market makers is the only indication of the volume flow in the NASDAQ market. The Instinet market has a dramatically different price and volume structure for this stock. The high BID and the low ASK prices for Dell on Instinet are $50\frac{3}{8}$ and $50\frac{1}{2}$. The institutions are bidding to sell 21,500 shares of Dell and offering to buy only 400 shares of Dell. Therefore, the ratio of BID to ASK volume is negative

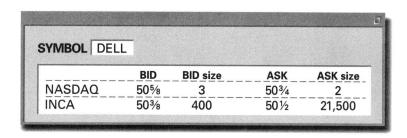

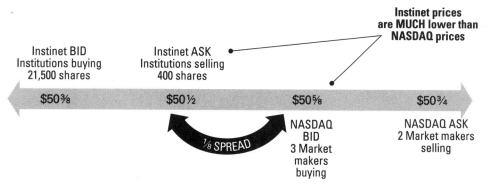

Figure 15.4 *Strong Bearish Signal: Crossed-Down Markets with a Large ASK Volume*

($^{400}/_{21,500}$), which is an indication of the adverse volume flow in the private market.

Both the Instinet BID and ASK prices are lower than the NASDAQ prices. The crossed market exists when the Instinet ASK price is lower than the current NASDAQ inside BID price. In fact, there is a $\frac{1}{8}$ spread between the Instinet ASK and NASDAQ inside BID prices.

Since there is a major difference in buying and selling prices between the two markets (the $\frac{1}{8}$ spread), there is the potential for a price arbitrage. That means an institutional trader could buy the stock on the Instinet at the lower ASK price and simultaneously sell it at the higher BID price on the NASDAQ. These would be riskless trading transactions. The arbitrage would result in a higher supply of Dell shares in the public market and increased demand of Dell shares in the private market. The ultimate result would be lowered Dell prices in the public market and increased Dell prices in the private market. The $\frac{1}{8}$ spread between the

Instinet BID and NASDAQ inside ASK prices would gradually disappear, and the markets would cease to be crossed.

Also, the selling volume on the Instinet indicates a strong potential for a price decrease. Once the 400 shares are bought on the Instinet, financial institutions that want to sell Dell will move to the public market. They would again start selling Dell shares to the three market makers on the BID side. Those three market makers would quickly lower the price (due to higher selling from the institutional customers). In other words, the three market makers would leave the inside BID price. The next NASDAQ inside BID price would be lower.

Figure 15.4 also displays a large Instinet ASK volume. The crossed-down market and the large Instinet ASK volume constitute a strong sell signal. The Instinet and NASDAQ markets can be crossed down, and the large Instinet volume can be on the BID side or buying side. Suppose that there are 40,000 shares in the Instinet BID book (rather than 400 shares) and 21,500 shares in the Instinet ASK book. That would mean that there are more Instinet buyers than Instinet sellers. The buying volume would act as a support level to any future price decrease.

Basic Trading Strategies Using Instinet

The basic day trading strategy using the Instinet tool is summarized in Table 15.1. The key is to be circumspect (that is, observant) and notice when the NASDAQ and Instinet markets are crossed or locked. However, that is not an easy task. Instinet and NASDAQ price quotes are updated and changed continuously. Crossed and locked markets can disappear in seconds. The trading software that filters the price information between the two markets can provide the color-coded alerts for the crossed and locked markets. That would help a trader visualize the trading opportunities.

As a rule of thumb, the larger the spread in the crossed-up or down markets, the stronger the trading signal. If the spread between the crossed markets is substantial, many professional traders will take the opportunity to profit from price arbitrage. Traders need to pay close attention to the actual volume being offered on the Instinet BID and ASK side. A large Instinet BID volume by itself is always a positive or bullish indicator. Conversely, a large Instinet ASK volume is always a negative or bearish indicator.

Table 15.1 *Day Trading Strategies and Instinet*

Markets	Prices	Volume	Trading Signal
Locked up	NASDAQ ASK = Instinet BID	Large Instinet BID volume	Bullish signal
Locked up	NASDAQ ASK = Instinet BID	Large Instinet ASK volume	Weak bullish signal
Crossed up	NASDAQ ASK < Instinet BID	Large Instinet BID volume	Strong bullish signal
Crossed up	NASDAQ ASK < Instinet BID	Large Instinet ASK volume	Weak bullish signal
Locked down	NASDAQ BID = Instinet ASK	Large Instinet ASK volume	Bearish signal
Locked down	NASDAQ BID = Instinet ASK	Large Instinet BID volume	Weak bearish signal
Crossed down	NASDAQ BID > Instinet ASK	Large Instinet ASK volume	Strong bearish signal
Crossed down	NASDAQ BID > Instinet ASK	Large Instinet BID volume	Weak bearish signal

Again, using the Instinet indicator is an advanced trading strategy. First, the day trader must have access to the Instinet market data or the software that would filter and process that information. Second, it is difficult to monitor trading activities on two different markets. The opportunities to observe the price differentials between the two markets are short lived. Day traders must continuously be alert to these opportunities.

NYSE Orders

THE NEW YORK STOCK EXCHANGE (NYSE) IS A MUCH DIFFERENT "animal" than the NASDAQ.

Every listed stock that trades on the NYSE floor is assigned a specialist. A specialist is the NYSE member firm that may handle one or more stocks traded at the same trading post. The role of the specialist is to maintain a fair and orderly market in specific securities. The specialist may act in a principal capacity (as a dealer) when trading for his or her own accounts or may act in an agent capacity (as a broker) when executing orders for the NYSE commission house brokers. The specialist will take on the role of the principal in order to maintain marketability and counter temporary imbalances in the supply and demand of a security.

The specialist must maintain a continuous market by standing ready to buy when there are no bidders (buyers) or sell when there are no offerers (sellers) at the trading post. By doing so, the specialist is said to maintain a market in the security. In essence, the specialist is the only "market maker" available for that security. There is no competition among different Wall Street firms to provide liquidity for that stock. A specialist is a monopolist.

When entering the trading crowd, a broker may ask the specialist for the "size of the markets." This information will tell the broker the current prices for the highest buyer and the lowest seller. The specialist will enter all buy and sell orders in his or her order book. The specialist is the only person who has the complete picture regarding the demand and supply of that stock. The specialist would then match buyers with sellers and thus maintain a fair and orderly market in that specific stock. The specialist may never compete with the public orders, but the specialist can bid higher or offer lower in order to reduce the spread between the bid and offer price.

Since there is only one "market maker" for the listed securities, there is no Level II screen information available for NYSE securities. A day traders who does not have a seat on the exchange would not know the depth of the market at any point of time—information that is available only to the specialist on the exchange floor. Thus day traders on the NYSE deal with a very limited set of stock information. Figure 16.1 displays what NYSE traders can observe on their screens.

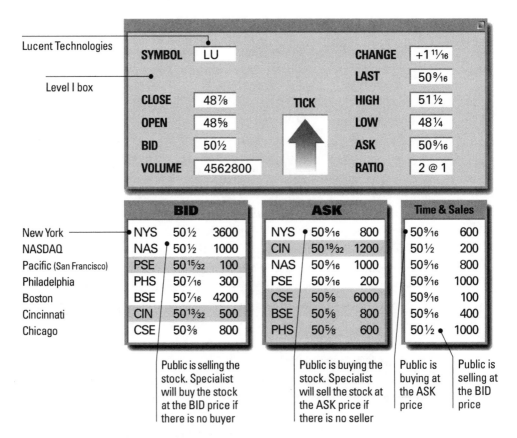

Figure 16.1 *NYSE Trading Information*

The first box is essentially the familiar Level I screen information. There is very little difference in the Level I information between the NYSE-listed securities and the NASDAQ's over-the-counter (OTC) stocks. The only difference between the listed securities and OTC stocks is the "ratio" field. The ratio field for the OTC stocks displays the number of marker makers on the inside BID and ASK side. In this example, with Lucent Technologies (LU), there is always only one specialist. However, there are several regional exchanges, in addition to the NYSE, that trade listed securities. In Figure 16.1, there are two exchanges that furnish the highest BID or the best selling price for Lucent Technologies. On the other side, only the NYSE has the lowest ASK or the best buying price. Thus the ratio field states that there are two exchanges with the best selling price and only one exchange with the best buying price. The probability is great that the NYSE will provide the best prices for the listed stocks among different regional exchanges.

Another important distinction between the NASDAQ Level II screen and the NYSE screen is the ability to view the size of the inside Market. In this example, the NYSE specialist has sell orders for 3,600 shares of Lucent Technologies. On the other hand, the NYSE specialist has buy orders for only 800 shares of Lucent. These shares are the actual size of the inside market. The day trader can then deduce that there are more sellers than buyers for the stock at this price level. That could indicate a potential for the price to decrease. In this case, the ratio of selling to buying is relatively small ($3,600/800$), so the downward pressure is relatively small. But, imagine if there is an order to sell 36,000 shares rather than 3,600 shares. That ratio alone would indicate a large potential for the price to decline in the near future. Many day traders state that this is why they decided to trade mostly NYSE stocks—there is less information to look at and they have the ability to see the true BID and ASK size.

The NASDAQ Level II screen does not show actual shares. Market makers are required to post only the absolute minimum of shares that they are willing to buy or sell. Consequently the bid for 1,000 shares by the market maker (on the inside BID) is misleading. The same market maker could be "sitting" on the inside BID refreshing the inside BID price and buying, for example, 100,000 shares. However, the NASDAQ Level II screen does show the depth of the market. It displays how many other market makers are willing to pay for the stock at different price ranges. The NYSE screen does not show any of that information. Day traders on the NYSE do not have access to "market depth" information.

The other useful information is the actual buy and sell orders that are being filled. That information is available in the Time and Sales window, which is also displayed in Figure 16.1. The day trader can see in real time whether the sales are being executed at the BID or the ASK price. The large number and size of executed sales at the ASK side would indicate a buying pattern. That would constitute a bullish sign. The large number and size of executed sales at the BID side would indicate a selling pattern; that would constitute a bearish sign. Occasionally, the Time and Sales window will display prices that are not the inside BID and ASK prices. The different prices might be old prices that are being reported with delay or the preferred trade orders.

Therefore, there is no real Level II screen information for the listed stocks of the NYSE screen. The different exchanges are color coded at the same price level, similar to the NASDAQ Level II screen. However, the probability is that day traders can only directly access the NYSE. The New York Stock Exchange uses a system called Designated Order Turnaround (DOT and Super DOT). The DOT system allows orders to be entered by day traders from the day trading firm's trading floor directly into the NYSE computer execution system. The order bypasses the floor broker and goes directly to the NYSE specialist for execution. Therefore, even if other exchanges have better prices than the NYSE, it is impossible to route that order electronically to different exchanges.

Super DOT

Super DOT or DOT is an efficient way to execute day trade orders on the NYSE. NYSE orders are a bit more expensive than NASDAQ SOES or Island orders. Small orders are matched and filled quickly by the specialist. However, it is estimated that the majority of orders on the NYSE go through the Super DOT or DOT electronic order execution system. Super DOT or DOT is fast and affordable, and thus day trading is technically possible on the NYSE.

If there is an exact price match between the Lucent buyers and seller, the Super DOT or DOT will match those orders quickly. Both the buyers and sellers will receive the trade confirmation in a few seconds. The specialist will only approve the trade by pressing a key in the Super

DOT system. A great majority of trades on the NYSE fit this description. The specialist, through the Super DOT, will pair or match the stock buyers with the stock sellers and collect a small commission. In about only 30% of all trades would the specialist step in and provide the other side of the trade order: play the role of the market maker and provide the liquidity for that stock.

The day trader may enter a number of different order types on the NYSE, such as market orders, limit orders, or stop orders. There are several order qualifiers that can be input by the day trader. Table 16.1 summarizes those order qualifiers. For instance, the limit orders can be limit on price, limit on close (LMT CLO), limit or better (LMT OB), stop (STOP), and stop-limit (LMT STP). Furthermore, the market orders can be current market price (MKT), market on close (MKT CLO), and mar-

Table 16.1 *Trade Order Qualifiers*

Order Qualifier	Order Description
LMT CLO	Limit order can be filled at the close of the market
LMT OB	Limit order that gives the specialist the authority to try to get the trader a better price, at his or her discretion
STOP	Specialist does not execute the order until it reaches a specified price and the order becomes the market order
LMT STOP	Specialist will execute the order at a specified price and will cancel it if the price changes
DAY	Specialist will cancel at the end of the day
GTC	Order is good until it is canceled
GTX	Order is good until it is executed
OPG	Specialist will send out the order at the open of the next day
FOK	If the quantity of shares requested is not available in the books at the time, the order will be canceled
IOC	Trader requests an immediate fill even though it could be a partial fill
GTD	Trader can specify a certain date when order can be canceled
AON	All or None: Fill the entire order at once or reject the order

ket price or better (MKT OB). The following time qualifiers apply to both the limit and market orders: good 'til canceled (GTC), opening (OPG), fill or kill (FOK), immediate or cancel (IOC), good through date (GTD), and day order (DAY).

Most trading software recognizes immediately when a listed stock order is being sent out to the NYSE. At that time, the NYSE order execution window will appear. The day trader can then select trade order qualifiers. Most of the time, day traders are inputting simple price limit orders. To cancel an open listed order on the Super DOT is a simple task. All trading software packages have user-friendly and simple command keys to cancel an existing open order.

NYSE Trading

It is my opinion that it is somewhat safer and easier to day trade NYSE stocks than NASDAQ stocks. The NYSE stocks are "slow" stocks. Trading them is conservative or "slow" day trading. The NYSE stocks are not as volatile as the NASDAQ stocks. NYSE stock prices tend to move in somewhat smoother fashion; there are fewer sharp price turns.

There are several reasons for the relatively higher intra-day price stability at the NYSE. First, the stocks listed on the NYSE tend to be large and established industrial corporations. Most NYSE stocks tend to be income stocks rather than growth stocks. The large and established companies of America tend to distribute dividends. The earnings and dividends tend to attract a different breed of long-term value investors. For instance, retirees are looking for stock price stability and income rather than growth. On the other hand, NASDAQ is laden with technology companies that are pursuing long-term growth strategies. Consequently, growth stocks attract stock speculators. Speculators tend to be short-term investors who are seeking capital appreciation rather than income. Speculative investors are always chasing the hot stocks, jumping in and out.

Second, the NYSE companies are simply too large and established to be very volatile. Large "blue chip" companies seldom issue news that can send stock prices skyrocketing up or down. It is a rare event for a NYSE stock to lose 50% of its capitalization value in a few days. That happens often on the NASDAQ. NASDAQ companies are relatively young companies; a single bad corporate announcement can send the stock price into a major descent.

Finally, the intra-day price volatility is lower with the NYSE stocks because there is only one specialist who controls the price volatility for each stock. The specialist can act to absorb and soften sharp price movements. The specialist knows the exact depth of the market (demand and supply) at any point in time because the specialist controls the order flow. There is little chance that the specialist will overreact.

On the other hand, NASDAQ market makers compete against each other and against day traders. The market makers do not know the complete order flow for a stock. They know what is in their individual order book, but they do not know the order flow of other market makers. Like any other day traders, market makers can see on the Level II screen the required minimum size of the BID and ASK made by the other market makers, but not the actual orders. With such uncertainty and lack of complete information, market makers might overreact and send a stock deeper in either price direction. Consequently, the average Beta value (which measures the relative price volatility compared to the industry average) is higher for NASDAQ stocks than for NYSE stocks.

Since the NYSE stocks do not move very fast in either direction, day traders have time to react. They can see that prices are going up or down. They are not easily whipsawed or whiplashed by sharp and sudden price reversals. Since there is no true Level II information available, the day traders must devote more attention to technical stock analysis. Here, charting becomes an important component of their trading style. In addition, the competition is much different on the NYSE. There are fewer day traders and more long-term investors at the NYSE. It is my opinion that one is better off trading against NYSE investors than NASDAQ market makers and other day traders. However, the day trading opportunities are much fewer and smaller at the NYSE.

Unfortunately, smaller risk brings smaller return. Successful and experienced day traders can potentially earn seven-figure incomes trading volatile NASDAQ stocks with a relatively small trading account of $100,000. Because the NASDAQ is so volatile, there are plenty of opportunities to make money.

Limit Orders Strategy on the NYSE

One important distinction between the NYSE and NASDAQ is the treatment of limit orders. In order to protect individual traders and investors, the NYSE enacted rules that assign priority to customer orders over those of the specialist. In other words, the customer's limit orders will be placed in front of the specialist's orders, even if the specialist was the first in line. The day traders trading on the NASDAQ market do not have that protection.

This feature affords many trading opportunities to day traders. The day traders can continuously buy the stock on the BID and sell it on the ASK. That is a tremendous advantage. In order for a limit order to be executed, someone has to be there on the other side of the trade buying or selling the stock at the market BID and ASK price through the market orders. Specialists seldom fill these orders. It is the investors on the NYSE who are sending the market orders closing the trade. In other words, when a day trader submits a limit order to buy a stock at the BID price, the investor is selling that stock at the BID price through the market order. Conversely, when a day trader submits a limit order to sell a stock at the ASK price, the investor is buying that stock at the ASK price via the market order.

That means that the day traders on the NYSE can trade without paying the BID and ASK spread. In fact, the day traders are making the spread. On slow moving NYSE stocks with substantial trading volume, day traders can buy the stock at the BID price and sell it a few minutes later at the ASK price. Since the NYSE rule grants the day trader's limit orders preference over the specialist's orders, there is a good possibility that the order will get filled.

The strategy is relatively simple. It works for the stable and somewhat liquid NYSE stocks, and if trading is done with large block shares. Since the stable and active NYSE stocks have usually a small spread of $\frac{1}{16}$, the trading profit potential is limited. However, with limited volatility the risk is limited as well. The day traders buy the stock from investors at the BID price and sell it to investors at the ASK price, and thus earn the spread. Since the intra-day price movement is limited, day traders need to have a substantial volume per trade in order to make any money. They need to trade the stock in increments of at least 2,000 shares. To afford trading in increments of 2,000 shares or more, the trader is likely to trade the less expensive NYSE stocks. Again, traders must use limit orders, and avoid order qualifiers such as the all or none.

The question remains as to where the trader's limit order is relative to the other orders on that price level. It is obvious that the trader's limit order is in front of the specialist's order. But what if other traders have already submitted several buy limit orders at the same BID price? That would place this limit order at the bottom of a computerized specialist's order book. It might take a long time before this limit order is executed. For stable NYSE stocks that are not being actively traded, this single buying transaction might take an hour. This is not glamorous and exciting NASDAQ day trading. It is grinding work of earning on every trade $\frac{1}{16}$ or "teeny." But "teenies" do add up at the end of the day.

Trading Against the Hedge Box

NASD, which governs NASDAQ, ruled in the summer of 1998 that the NASDAQ market would no longer allow trading against the hedge box. Until then, trading against the hedge box was a widespread practice among professional day traders. It was a cleaver tool used to bypass the NASD short selling up-tick rule, which stipulated that legal short sell must occur on the last up-tick price. The NASD stipulated that an investor or trader can short sell a stock only when the BID price bar on the software screen is green, which indicates that the last price tick is higher than the previous tick.

Unfortunately, that is the most difficult part of short selling. The day trader must bet on the stock price going down even though the last price information shows the opposite—a price increase. Wouldn't it be a lot easier if the day trader could short sell that stock on a down-tick, when the price is already declining? Fortunately, this can be accomplished on the NYSE by "trading against the hedge box." The NYSE is an independent and self-regulated organization, which never officially adopted the NASDAQ rule prohibiting trading against the hedge box. Until the NYSE adopts that rule, grading against the hedge box is legal on NYSE.

There are three types of trading accounts:

1. The Type I account, which is a cash account;
2. The Type II account, which is a margin account; and
3. The Type III account, which is a hedge account.

Most day traders will open a Type II account and trade using money deposited in that margin account. Most likely, the established margin account will be in the name of the day trader and will carry his or her social security number as a tax identification number.

In addition to a margin account, the day trader will need another account, which will be the Type III account or "hedge account." However, the Type III account must be in the name of another person and must carry a different social security number as a tax identification number. Most likely, the day trader will use the name and social security number of his or her spouse or parent. Finally, the two accounts will be linked, or as securities industry folks would say, "cross-guaranteed." Equity from one account will be used to offset equity in the other account.

To create a hedge box, the day trader needs to complete two separate trading transactions. Suppose that Lucent Technologies (LU) is trading on the NYSE at $49^{15}/_{16}$ and 50. The first transaction would be to open 1,000 shares in a long position in LU at the ASK price of 50. The second transaction would be to short sell the LU stock. To sell short the stock, the day trader must ensure that:

1. LU is on the broker's "short list" (that is, the shortable stocks that can be borrowed from the broker); and
2. The short sell must be legal, or the last BID price must be on the up-tick (suppose that $49^{15}/_{16}$ was an up-tick and thus had a green BID price). Figure 16.2 depicts that starting point.

The second step is to journal (transfer) the short sell trade (1,000 LU $49^{15}/_{16}$) from the margin account into the hedge account. This is a relatively simple process. The day trader simply tells the day trading firm's office manager to journal the short sell trade from the Type II account to the Type III account. Since both accounts are linked (cross-guaranteed) and serviced (or cleared) by the same broker, this is a simple and cost-free accounting procedure. Figure 16.3 depicts this step.

The hedge box is now completed. The position in the margin account is 100% hedged, or covered by the equivalent and opposite position in the hedge account. The day trader has two opposite open positions in two separate linked accounts:

1. The margin account has one open long position for 1,000 shares of LU; and
2. The hedge account has one short position for 1,000 shares of LU.

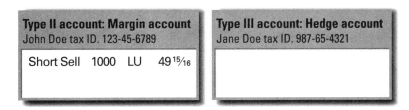

Figure 16.2 *Creating the Hedge Box: Step #1*

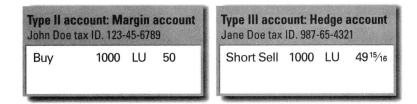

Figure 16.3 *Creating the Hedge Box: Step #2*

If the stock declines in price by 1 point, this would mean a $1,000 loss in the margin account and a $1,000 gain in the hedge account. Conversely, if the stock price goes up by 1 point, there would be a $1,000 gain in the margin account and a $1,000 loss in the hedge account. Either way, the day trader is 100% covered or hedged. The trader will not make or lose any money by keeping the equivalent long position in the margin account and short sell position in the hedge account.

If the day trader decides one day to close the hedge box, the trader would instruct the office manager to journal back the short sell position from the hedge account into the margin account and close both positions. The short sell position is essentially a sell position that will close the equivalent long position. In essence, the trader bought LU at 50 and sold it at $49^{15}/_{16}$, thus losing $^{1}/_{16}$ or $62.50 on that trade. When the transaction cost (the commission) is taken into account, the trader lost approximately $100 in creating this hedge box.

The NASD recognizes that the day trader's long position is 100% covered with the equivalent and opposite position in the hedge account, and thus the margin maintenance requirement is only 5% of the value of the long position and not the 50% margin requirement for Regulation T. To clarify, Regulation T is the federal decree governing the amount of credit that may be advanced by the NASD brokers or dealers to customers for the purchase of securities. In other words, the day trader will lose 5% of the purchasing power or approximately $2,500 by establishing this hedge box. If there are no *opportunity costs* for creating hedge boxes, such as the 5% loss in purchasing power, a day trader could establish hundreds of different hedge boxes. In other words, the day trader can open the maximum of 20 hedge boxes. The 5% loss in the purchasing power is the *opportunity cost* for opening the hedge box. In essence, the 5% of the purchasing power could have been used to purchase more stocks. Finally, professional day trading software packages are capable of monitoring hedge boxes and reminding (or informing) the day trader if a particular stock is "hedged."

What is the benefit of creating a hedge box? Assume that the stock market is facing a major correction, and that most stocks, including Lucent Technologies, are declining in value. The only way a day trader can make money in a down market is to short sell. Since stock prices tend to fall at a faster pace than they tend to increase, a day trader can earn substantial sums of money in a short period of time by taking short sell positions. However, it is difficult to make a legal short sell if prices are continuously on a down-tick (a red BID price). But if the day trader has created a hedge box, the trader does not have to wait for an up-tick to make the short sell. Figure 16.4 depicts how this is done.

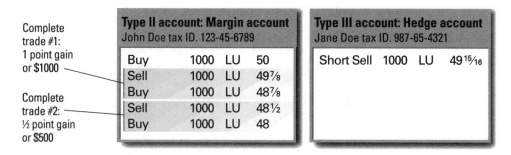

Figure 16.4 *Trading Against the Hedge Box*

Since the margin account has only one long position, the day trader is allowed to close the long position and sell the stock at any time. The day trading software will recognize that the trader has a 1,000 long position in LU, and it will process the sell order for 1,000 shares of LU at $49\frac{7}{8}$. In essence, the day trader does not need to short sell the stock, but rather only to sell the stock. The day trader can simply sell the Lucent Technologies on a down-tick and then a few hours (or minutes) later purchase the same stock at the lower price ($48\frac{7}{8}$). Selling a stock at $49\frac{7}{8}$ and then buying it at 48 will constitute one round-trip trade (trade #1). In essence, the day trader earned 1 point by selling the stock at $49\frac{7}{8}$ and later buying it at 48.

Suppose that the price decline for LU continues. With the completed trade #1, the margin account shows again a 1,000-share long position in LU. Again, the day trader does not have to wait for an up-tick to short sell Lucent Technologies. The day trader can sell LU at $48\frac{1}{2}$ and then buy it a few minutes or hours later at the lower price of 48. That would constitute the second complete trade (trade #2), and this time the trader earned $\frac{1}{2}$ point or $500. At the end of the trading day, the hedge box for LU will look exactly the same as it did in Figure 16.3: 1,000 shares long position in the margin account and 1,000 shares short sell position in the hedge account. When the NYSE opens for trading on the next day, the day trader is free to pursue this trading strategy again and again.

V

Introduction to Day Trading Techniques

Do you remember seeing a warning sign in bold capital letters—"Danger, High Voltage"—on an electrical transformer or a high voltage power line? It dawned on me that a similar sign—"Danger, High Volatility"—could be placed on any computer that is used for day trading. In section V, we describe the tools, concepts, and trading techniques that are used by successful day traders to manage such high price volatility.

➤ We begin with an overall strategy for day trading, which is followed by general suggestions for successful day trading. A chapter of this section will summarize all the signals that indicate the potential for price increases and decreases, as well as the indicators for overbought and oversold markets.

➤ The following chapter in this section explains risk management skills and tools for day traders, which is crucial information for this business. We suggest several alternative approaches to day trading: slow, intermediate, and fast trading. We also explain in section V how day traders deal with losing streaks. Finally, we identify and differentiate among several day trading styles: specialist, scalper, market maker, and position trader.

➤ The psychology of day trading and the psychological characteristics of day traders is the next topic of this section. The author will emphasize the need to develop a day trading plan and the ability to "visualize" trading. In addition, the topic of stress associated with day trading is introduced, as well as the potential stress reducers.

➤ The issue of "where to trade" is addressed next. We differentiate between the two choices: day trading firms and Internet-based brokers. Additional topics that go with the selection of the day trading broker are covered as well: trading remotely with the day trading firm, day trading on a full-time versus part-time basis, Securities Investor Protection Corporation (SIPC), and how the trades are cleared. The author will also reiterate the issue of suitability for day trading. Finally, this section will describe the features of the trading software used by the day trading firm.

➤ Since almost all day traders open margin accounts, the Regulation T and long, short, and combined margin accounts are described in detail. In addition, the topics of restricted margin accounts, margin maintenance requirements, and intra-day margin calls are explained.

➤ In addition to dealing with price volatility, day traders must also deal with the IRS. The good news is that the probability of being audited by the IRS is very low. Several tax issues are briefly discussed, such as defining the tax rates, income, capital gains and losses, trading expenses, and the three IRS tax classifications: market maker, investor, and trader.

17

Day Trading Strategies

I N MY OPINION, IT IS MORE IMPORTANT TO DO THE RIGHT TRADES THAN TO do the trades right. Many traders become preoccupied with trade order execution mechanics. They become very proficient in understanding the NASDAQ and NYSE market order execution systems. They have learned the rules of trading and they have mastered trading execution software. They know how to enter and exit trades efficiently, but these skills alone do not make them good day traders.

The most important half of the equation is the ability to pick the right trades. A day trader could master the order execution system and still lose money day trading. If the day trader consistently has a majority of losing trades, then he or she might not be in the business very long. It is possible to be a profitable day trader even with a majority of losing trades, but one would need to limit one's losses and maximize one's profits, which requires a great deal of trading discipline.

The Overall Strategy

Day trading success ultimately depends on the overall impact of two trading factors:

1. The day trader must have a higher percentage of winning trades than losing trades. Let us assume that the ratio of winning to losing trades is 60% to 40%, which is a realistic assumption given the quality

and quantity of financial information available to day traders. The long-term objective is to improve that winning percentage through time and experience.

2. The day trader must maximize the financial value or benefits derived from his or her winning trades and minimize the financial cost of losing trades. In other words, the dollar value from the 60% winning trades should be substantially higher than the dollar value derived from the 40% losing trades. This is when risk management becomes a crucial skill.

To improve the overall percentage of winning trades, the day trader should trade only when the odds of winning are in the day trader's favor, or when the probability of winning has increased. It is my opinion that the probability of winning will increase when the following events occur:

➤ The day trader trades on the same side of the stock trend. As day traders often state, "Trend is a friend." Again, a day trader does not need to anticipate or predict the future market trend. All a day trader needs to do is react to existing and observable price trends. The trend can be seen on the Level II screen and on real-time technical analysis charts. There is no need to time the market turns perfectly and buy at the bottom and sell at the peak of the cycle. Also, the trader does not need to be contrarian and buy a stock when everyone else is selling it, or short the stock when everyone else is going long. That is one investment strategy, but it is not day trading.

➤ The day trader trades on the same side of the market as the Wall Street professionals. The probability is greater that the market makers can predict future market prices more accurately than can the average day traders. If key market makers are accumulating a stock, the probability is that the stock will increase in value. Conversely, if key market makers are disposing a stock from their inventory, the probability is that the stock will decrease in value. A common expression among day traders is, "Shadow the ax." Again, this action can be observed on the Level II screen.

➤ The day trader does not buy overbought stocks or short the oversold stocks. In other words, the day trader is always cognizant about a stock's intra-day price resistance and support levels. That information is again observable on technical analysis charts such as the Bollinger bands. (This does not preclude buying the 52-week High and short selling the 52-week Low. This can be a profitable trading strategy—many good day traders simply buy higher the 52-week High and short sell lower the 52-week Low.

➤ The day trader attempts to buy the stock at the BID price and sell at the ASK price, which is the basic trading strategy of the Wall Street professionals (the market makers and specialists). By cutting or eliminating the BID and ASK spread, the trader's profitability of the trades will increase by the amount of the eliminated spread.

➤ The day trader should take a trading position only after observing a clear trading signal to buy or short sell the stock. Without a clear signal, the trader is gambling.

Trading Recommendations

The following trading suggestions are based on the author's personal opinions. Day trading is not an exact science, and there is no "bullet-proof" trading method or strategy that can sustain scientific scrutiny. The trading recommendations are presented as a list, not necessarily in order of relative ranking. Readers might disagree with one or more suggestions, and that is OK. Every trader develops his or her own style.

The author is not advocating that a novice trader should incorporate all of the following recommendations immediately. Only experienced day traders should utilize some of the recommendations, such as the recommendation to trade expensive and volatile NASDAQ stocks in increments of 1,000 shares. Chapter 18, on risk management, will elaborate further how the novice trader should move along the ubiquitous learning curve. All of the suggestions have been mentioned previously throughout the book; the list can serve as a summary of day trading recommendations.

Day traders should consider the following:

1. Consider trading volatile stocks. The stock's relative *volatility* is measured by the *Beta coefficient*, which tells how much a stock moves in relation to the S&P 500 Index. A stock with a Beta value of 1.5 or higher (that is, the stock is 50% more price volatile than the S&P 500 Index) would be a good start. Technology stocks usually fit this requirement. Appendix 2 lists the 100 NASDAQ and NYSE stocks with high price volatility and daily trading liquidity. Many traders attempt to trade stocks that are not volatile. It is difficult to make money day trading if the trading stocks are not moving, and there is no point in monitoring stocks tick by tick if prices are historically stable.

2. Consider trading stocks that have high *absolute price volatility*: stocks with a daily price range of at least 2 points. The difference between the intra-day high and low stock prices should be 2 points or higher. That is how day traders make their money—through high absolute intra-day price movement. It is possible to have high relative price volatility (high Beta) and low absolute volatility (low intra-day price range) if a stock is inexpensive. Again, technology stocks tend to be expensive and volatile; thus they have both high relative and absolute volatility.

3. Consider trading stocks that have high *absolute liquidity*. A stock's liquidity is measured by the average daily trading volume statistics, which tell how many shares are traded on average every day. The daily trading volume should be at least 500,000 shares. It is crucial to have many buyers and sellers for a stock. If there is no liquidity (if fewer than 500,000 shares are traded daily), traders could have a difficult time getting out of the trade at the desired price. For instance, the price could drop very quickly, and the trader might simply get stuck in a long and losing position.

4. Consider trading stocks in the right size. Traders should start day trading with 100-share increments, but eventually they need to graduate to trading in increments of 1,000 shares. Ultimately, the objective of day trading is to trade the NASDAQ and NYSE stocks in increments of 1,000 shares and to profit from the small intra-day price movement. A small relative gain of $\frac{1}{8}$ or 12.5 cents per share would result in a large absolute profit of $125 if 1,000 shares were purchased in that single trade. If the trader were to purchase only 100 shares, the profit would be only $12.50. That would not even cover the transaction cost.

5. Trade stocks that are expensive. Again, the objective of day trading is to profit substantially in absolute dollar terms from relatively small intra-day price movements. For an expensive stock ($100 or more per share), a small relative change of 1% is 1 point, which would constitute $1,000 potential profit if 1,000 shares were purchased that day. And this is quite common and feasible. Stocks move up or down easily 1% during the trading day. On the other hand, for an inexpensive stock ($10 per share), a 1-point price change would be a large relative change of 10%. If 1,000 shares were purchased, the stock price would need to change up or down 10% to earn $1,000 potential profit. This, on the other hand, does not happen very often.

6. Trade stocks that have a small spread. If the day trader is looking for quick order execution and a guaranteed price (for example, using SOES), then he or she would buy the stock from the market makers at the higher ASK price and sell the stock to the market makers at the lower BID price. If the spread is small, such as $\frac{1}{16}$, the day trader does not have to wait long for the $\frac{1}{16}$ price movement just to break even. A day trader needs to detect a small price movement, wait for the price to go up $\frac{1}{16}$, and the trader is already "in the money." On the other hand, if the spread is large, such as $\frac{1}{2}$, the day trader must wait for the $\frac{1}{2}$ price movement just to break even. And that can be a long and risky wait. The only exception is if the day trader employs a specific strategy to cut the spread (for example, buy and sell in between the BID and ASK prices) through execution on the ECNs; then the stock must have a large spread.

7. Trade stocks that have substantial depth on the BID and ASK side on the Level II screen. The stock should have several market makers on both the BID and ASK sides. There should be many buyers and sellers for that stock. That would promote and ensure an easy entry and exit for that particular trade.

8. Have a reason to trade that particular stock at that particular point in time. Day traders should observe trading signals to buy or sell a stock. A trading signal could be a combination of several events occurring simultaneously: some would be observed on the Level II screen, and some are technical analysis indicators.

9. Trade stocks that have a momentum or price trend. Do not purchase or sell short a stock that is not moving at that point in time. Otherwise, the day trader is just hoping for an appropriate outcome. The day trader would have only 50% probability of guessing and making a winning trade if there is no observable price momentum or direction. Before the day trader takes a long or short stock position, he or she needs to observe a series of up-ticks or down-ticks that would indicate or prove a price trend. Day traders do not need to be proactive and anticipate the

price movement; they need only be reactive and follow the observable price movement.

10. Take the stock position (long or short) that coincides with the broad market price movement (for example, S&P 500 Index) or the industry sector market movement (such as the Semiconductor Index). At least, a day trader should be cognizant of the S&P 500 Index or the NASDAQ 100 Index price movement. It would be difficult to expect that one stock would appreciate in value if there were a broad stock market sell-off. The probability of making a winning trade declines if the day trader takes a position against the broad market.

11. Be cognizant of the stock's intra-day price support and resistance levels before entering the trade. The Bollinger bands indicator is an excellent and dynamic technical analysis tool that shows real-time intra-day price support and resistance levels. The problem is that day traders often enter a long or short trading position too late. The price was already at the upper or lower Bollinger band level (at the intra-day support or resistance level) when the day traders decided to open the position. A day trader should not purchase a stock if the stock is at the price resistance level or at the upper Bollinger band at that point in time; this is the time to seek short selling opportunities. Conversely, the day trader should not sell short a stock if the stock is at the price support level or at the lower Bollinger band at that time; instead, the day trader should look for buying opportunities.

12. Be cognizant of the stock's intra-day price support and resistance levels when preparing to exit the trade. Again, some day traders often wait too long to exit or close their long or short trading positions. For example, the price may have already peaked and started to decline when the trader decided to exit the long position. By then, it could be too late. The price could be declining too fast, and a small profit could turn into a small loss. It is always better and easier to sell at the price strength, when the price is still increasing or stable and not declining. Day traders should look to exit their short positions when the price is at the price support level or the lower Bollinger band level. Conversely, the day traders should seek to close their long positions when the price is at the upper Bollinger band or the price resistance level.

13. Consider using predominately limit buy orders rather than market buy orders, thus controlling the entry price. In addition, limit orders

will help to obtain a better price by attempting to buy at the BID price and sell at the ASK price.

14. Consider using the ECNs rather than SOES when trading on the NASDAQ. That would help in buying the stock at the BID price and selling it at the ASK price.

I have mentioned before that the day trader must first observe a signal to buy or sell a stock before executing the trade. Too many times, day traders enter a trade based on a gut feeling. Gut feeling is not good enough. Since there is no such thing as a crystal ball to predict future outcomes, the next best device would be a signal that indicates a potential for price movement. Some trading signals are observable on the Level II screen, and some are derived from technical analysis indicators.

It is unrealistic to expect that all signals must occur simultaneously to generate a clear buy or sell signal. The trading universe does not have to be lined up perfectly for the day trader to decide to buy or sell a security. However, the day trader must be able to recognize and understand the majority of listed signals in order to detect the price trend.

Potential for Price Increase

The following is a summary of observable events that characterize potential for price increase for a particular stock. If there is a reference to Level II information and market makers, the listed events apply to NASDAQ stocks. When there is no reference to the Level II screen or to market makers, the event can be applied to the NYSE as well. In other words, the following are the buy signals to open a long position and close a short position:

1. A series of green or up-tick BID and ASK prices showing on the Market Ticker window for a particular stock. That is the alert that prices are moving up.

2. A day trader should be able to observe the counterclockwise movement on the Level II screen as more market makers leave the inside ASK and join the inside BID. For example, a day trader should be able to detect on the Level II screen any price quote that is moving up from the bottom of the ASK side to the top of the ASK side. Then, that price quote would "jump" over from the ASK side to the top of the BID side, and eventually move down to the bottom of the BID side.

3. The first market maker enters a new high BID price. That would create a new higher BID price. That would clearly state that one market maker is willing to pay more for that security than the other market makers.

4. The last market maker leaves the inside ASK price. Thus the higher ASK becomes the new inside ASK price. The new higher inside ASK price becomes the best selling price, which would mean that the public is buying and the market makers are selling at the higher price.

5. An "ax" or a key market maker has joined the inside BID price on the Level II screen. That would mean that the "ax" is buying the stock.

6. An "ax" or a key market maker has refreshed the inside BID price on the Level II screen. That would mean that the "ax" continues to buy that stock. After being hit for the order, the market maker chooses to maintain the same inside BID price.

7. An "ax" or a key market maker has left the inside ASK price on the Level II screen. That would mean that "ax" has stopped selling that stock. After being hit for the order, the market maker chooses not to maintain the same inside ASK price.

8. A market maker simultaneously leaves the inside ASK and joins the inside BID price. That would mean that the market maker has stopped selling the stock and has instead become the buyer of that stock.

9. The buying trades are going off at ASK price on the Time and Sales window. That would indicate that the public is buying the stock.

10. The buying trades are going off at 500 or 1,000 shares volume on the Time and Sales window. That would indicate substantial acquisition volume. In other words, it would indicate that the public is buying a substantial quantity of shares.

11. There is a crossover between the Fast Exponential Moving Average (EMA) line and the Slow Exponential Moving Average line. In other words, the Fast EMA, which in our earlier example consisted of three observations of one-minute interval data, has crossed over and above the Slow EMA line, which in our earlier example was built from nine observations of one-minute interval data.

12. The MACD line is positive and is increasing at an increasing rate. That would indicate divergence between the Fast and Slow EMA lines. In other words, the Fast EMA is increasing at a faster rate than the Slow EMA line. Bulls in the stock market are getting stronger.

13. The price has reached the lower Bollinger band, which constitutes the intra-day price support level.

14. The momentum (MOM) indicator is positive and is increasing at an increasing rate. That would mean that there is a price increase momentum at this point in time. From the earlier example, the current stock price is higher now than the stock price nine minutes ago.

15. The price and On-Balance Volume (OBV) indicator move in the same direction. If both the price and OBV are moving up, the trend is considered strong. However, if the current price is going up and the running cumulative OBV line is declining, then divergence exists, and there is a distinct possibility of price reversal.

Figure 17.1 summarizes and displays graphically the information on a Level II screen that would characterize potential for a price increase for a particular stock.

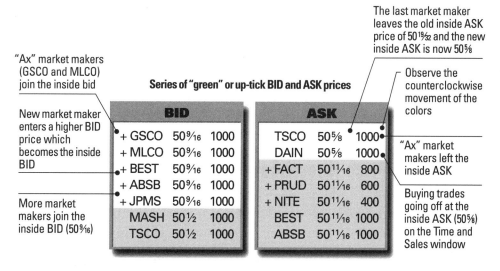

Figure 17.1   *Level II Information that Indicates Potential for Price Increase*

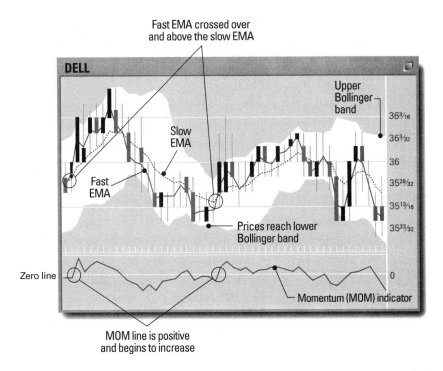

Figure 17.2 *Technical Analysis Information that Indicates Potential for Price Increase*

Figure 17.2 displays graphically the information available on technical analysis screens that would characterize potential for a price increase for a particular stock.

Potential for Price Decrease

The following list is a summary of observable events that characterize the potential for a price decrease for a NASDAQ stock. In other words, these are the sell signals to open a short position and close a long position.

1. There are a Series of red or down-tick BID and ASK prices showing on the Market Ticker window for a particular stock. Prices are going down.

2. The day trader should be able to observe the clockwise movement on the Level II screen as more market makers leave the inside BID and join the inside ASK price. For example, a day trader should be able to detect on the Level II screen any price quote that is moving up from the bottom of the BID side to the top of the BID side. Then, that price quote would "jump" over from the BID side to the top of the ASK side, and eventually move down to the bottom of the ASK side.

3. The first market maker enters a new lower ASK price. That would create a new lower ASK price. That would clearly indicate that one market maker is willing to sell that security for less than the other market makers.

4. The last market maker leaves the inside BID price. Thus the lower BID becomes the new inside BID price. The new lower inside BID price becomes the best buying price, which would mean that the public is selling and market makers are buying at the lower price.

5. An "ax" or key market maker has joined the inside ASK price on the Level II screen. That would mean that the "ax" is selling the stock.

6. An "ax" or key market maker has refreshed the inside ASK price on the Level II screen. That would mean that the "ax" continues to sell that stock. After being hit for the order, the market maker chooses to maintain the same inside ASK price.

7. An "ax" or key market maker has left the inside BID price on the Level II screen. That would mean that the "ax" has stopped buying that stock. After being hit for the order, the market maker chooses not to maintain the same inside BID price.

8. A market maker simultaneously leaves the inside BID and joins the inside ASK price. That would mean that the market maker has stopped buying the stock and has instead become the seller of that stock.

9. The selling trades are going off at the BID price on the Time and Sales window. That would indicate that the public is selling the stock.

10. The selling trades are going off at 500 or 1,000 shares volume on the Time and Sales window. This would indicate substantial stock distribution volume. In other words, it would indicate that the public is selling a substantial quantity of shares.

11. There is a crossover between the Fast Exponential Moving Average (EMA) line and the Slow Exponential Moving Average line. In other words, the Fast EMA has crossed over and below the Slow EMA line.

12. The MACD line is negative and is decreasing at an increasing rate. This would indicate divergence between the Fast and Slow EMA lines. In other words, the Fast EMA is decreasing at a faster rate than the Slow EMA line. Bears in the stock market are getting stronger.

13. The price has reached the upper Bollinger band, which constitutes the intra-day price resistance level.

14. The day trader should be able to observe that the momentum (MOM) indicator is negative and is decreasing at an increasing rate. That would mean that there is a price decrease momentum at this point in time.

15. Finally, the day trader would like to observe that the price and On-Balance Volume (OBV) indicator are moving in the same direction. If both the price and OBV are moving down, then the downward trend is considered strong. However, if the current price is going down and the running cumulative OBV line is increasing, then divergence exists, and there is a distinct possibility of a price reversal.

Figure 17.3 summarizes and displays graphically the information on a Level II screen that would characterize potential for a price decrease for a particular stock.

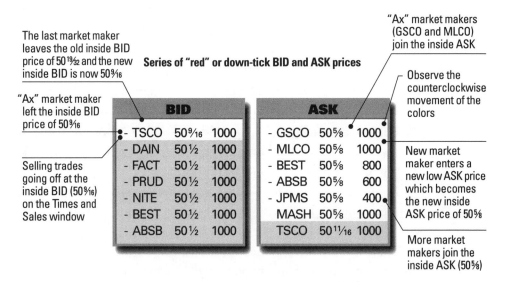

Figure 17.3 *Level II Information Indicating Potential for Price Decrease*

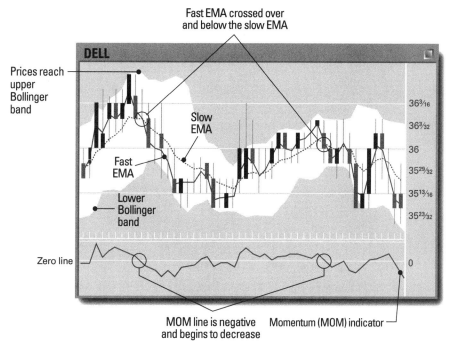

Figure 17.4 *Technical Analysis Information Indicating Potential for Price Decrease*

Figure 17.4 displays graphically the information on a technical analysis screen that would characterize potential for a price decrease for a particular stock.

Overbought and Oversold Indicators

The following are alerts for overbought and oversold markets. An overbought market means that prices have risen too steeply and too fast; an oversold market means that prices have fallen too steeply and too fast. The two overbought and oversold indicators are the MACD and stochastic indicators. They show when prices have moved too far and too fast in either direction and thus are vulnerable to a reaction.

When the MACD line is negative and moving up toward the zero line, that would indicate convergence between the Fast and Slow EMA lines. In other words, the Fast EMA is decreasing at a slower rate than the Slow EMA line. It is an indicator of an oversold market; bears in the stock market are losing steam. The oversold indicator occurs when the Fast Stochastic (%K) line has reached 25 or goes below 25.

Conversely, an overbought indicator would be a positive MACD line that is decreasing and moving down toward the zero line, indicating convergence between the Fast and Slow EMA lines. In other words, the Fast EMA is increasing at a slower rate than the Slow EMA line. Bulls in the stock market are losing steam. An indicator of the overbought market occurs when the Fast Stochastic (%K) line has reached 75 or goes above 75.

CHAPTER
18

Risk Management

THE MANTRA IN REAL ESTATE MAY BE "LOCATION, LOCATION, AND location." But in the day trading business the most important ingredients for success are risk management, risk management, and risk management. This is probably the most important topic of this book. The day trader's risk management skills will make the difference in whether he or she succeeds or fails in this business. And those skills are particularly relevant for new day traders.

In my opinion, the mission for new day traders is not to make money initially. In fact, the novice day trader should expect to lose money at the beginning. The learning curve for the day trading profession is steep and expensive. The day trader's objective should be long-term survival. If a novice day trader stays in the business six months from the opening of the trading account, there is a distinct probability that the day trader is making a profit. If the novice day trader stays in this business after one year from the opening of the trading account, then there is a strong probability that the day trader is making a six-figure annual income.

It is easy to lose money day trading. Day traders commonly trade the most volatile and expensive high tech NASDAQ stocks in increments of 1,000 shares. A 1-point loss when trading 1,000 shares of a volatile Internet stock translates into a $1,000 loss. Before one is ready to day trade the expensive and volatile Internet stocks in large increments, one has to go up the learning curve, and that learning curve is steep. However, the learning curve does not have to be expensive. It is my opinion that most people lose money day trading because they start live day trading before they are ready. Furthermore, when they do start day trading, they start trading volatile and expensive stocks in large increments. That is a recipe for losing a lot of money quickly.

The key to survival is to start slow, and gradually move up. A child has to learn to crawl before that child can walk. Only after the child has mastered walking can that child attempt to run. I remember how long it took my son to learn to hold a pencil properly. For years, he would hold a pencil as a stick. It took three years or so for my son to master a skill that seems by adult standards to be notably elementary. The same analogy can be applied to day trading. What seems simple and obvious for experienced day traders is obscure and complex for the novice trader. It takes time to pick up those trading skills.

Starting slowly is the paramount consideration. It is the best way to ensure that the novice day trader does not "blow up" in the first few months of day trading. It is very easy to blow up at the beginning. The novice day trader will make many errors and mistakes. Those mistakes could be inputting order errors (pressing the wrong key) or misreading the market direction (making the wrong trade). The novice day trader could not possibly eliminate all the errors and mistakes; mistakes are part of the learning process. Thus, the first objective is to minimize the number of mistakes. The second objective is to minimize the cost of those mistakes and to learn from them. Those mistakes do not need to be expensive.

The Slow Trading Approach

The "slow" day trading approach is the conservative approach. This slow approach provides an opportunity to learn the business gradually without losing a lot of money. The first step is to select "slow" stocks. Those stocks do not move very fast. They tend to be relatively stable and do not move very much or fast in either price direction, so the reaction time is much longer. And thus the novice day trader has plenty of time to react to the price movement and to get the order executed.

In other words, the color-coded price levels as seen on the Level II screen would not "fly" as fast as those of more volatile stocks. BID and ASK prices would move at a slower pace, so the novice day trader can visualize the price movement. The point is that the novice day trader can see and interpret the price movement on the Level II screen. It is possible to visualize and determine who among the market makers is buying and selling that particular stock. And once the price trend is ascertained, the novice day trader has time to react and execute an order before the price moves away.

On the other hand, "fast" stocks such as the expensive Internet stocks simply move too fast. The day trader does not have time to react. At one moment the price is going up, and a few moments later the price is going down. It is difficult to ascertain a trend. A good analogy would be that the day trader is surrounded by trees (that is, the real-time stock price ticks) and cannot see the forest (that is, the stock price trend). Furthermore, since the price is moving fast, it is difficult to get the order filled at the desired price level. A novice day trader could submit a limit buy order, and by the time the trader gets the time and courage to press the correct execution key, the stock price has already moved up, and the order does not get filled.

Slow stocks tend to be inexpensive stocks with a price less than $20 and more than $5 per share (there is no point in day trading "penny stocks"). Because they are relatively inexpensive, the stocks do not move a lot in absolute dollar terms. The slow stocks might be as volatile as the fast stocks in relative (that is, percentage change) terms. The slow stocks might have a high Beta, just like the fast stocks, so the relative volatility might be the same. Although the slow stocks' prices might move with the same percentage magnitude as the fast stocks. It is the absolute dollar change that counts. The 5% price change for the $20 stock is only 1 point. On the other hand, a 5% price change for a $100 stock is 5 points. For the novice day trader, it is easier to follow stocks that move 1 point in a day than those that move 5 points in a day.

A price movement of $\frac{1}{4}$ or $\frac{1}{2}$ is a real price trend for the slow stocks because it represents a relatively high percentage change in price. That is a real price movement, so it is possible to observe the market forces of supply and demand that generated the price movement. For example, one could observe a buildup of market makers on the inside BID side and a reduction in the number of the market makers on the inside ASK.

On the other hand, the $\frac{1}{4}$ or $\frac{1}{2}$ is a relatively small percentage change in price for fast, expensive stocks, such as the Internet stocks. That is a simple noise in the market and is not the real price movement. It is more difficult to detect the market forces of supply and demand that generated price movement for fast stocks. The fast stocks could continuously gyrate up and down without any discernible price pattern. And thus it is easy to get "jiggled out" when trading the fast stocks.

For example, a novice day trader opens a long stock position after observing on the computer screen a few price up-ticks and anticipating continued price increase momentum. A few minutes (or seconds) after the order confirmation, the novice day trader observes a few price down-ticks on the screen. The novice day trader quickly gets out of the long position at a small loss, but a loss nevertheless. The novice day trader then decides to open a short position, anticipating a continued downward price movement. After the short sale order confirmation has been received, the novice day trader discovers a few price up-ticks on the screen for that stock. In order to minimize the loss, the novice day trader quickly gets out of the short position at a small loss. Two trades later the novice trader is down a few hundred dollars. The novice trader was jiggled out of a few hundred dollars by the market makers.

The slow approach, which consists of trading the slow, inexpensive stocks, would assure that the novice day trader would not get easily jiggled out by market gyrations. The novice day trader would be able to ascertain or visualize real price movement. At that time, the novice day trader would go with the trend.

In addition, trading the slow stocks would also limit the initial number of trading transactions. Fewer transactions would limit the number of possible mistakes, which would further enhance the probability of long-term survival. Fewer transactions, of course, would also limit the potential to make money. However, the objective of the novice day trader is not to make money initially, but to learn to day trade. Again, the focus is on the long-term trading continuation. In order to make money day trading in the long run, the novice day trader must survive in the short run.

The most important step that the novice day trader can undertake initially is to start day trading in increments of 100 shares. Trading the slow stocks will minimize the total number of losing trades. Trading in increments of 100 shares will minimize the cost of those mistakes. The novice day trader cannot avoid making losing trades. It is realistic to expect that a novice day trader will have $2/3$ winning trades and $1/3$ losing trades. With time and experience, the percentage of winning trades should increase. If the novice trader starts day trading in increments of

1,000 shares, then one small trading mistake with a price change of $\frac{1}{8}$ would translate into a \$125 loss. It is easy to make a $\frac{1}{8}$ mistake, and \$125 mistakes can quickly add up.

It is much preferred to trade in increments of 100 shares. Then one small trading mistake with a price change of $\frac{1}{8}$ would translate into only a \$12.50 loss, which the novice day trader can afford to absorb. The novice day trader can afford to make many small mistakes (that is, $\frac{1}{8}$ price change mistakes), learn something from each mistake, and still be as well off as with one $\frac{1}{8}$ small mistake when trading in 1,000 share blocks. It is my firm advice to all new day traders to start trading in increments of 100 shares.

It is also true that it is very difficult to make money day trading if one trades in increments of 100 shares. If the round-trip trading transaction cost (commission) is \$37.50, and if the day trader is trading in increment of 100 shares, then the stock price needs to go up (or down for the short sell) $\frac{3}{8}$ just to break even on that trade. The price movement of $\frac{3}{8}$ is a substantial and real price movement for the inexpensive slow stocks. But then, the objective of the novice day trader is not to make money initially, but to learn to day trade. Again, the focus is on long-term day trading existence.

It is my recommendation that a novice day trader start with 100 shares and increase the trading allotment 100 shares each week. With each passing day, the novice day trader should learn something from past mistakes. Trading in allotments of 100 shares would ensure that mistakes are not expensive, and the trading capital would be preserved. The second week, the novice day trader could increase the allotment from 100 shares to 200 shares. That would be my recipe for minimizing the overall cost of learning the day trading business.

The Intermediate Trading Approach

The "intermediate" trading approach is somewhere in between the slow and fast approaches. It is risky to jump from the slow to the fast approach overnight. However, the intermediate trading approach provides a soft landing. The first step is to select intermediate stocks, which do not move as fast as some of the expensive Internet stocks. They tend to be somewhat stable and do not move extremely fast in either price direction, so the trader's reaction time is somewhat manageable. Thus the intermediate day trader has sufficient time to react to the price movement and to get the trade order executed.

Intermediate stocks—stocks with prices between $20 and $50—are more expensive than slow stocks. They might be just as volatile as the fast stocks in relative percentage change terms. The intermediate stocks might have a high Beta value, but it is the absolute dollar change that counts. A 5% price change for a $50 stock is 2.5 points. On the other hand, a 5% price change for a $100 stock is 5 points. The intermediate day trader would have an easier time following the stocks that move 2.5 points in a day than those that move 5 points in a day.

Since the intermediate stocks are more expensive, the $\frac{1}{4}$ point is a relatively small percentage change in price. The $\frac{1}{4}$ price movement is a noise in the market. It is not a real price trend. My point is that the $50 stocks continuously gyrate up and down without any discernible price pattern. Thus, it is easy to get jiggled out when trading those stocks. Day traders should always be aware of that danger.

The next step that the intermediate day trader can undertake is to trade in increments of 500 shares. This will somewhat limit the cost of wrong trades. If the day trader trades in increments of 500 shares, one small trading mistake with a price change of $\frac{1}{8}$ would translate into only a $62.50 loss. It is better to lose $62.50 than $125.

It is also possible to make money day trading if the day trader trades in increments of 500 shares. If the round-trip trading transaction cost is approximately $32, and if the day trader is trading in increments of 500 shares, then the stock price needs to go up or down only $\frac{1}{16}$ to break even on that trade. A price movement of approximately $\frac{1}{16}$ is immaterial and quite common. Trading in allotments of 500 shares would ensure that mistakes do not add up quickly into an enormous loss.

The Fast Trading Approach

The "fast" trading approach should be the domain of experienced day traders. The fast day trading approach is an aggressive trading approach. The focus of attention is on "fast" stocks: those stocks whose prices move extremely fast. The stocks tend to be the expensive (greater than $50 per share) and volatile Internet and high technology stocks. They are extremely volatile and move notably fast in either price direction.

Consequently, the trader's reaction time is very short. The fast day trader does not have much time to react to the price movement and to get the order executed.

Again it is the absolute dollar price change that counts. A 5% price change for a $150 stock is 7.5 points. The fast day trader must be attentive throughout the day in order to follow the stock that moves 7.5 points in a day. A $\frac{1}{2}$ point is a relatively small percentage change in price for stocks priced at $150. It is a noise in the market and not a real price trend. The $150 stock would continuously gyrate up and down without any discernible price pattern. It is very easy to get jiggled out when trading those stocks.

The fast day trader usually trades in increments of 1,000 shares. Trading in increments of 1,000 shares exposes the day trader to substantial loss due to bad trades. But, high risk is associated with high returns. Day trading in increments of 1,000 shares is the best way to make a lot of money. If the round-trip trading transaction cost is approximately $32, and if the day trader is trading in increments of 1,000 shares, then the stock price needs to go up or down only $\frac{1}{32}$ to break even on that trade. Again, the price movement of approximately $\frac{1}{32}$ is immaterial and common. It happens all the time. However, a $\frac{1}{32}$ price movement can go in the wrong direction as well. Trading in an allotment of 1,000 shares would guarantee that trading mistakes would be expensive.

Losing Money

I have always wondered why so many people have failed with day trading. Why is it that so many people have lost money when, on the surface, day trading is deceptively simple? The core of day trading is to exploit short-term price volatility of stocks and earn small incremental profits by trading in increments of 1,000 shares. Trading in 1,000-share increment is a double-edged sword. On the upside, a day trader can quickly earn $125 profit if the price goes in the favorable direction by a single $\frac{1}{8}$ of a point. Conversely, the day trader can quickly lose $125 if the price goes in the opposite direction by $\frac{1}{8}$ of a point.

This is where the trader's discipline comes in! The key is to minimize or control the losses. If $\frac{1}{8}$ is your loss limit, then do not lose more than $125 on a trade. Minimize the downside, and maximize the upside. That is the secret to success. However, many new day traders do not have required discipline. They allow a small loss to turn into a large loss. They wait too long, so that an initial $\frac{1}{8}$ loss turns into a $\frac{1}{4}$ or $\frac{3}{8}$ loss or an even larger loss.

If a price drops $\frac{1}{8}$ of a point, get out of the trade. Do not wait for your $\frac{1}{8}$ loss to turn into $\frac{3}{8}$ or more! Know your exit price points in advance for your losing trades (as well as your winning trades). Visualize your trade before you make it. If the trade is a winning trade, plan your exit price. More important, if the trade is a losing trade, stick to your loss limit strategy.

In addition, all accounts are margin accounts. So there is an issue of 2 to 1 financial *leverage* (the 50% Reg. T margin requirement). For instance, a $10,000 initial deposit creates $20,000 buying power. However, leverage works in both directions. Positive leverage happens when a day trader quickly picks up $\frac{1}{4}$ point or $250 gain on a relatively small initial investment (the initial account deposit). Conversely, negative leverage occurs when a day trader quickly loses a $\frac{1}{4}$ or $250 loss. If the day trader lost only $250 every trading day, the entire equity would be wiped out in two months. Because of 2 to 1 leverage, it is possible to lose more money than one's initial account deposit.

Risk Management Tools

The following six measures are the day trading risk management tools. All day traders regardless of their relative day trading experience can easily apply them. These measures are my suggestions, and will only limit risk exposure, not eliminate all day trading risk. Furthermore, the measures will not guarantee that a day trader will be successful. The risk management measures are also ranked, although the ranking is only my personal opinion.

1. The first and foremost risk management measure is to go flat at the end of the trading day. The day trader should close all of his or her open positions at the close of the market. There are many reasons for doing so. First, this eliminates any overnight risk exposure, since the market forces of supply and demand remain active after market close. Institutional investors and traders continue to trade after the market hours through Instinet. Corporations wait for the market to close to announce corporate

news. The federal government issues economic reports at 8:00 A.M. Eastern Time. There are many exogenous reasons that can influence a stock to open with a price gap.

By keeping an overnight position, the day trader risks a lot to save a little. All the day trader could possibly save is the commission cost. And since the commissions are deeply discounted, the day trader is not saving a lot. If the day trader believes that the stock will continue to appreciate in value, the trader always has an option to buy the same stock when the market opens. If the stock opens with the gap up, the day trader is also forgoing the value of that upward gap. But that is a big *if*. The potential reward of earning additional money from the gap does not justify the substantial risk that comes with overnight long or short positions.

One of the most important advantages that day traders have is the ability to be in control of the trading portfolio. Day traders can observe price momentum tick by tick, and if the traders are wrong they can get out of that position quickly. The day trader is always in full control. If the day trader keeps an overnight long or short position, the trader has abdicated that trading control. He or she has to wait for the next day to resume control over their money.

In essence, if you are a day trader, then do not let yourself become an investor.

2. The second crucial risk management tool is to get out of losing trades. The day trader must react to the market activity. If the price is going up, the day trader should open the long position. Suppose that the day trader is wrong. The long position is losing money. The price of the stock has reversed its trend, and now it is going down. The day trader has received a clear signal to get out. In fact, every down-tick is a signal to the day trader to get out. The day trader then has two distinct choices: (1) Get out of the stock immediately and minimize the loss, or (2) hold on to the long position and hope for a price reversal.

Hope is a four-letter word. It is not good to hope. A day trader who hopes that the open stock position will turn around has abdicated control over his or her trading money. Yes, it is possible that the position could reverse and the stock price might bounce back. Yes, it is even possible that the losing position could turn into a profitable trade. Yes, everything is possible. But how likely is that to occur? What is the probability that the stock will bounce back? If a day trader can not logically ascertain the probability of a price reversal occurring, the day trader should close that position immediately. It is the only prudent thing to do.

The day trader should not wait for a small loss to turn into a bigger loss. The trader needs to get out of that losing long position as quickly as possible. How many price signals (price down-ticks) does it take to convince that trader that he or she was wrong on that trade? Is it $\frac{1}{8}$ or $\frac{1}{4}$ or $\frac{3}{8}$? If he or she is trading in 1,000-share blocks, does the trader need to lose $125 or $250 or $375 before admitting that he or she was wrong?

My advice is not to "marry" the losers. In other words, do not get attached to losing stock trades. The stock price is going in a different direction than anticipated. Listen to the market. See the obvious. Do not fight the ticker tape. Get out of that position! New day traders must learn to admit they were wrong—and that is the key—admitting that your trade was wrong and moving on to the next trade.

3. The day trader must set loss limits. The levels of loss limits will vary among day traders. The loss limit depends on the day trader's trading style, the amount of trading capital available, the level of day trading experience, and individual willingness to assume risk. Nevertheless, the day trader must retain those self-imposed loss limits throughout the trading day. The loss limit could be $\frac{1}{8}$ or $\frac{1}{4}$ or $\frac{3}{8}$ or $\frac{1}{2}$ of a point, or even higher such as 1 point. However, 1 point should be the maximum loss that a day trader would lose on a single trade.

The circumstance that the day traders can control in their day trading endeavor is the amount of their losses. They can somewhat influence the profits or the upside aspects of the day trading business. They can decide whether to enter a stock position or not. They can decide when to close an open a position so they have control over the exit strategy. But the day trader does not know how much money he or she will make on any position. If prices are going up, the day trader will continue holding that position. The amount of profit will depend on the strength of that price increase momentum. However, day traders must manage their losses or the downside aspect of the business. That is the key to trading success: control to minimize the downside, and try to maximize the upside.

Another loss limit device is to set an absolute dollar amount that the day trader is willing to lose for one day of trading. As stated, the absolute dollar loss amount will vary among day traders; it will depend on the day trader's available trading capital and individual willingness to assume risk. The amount could be $500 or $800 or $1,000 or higher. Everyone will have bad trading days. The key is to contain how expensive the bad trading days are. They do not have to be expensive. If trading is not going in the right direction one day, close your open positions and go home to reenergize. The next day might be different. There is always the next day.

Furthermore, the day trader should also set an absolute dollar amount that the day trader would be willing to lose for one week of trading. That amount should be higher than the loss limit imposed for the day losses. However, it should not be proportionately higher (for example, five times higher). It would be unrealistic to expect that the day trader will lose the maximum loss amount every single day. If that is the case, the day trader does not know what he or she is doing. Go back to the drawing board. The day trader should reassess his or her entire day trading strategy. Ultimately, appraise whether day trading is a suitable business.

4. If the stock price is moving quickly against the trader's position, then the trader should get out of that position quickly. Too often, the day trader admits that a trade was bad and decides to get out, but instead of getting out in the fastest possible way, which is through the SOES market order, the trader tries to extract a better price. Instead of selling the stock at the best BID price via the SOES market order, the trader attempts to submit an offer to sell at the inside ASK or lower ASK price (that is, $\frac{1}{16}$ lower ASK) through an ECN such as Island.

Since the stock price is dropping fast, the probability is low that the offer to sell at the ASK will get filled. At that time, the trader will attempt to resubmit a new offer to sell at the new ASK, which is lower than the previous ASK price. Again, the probability is low that the offer to sell will get filled, because the stock price is falling quickly. By the time the trader drops the idea of offering the stock for sale through the ECNs and executes the SOES market order at the inside BID price, the BID price is already down. The trader has lost money trying to pick up a $\frac{1}{16}$ higher selling price. The inside BID price is now lower than it was a few moments ago.

5. Another common risk exposure is to *pyramid* the stock position. The day trader would start with a 1,000-share long or short position. Then the trader would quickly add a few thousand more shares to the

existing open position. (Obviously, that is subject to availability of trading funds.) If the stock price quickly reverses its course, the trader would have trouble selling several thousand shares quickly. The day trader would eventually sell all the shares, and it is likely that the obtained average selling price would be lower than the price obtained if the block had only been 1,000 shares.

6. Another risk exposure is to open multiple stock positions. The day trader would start with a 1,000-share long or short position, and then add several other different stocks to the existing open position. (Again, that is all subject to availability of trading funds.) It is not a simple task to monitor numerous open positions. Experienced traders can do it because they have been doing it for a long time. Inexperienced traders would have a difficult time. The probability is that they would miss several opportunities to close the open positions at a better price. They might miss the trading signals. They might miss the price reversals. It is my opinion that new day traders should stick with only one open position at a time. With time and experience, day traders can add one or two more open positions.

The Losing Streak

Every day trader will sooner or later face the losing streak. Sometimes that losing streak can be so pronounced and severe that it challenges the trader's confidence. The question is not whether the losing streak will happen, but what to do when it does happen. So what can be done?

1. My advice would be to stop losing money. At first sight, this advice seems comical. But bear with me. If the losing streak is pronounced, stop trading for a few days. Take a break. Take the time off and recharge your batteries. The market will be there when you come back. With a fresh, reenergized mind, you might find the trading outcome to be different. The point is that you have stopped losing money. During the time off from day trading, take a look at your losing trades. Print a price chart of the stock(s) that are responsible for the losing streak that day, and mark all of your buy and sell points. Examine the buying and selling decisions. Try to understand why those trades were bad. Try to learn from your mistakes.

2. Also, go back to the basics. Reexamine and reevaluate your trading style. Keep a trading diary. Write down the reasons for entering the trades. See whether those reasons passed the reality test. Write down the reasons for exiting the trades. See whether the exit strategies are efficient. Look for your individual trading patterns. The worst option is to blame something or someone else for the losses. Do not blame the losses on bad luck. Luck has nothing to do with the recurring losses. Traders are individually responsible for their own losses.

3. When the day trader comes back to trade reenergized, the key is to reverse the losing streak. The objective is to score profitable trades, regardless of how small the profit is. In other words, place anything green on the board. If it is a $\frac{1}{16}$ gain—take it. Sell it for the small gain. The focus is to rebuild confidence. Again, the objective is to stop bleeding, or stop losing money. Any trading gain is a step in the right direction.

4. Reduce the trading share size. If the day trader is commonly trading in increments of 1,000 shares, then drop the size to 500 shares. That would alleviate some of the pressure of losing a lot of money. If there is a loss, it is not dramatic. Again, the focus is to stop losing money. If the trader is losing money, it is not a lot of money lost. With a few profitable days, the trader's confidence will be regained. At that time the day trader can resume trading the normal lot size of 1,000 shares.

5. Do not double the risk exposure. The worst thing a day trader can do is to double the money in order to recover losses quickly. Do not start pyramiding trading positions and trading in increments of 2,000 shares. Adding additional shares will only add additional psychological pressure. Also, the loss potential is now much greater. Doubling the shares will not stop the losses. Instead, the day trader has increased exposure to potentially higher losses. How would an additional large trading loss help the day trader to regain lost confidence?

19

Day Trading Styles

Every day trader eventually develops his or her own trading style that reflects his or her risk tolerance and individual personality. Many different trading techniques can be generalized into four distinct day trading styles. Those styles are the "specialist," "scalper," "market maker," and "position" day traders.

In reality, many day traders use hybrids of different styles. During any portion of the trading day, a day trader could be a specialist. But when the opportunity arrives, the trader could quickly become a scalper. He or she would take advantage of a price jump for a stock that is suddenly moving up due to some exceptional good news. Yes, day traders are opportunists. Day traders can start the day trading business with one style and discover quickly, after losing some money, that the style is not working for them and try another trading style. Day traders are continuously in the process of evolving and modifying their approaches.

The "Specialist" Day Trader

This group of day traders specializes in a few NASDAQ or NYSE stocks that are actively traded and have substantial intra-day price volatility. Those stocks are usually well-known stocks such as Dell, Intel, Microsoft, Cisco, or similar high technology stocks. Some day traders specialize in one or two stocks from each technology industry sector, such as semiconductors, networks, Internet, software, hardware, and database providers. Since those high tech stocks and industry sectors have significant intra-day price volatility, there are plenty of opportunities to day trade. If nothing is happening in one industry sector, other sectors might be active and volatile.

A specialist day trader would select five or ten stocks and input the symbols of those stocks into the Market Ticker window. Then he or she would watch for price momentum. The moment the day trader is alerted to any kind of price movement on the Market Ticker window, he or she would input that stock symbol into the Level II, Time and Sales, and the technical analysis chart windows. The trader would start to analyze that stock closely. In essence, he or she would look for a trading signal to open a long or short position.

Because day traders specialize in a few stocks, they develop a very good feel for these securities. Specialists monitor the stocks' performance continually, and thus know about the stocks' monthly, weekly, and intra-day price data. For instance, the day traders develop a good feel about the stocks' intra-day price support and resistance levels. In addition, specialists read and monitor everything written or published in the mass media or Internet on their stocks. For example, the specialist day traders would know when the companies they monitor plan to announce earnings reports.

Because of the intense concentration on a few stocks, specialists are willing to take on additional risk. If the stock price momentum is there, they are willing to purchase or short sell additional shares—to pyramid or increase their position from 1,000 shares to several thousand shares. Specialists believe that the additional risk associated with the higher number of shares is a calculated risk. Due to their intense monitoring of a few stocks, specialists develop a higher tolerance for the risk. A particular stock could reverse the trend $\frac{1}{2}$ point or higher, and the day trader would hold onto the position. A specialist would be willing to absorb a $\frac{1}{2}$-point loss and wait for the stock to reverse a losing trend because he or she feels confident that they know the stock behavior well.

Being a specialist day trader has its advantages. Traders develop a great deal of knowledge about their stocks, so they tend to have a greater percentage of winning trades. Specialists occasionally hold an overnight position. They justify that additional overnight exposure risk with the explanation that they know the stock well. Since they monitor only a few stocks, specialists tend to make fewer trades and thus they save on commission costs.

It is my opinion that specialists assume lower risks. They make fewer trades each day, and when they do trade, they take positions in the stocks that they know well. On the other hand, specialists have lower profit potential. Since the specialists monitor only a few stocks, they miss many opportunities elsewhere in the market, where stock prices could be extremely volatile. Consequently, specialists seldom have "fabulous" trading days. They assume lower risk and thus the potential for a lower rate of return.

TRADER PROFILE: SPECIALIST DAY TRADER

Ted Giattina, Age 58, Sacramento, California

Ted is a profitable new day trader. He started day trading in February 1999. Ted is an attorney who decided to leave the practice of law and pursue day trading. Like many others, he was attracted to day trading because of its high income potential and the ability to work for himself. He opened a trading account with $75,000, and like most other newcomers he lost money at the beginning. Ted learned the day trading business by taking classes, reading day trading books, and paper trading. Ted's best one-day profit was $3,500, and his worst one-day loss was $1,500.

Ted is a specialist day trader. He specializes in the NYSE stocks, and furthermore he closely monitors the NYSE airline and financial institution stocks. Some of his favorite stocks are UAL, LEH, MER, ONE, CMB, C, and LU. He initially started trading NASDAQ stocks, and he lost money. Ted claimed that the NASDAQ market was simply too fast for him, making him always tense and stressed out. He decided to switch to the NYSE because it moves at a much slower pace than the NASDAQ market. Ted claims that the NYSE market fits his age and personality much better. He points out half-jokingly that NASDAQ is "for the young day traders."

Ted makes a few round-trip trades (approximately eight to ten) per day. The holding period for his trades is somewhat longer than the short-term holding period of other day traders. He sometimes carries overnight open positions. Ted believes that this is a relatively safe practice, because he specializes in a few stocks that he knows well and does not mind carrying them for the long-term as an investment.

Ted claims that 75% of his trades are winning trades, with 85% of all trades being on the NYSE market and 15% on the NASDAQ. Ted buys stocks that are near the intra-day price support line (the lower Bollinger band). If the stock moves up, he will sell to take the profit. If the stock does not move up, he will patiently wait for upside movement. Ted pays close attention to the S&P Futures market and what is being "printed" on the Time and Sales window. He will also make sure that he takes an open stock position in the same direction as the broad market. If the stock price trading range is narrow and the S&P Futures market is not trending, Ted will stay out of a trade altogether.

Ted's recommendations to new traders to improve their success rates:

➤ Establish a discipline that works for you.

➤ Avoid hasty trading decisions—there are always other trading opportunities.

➤ Stay with the trend of the S&P Futures market.

➤ Specialize initially in a few stocks.

The "Scalper" Day Trader

Day traders who are known as "scalpers" are the original Harvey Houtkin's "SOES bandits." Harvey Houtkin is a pioneer of the day trading business who coined the unfortunate term "SOES bandit" to depict an anti-establishment image of day trading. The term *bandit* connotes that day traders are somehow taking something that does not belong to them. That is untrue. Day traders take risks like any other professional stock trader. When and if they earn money trading stocks, they earn it because they are smart, quick, and efficient. They are not "bandits."

Scalping is the most common day trading style. As the word implies, the scalper monitors a great number of volatile stocks that have decent daily trading volume (at least 500,000 shares per day). Scalpers look for any stock that is moving up or down. They sift through a sea of financial information to pick up on any stock that is moving. They watch CNBC reports, and observe the real-time and dynamically updated Top

NASDAQ and NYSE Advances and Declines reports and the 52-week High and Low price breakouts window.

In addition, scalpers often spend many hours on the Internet searching and sifting through different financial information Web sites. They look for clues about any stocks that might be in play the following trading day, to obtain early insights about which stocks might be volatile the next day.

The Internet has several chat rooms designed specifically for day traders. Those Internet chat rooms offer rumors, tips, and advice. Beware of the quality of information available in those chat rooms. The chat rooms are often the source of "pump and dump" stock schemes. Unscrupulous stock promoters and manipulators use the Internet chat rooms to talk up a stock's price, and then sell or "dump" the stock at an inflated price. The author's advice is *caveat emptor*—buyers beware!

Day trading stocks on news can be extremely lucrative. There are numerous events, such as stock upgrades (or downgrades), mergers and acquisitions reports, or stock splits that could cause an immediate public reaction in the price of a stock. Most likely, the market (that is, the public) will overreact, and the stock price will move greatly. A word of caution—the day trader should avoid submitting a market buy order during a time when the market is absorbing positive news, because the order could get filled near the stock's high intra-day price. The ensuing profit taking (that is, selling) could quickly lower the price of that stock. The day trader could end up selling the stock at a loss. (It is always a good idea to utilize a limit buy order.)

When a stock price has upward momentum, the most common execution strategy employed by scalpers is to buy the stock at the inside ASK price via SOES. There is no point in submitting an offer to buy a stock at the inside BID, or to try to cut the spread (by submitting the high bid). The market makers and other day traders would not be interested in selling a stock with a positive (upward) momentum at a lower price than the ASK price. Once the day trader owns the stock (that is, has a long stock position) and after the price increases, if there is still a positive price momentum, the day trader could attempt to sell the stock by offering to sell it at the inside ASK or near the inside ASK price.

If the scalpers believe that particular stocks have the potential to move up or down that day, they would add these stocks into the Market Ticker window. From that time on, they would monitor these stocks for any price momentum. If there has been no price movement that day or that week, the day trader would simply delete that stock symbol from the Market Ticker. If price movement has been detected, scalpers would input that stock symbol in the Level II, Time and Sales, and technical analysis chart windows. They would quickly analyze the stock to determine whether to buy it or sell it short.

Because scalper day traders do not specialize in trading any particular stock, they do not develop a good feel for any securities. Scalpers do not closely and continuously monitor all stocks' performances, and thus they do not form a strong opinion about the stocks' intra-day price support and resistance levels. As a rule, scalpers do not have a high tolerance for loss. They get in and out of trading positions quickly. If they are right about a stock, they will stay in that trading position long enough to pick up $\frac{1}{4}$ or higher profit. If the scalpers are wrong, they will quickly leave with a minimal loss of $\frac{1}{8}$ or $\frac{1}{4}$.

Scalpers are not willing to absorb higher risk. They do not want to hold and wait for a stock to reverse a losing trend, because they do not feel confident that they know the behavior of that stock that well. A scalper would seldom hold an overnight position. That is not their style. Because they don't focus on any particular stock, scalpers are not willing to take any additional risks. Thus scalpers would seldom pyramid or increase their position from 1,000 shares to several thousand shares.

Scalpers tend to make a lot of trades. Sometimes, the trades are only a few minutes long. It is not uncommon to find scalpers who make 100 trades per day. Sometimes, a winning trade of $\frac{1}{16}$ would suffice. That is $62.50 gross profit on a trade of 1,000 shares. A day trader is "scalping" $\frac{1}{16}$, $\frac{1}{8}$, or $\frac{1}{4}$ from the existing price momentum. Since this style generates many trading transactions, $\frac{1}{16}$ and $\frac{1}{8}$ and $\frac{1}{4}$ could add up to a substantial sum at the end of the trading day.

Since scalpers do not acquire a great deal of knowledge about any particular stock, they tend to have a lower percentage of winning trades. They simply surf the NASDAQ and NYSE markets looking for intra-day price volatility. If a stock is moving up, a scalper would buy that stock. They sometimes take a position in a stock that they know nothing about. In my opinion, scalpers assume greater risk than specialists. However, since scalpers monitor many stocks, they have opportunities to score more "home runs." A home run would be a winning trade with 1 point or more. On 1,000 shares traded, that would translate into $1,000 profit or higher. Consequently, scalpers have the potential to enjoy "fabulous" trading days. Since scalpers monitor a great number of stocks, they tend to make many trades and they pay a lot in commissions. Day trading shops love to have successful scalpers in their trading rooms. They are simply good for business. In summary, scalpers assume higher risk and thus higher potential for profitability.

TRADER PROFILE: SCALPER DAY TRADER

Mark Jones, Age 33, Boise, Idaho

Mark is a profitable day trader. He started day trading in March 1997 in Boise, Idaho. He came into this field with a few years of industry experience as a stockbroker. Like many other day traders, Mark was attracted to day trading because it has the potential for extreme profitability.

He opened a trading margin account with a $30,000 deposit, and at first he lost a little money. Mark learned the day trading business on his own. Mark's best one-day profit was $9,800, and his worst one-day loss was $2,300. Mark claims that every trading day he nets after commissions on average approximately $600. Since he keeps his account relatively small ($60,000 purchasing power), Mark commonly receives intra-day margin calls from his clearing firm.

Mark is a typical scalper day trader. He makes many round-trip trades (approximately 60 or more per day). The holding period for his trades is extremely short (a few minutes to one hour). He seldom, if ever, carries overnight open positions. Mark states that 65% of his trades are winning trades, while 35% are flat trades or losers. Ninety-five percent of his trades are on the NASDAQ market. His trading style can be summarized as scalping and trading on the news. Before the market opens, Mark watches CNBC and surfs Internet financial sites and chat rooms searching for companies that might have the potential for their stock prices to move up or down that day.

Mark pays close attention to the S&P Futures market and what is being "printed" on the Time and Sales window. He makes sure that his open stock positions are in the same direction as the S&P Futures market. If the S&P Futures market is up at that moment, Mark will go long with his "strong" stocks. The strong stocks are those that have favorable (upside) movement on the Level II screen (that is, counterclockwise movement), favorable prints (that is, buy orders at the ASK price in the Time and Sales window), or large bidding on Instinet. If the S&P Futures market is down, Mark will go short with his "weak" stocks, which are the stocks that have unfavorable movements on the Level II screen, Time and Sales window, and on Instinet trading.

Mark's buy signals come mostly from the information on the Level II screen and watching the actions of the "ax" market makers. He monitors closely the trading on Instinet, as well as observing the stochastic oscillator for overbought and oversold market conditions. Mark prefers to enter the market through the SOES limit order (buying on the ASK price or selling short on the BID price), and, to cut the spread, exit the market through Island (that is, in the case of long positions—offer at the ASK price). Mark's favorite NASDAQ trading stocks are WCOM, AMAT, INTC, MSFT, ALTR, and SUNW.

Mark's recommendations to new traders to improve their success rates:

➤ Cut your losses.

➤ Stay with the stock trend.

➤ Stay with the overall S&P Futures trend.

➤ In an up market, go with strong stocks; in a down market, go with weak stocks.

➤ At the beginning, specialize and trade a limited number of stocks.

The "Market Maker" Day Trader

This group of day traders tries to exploit the large spread between the BID and ASK prices. The spread varies from stock to stock. It depends mostly on trading volume. Thinly traded stocks always have a larger spread. First of all, there are few NASDAQ market makers making the market for inactive stocks. That means lower competition. There is also little inflow and outflow of funds (that is, order flow) for those stocks. Thus it is difficult to ascertain any visible supply and demand. Consequently, thinly traded stocks carry substantially larger trading risk. The large spread is the compensation to NASDAQ market makers for providing liquidity for those illiquid stocks.

Most day traders do not trade thinly traded stocks. The stocks are simply too risky. For instance, upward price movement can be quickly reversed. The prices could start declining sharply, and the trader could have a hard time getting out. Since there is little liquidity (that is, few buyers entering the market for that stock), the trader would have to sell the stock to the few existing market makers for that stock who are buying the stock for their own portfolios. But the market makers have already adjusted the price to a lower level. The trader would end up selling the stock at a loss.

On the other hand, actively traded stocks such as Dell, Intel, Microsoft, or Cisco have very small spreads. There are plenty of market makers making the market for those stocks. There is a substantial inflow and outflow of funds. In essence, there is visible supply and demand. It is easier and safer to trade such liquid stocks. The spread tends to be narrow ($\frac{1}{16}$ or $\frac{1}{8}$) for actively traded stocks.

For expensive stocks that trade in the $100-plus range, the spread tends to be larger ($\frac{1}{4}$ or $\frac{5}{16}$). However, the value of a $\frac{1}{4}$ spread for a $100 stock is smaller in relative terms than the value of a $\frac{1}{8}$ spread for a $20 stock. For example, a $\frac{1}{4}$ spread for $100 constitutes $\frac{1}{4}$ of 1% of the stock price, or 0.25%. On the other hand, a $\frac{1}{8}$ spread for a $20 stock constitutes $\frac{5}{8}$ of 1% of the stock price, or 0.63%. In essence, a $\frac{1}{4}$ spread for the expensive stocks is a smaller spread in relative terms than a $\frac{1}{8}$ spread for the inexpensive stocks.

The level of spread depends on the forces of supply and demand for that stock. Often during the trading day that spread widens. The spread can go up to $\frac{1}{2}$ to $\frac{5}{8}$ for expensive stocks such as Yahoo (YHOO) and Amazon.com (AMZN). An astute and smart day trader can decide at that time whether to play the market maker's game. Figure 19.1 illustrates this point.

Figure 19.1 *Day Trader Acting as Market Maker*

NASDAQ market makers buy stocks from the public at the lower BID price and sell the same stock to the public at the higher ASK price, and thus earn the spread. In the example in Figure 19.1, that spread of $\frac{5}{16}$ is substantial. Perhaps, the spread widened at that point because all market makers (sellers) left the lower ASK price of $150\frac{5}{8}$, and thus the higher ASK price of $150\frac{11}{16}$ became the best ASK price. Conversely, the spread could also be widened if all market makers (buyers) left the previously highest BID price of $150\frac{3}{8}$, and the lower BID price of $150\frac{5}{16}$ became the best BID price. The bottom line is that the spread for a variety of supply and demand conditions had widened to $\frac{5}{16}$.

The astute day trader would notice that development. The day trader would then offer to buy that stock at a price higher than the current best BID price. The day trader would submit a "High Bid on Island for $150\frac{3}{8}$." In other words, the day trader would submit a bid through an Electronic Communications Network, such as Island, to buy the stock for the higher price of $150\frac{3}{8}$. The $150\frac{3}{8}$ bid would be posted electronically through the Island system nationwide. That price would constitute the best BID price in the nation at that point in time. The chances are that the bid would get filled. If one were selling that stock, then one would rather sell the stock for the higher price of $150\frac{3}{8}$ than the lower price of $150\frac{5}{16}$.

After the bid has been accepted and the buy trade confirmed, the day trader acting as the "market maker" would immediately offer to sell that stock at the price lower than the current best ASK price. The day trader would submit a "Low Offer on Island for $150\frac{5}{8}$." In other words, the day trader would submit through an ECN such as Island an offer to sell the stock for the lower price of $150\frac{5}{8}$. The $150\frac{5}{8}$ offer would be posted electronically through the Island system nationwide. That price would constitute the best ASK price in the nation at that point of time. Again, chances are that the offer would get filled. If the public were buying that stock, then the public would rather buy that stock for the lower price of $150\frac{5}{8}$ than the higher price of $150\frac{11}{16}$.

The astute day trader could be rewarded handsomely for this activity. In this hypothetical example from Figure 19.1, if the day trader were trading in 1,000-share increments, the gross profit would be $\frac{1}{4}$ or $250. Also, the net result would be that the spread would have been reduced from $\frac{5}{16}$ to $\frac{1}{4}$. If the spread remains at $\frac{5}{16}$, then many more day traders would be attracted to this opportunity. In short, a large spread such as

$^5/_{16}$ would attract many day traders who would continuously attempt to bid and offer at a better price. They would repeat this process again and again. The ultimate result will be a cut in the spread.

This strategy can work if the spread is large or wide. If the spread is small, such as $^1/_{16}$, there is little potential for cutting the spread: to offer to purchase the stock at any price higher than the current best BID price. The day trader could submit an offer to buy the stock at the current BID price through an ECN such as Island. However, there is no guarantee that the order would get filled. At that time, the day trader would be competing with other market makers to purchase the same stock at the same quoted price as other market makers.

Cutting the spread would be an example of a day trader doing something that is "socially redeeming." That does not mean that day traders are a benevolent group of people. Day traders are pursuing their own self-interest, which is to make as much money as possible. However, the ability to submit better BID and ASK prices through the ECNs would end up generating a socially beneficial result: a lower spread between the BID and ASK price.

It is not surprising that NASDAQ market makers and the Wall Street establishment do not like this type of day trading activity. Cutting the spread cuts into market-making profitability. However, this type of day trading has generated favorable media attention. Several reporters have portrayed this activity as a story of "David versus Goliath" or a story of small day traders wrestling with the established NASDAQ market makers.

TRADER PROFILE: MARKET MAKER DAY TRADER

Jan Zomat, Age 49, Rocklin, California

Jan is a former day trader. Jan left the day trading business somewhat dissatisfied after only six months of live trading. Although he had started to make money and was breaking even, Jan felt that the day trading business was not for him. He found it to be stressful and demanding and more difficult than he had initially envisioned. Jan thought that he had not received adequate support and assistance from the local day trading brokerage firm. A self-employed businessman who owns and operates a local hair-styling salon, Jan ultimately felt that day trading interfered with his primary business. Since Jan lives in California, he would start day trading early—at 6:30 A.M. After the market closed—at 1:00 P.M.—Jan would go to his hair-styling business and work for several more hours.

Initially, Jan was dissatisfied with the performance and relative expense of his full-service stockbroker. He felt that he could do a better job on his own. He saw an advertisement for a day trading broker on CNBC and decided to try his hand. Like many others, Jan was attracted to day trading because of its high income potential and the ability to work for himself. Jan started day trading in June 1998 in the Sacramento branch office of GO Trading; later he transferred his account to On-Line Investments. Presently he trades options because it provides greater leverage and does not require any time commitment. He also maintains an investment account with E*Trade.

Jan opened a trading margin account with $85,000, and like most other newcomers he lost money at the beginning. Jan learned the day trading business by taking classes, reading day trading books, and paper trading. Jan's best one-day profit was $4,000, which happened on a day that Internet stocks were running wild. His worst one-day loss was $5,000; it happened also when he bought Internet stocks at the market peak. (Jan remembers that this particular losing trade was a "tip" from a fellow day trader.)

Jan was something of a market maker day trader. He preferred to buy stocks at the BID price, and he tried to sell at the ASK price through Island, thus earning the spread. The Island was his primary trading platform. Trading as a market maker is a difficult task. For each trading transaction, Jan needed another trader on the other side of the trade. In addition to his market making trading style, Jan was also a scalper who would jump on an opportunity to make some money on a stock that was moving. He watched CNBC closely and browsed Internet financial sites in search of companies that might have the potential for stock prices to move up or down that day. When Jan would identify a price movement, he would jump in and buy the stock at the ASK price (through Island or SOES) and after the stock had moved up, he would try to sell it at the ASK price (through Island).

Jan made many round-trip trades (approximately 30 or more per day), and the holding period for his trades was rather short (a few minutes to one hour). He sometimes carried overnight open positions. Jan justified doing this because he traded stocks of large and established companies. If Jan were too late to exit a losing trade, he would refuse to take a large loss. Jan would hold the stock in his portfolio until the stock rebounded. Jan stated that only 55% of his trades were winning trades, while 45% were flat trades or losers. Seventy-five percent of his trades were on the NASDAQ market.

Interestingly enough, Jan did not pay much attention to the broad market (the S&P Index). Jan bought stocks that were near the intra-day price support line (lower Bollinger band) or the intra-day low price. He used Fast and Slow Moving Averages to monitor stocks. He also paid attention to what was being "printed" on the Time and Sales window. Jan would sell the stock when it reached its intra-day price resistance level (upper Bollinger band).

Jan's recommendations to new traders to improve their success rates:

➤ Try live day trading for at least six months. Paper trading does not count.

➤ Use your own risk money. Do not borrow funds to start day trading.

➤ Start slowly with slower moving stocks.

➤ Specialize initially in a few stocks.

➤ Pay close attention to news that can move a particular stock.

➤ You do not have to be in the market all of the time. It is OK to sit on the sideline.

The "Position" Day Trader

This group of day traders is a hybrid between the aggressive investors and the passive day traders. The position trader pays close attention to the technical analysis indicators and studies a stock closely before opening a position. If the trader is right, he or she would keep that position open for a longer period of time than usual. The time frame of analysis for a position trader is much longer than that of the typical day trader. Sometimes that time frame is one day, and sometimes it is a few days. Position traders often keep overnight positions. They tend to make fewer trades and keep those trades open for a longer period of time. They also seek higher price movement than the typical day trader. They wait for the stock to move a few points higher before closing a position.

Position traders tend to have trading accounts with high capital. Subsequently, they can afford to purchase more than 1,000 shares at a time and often pyramid their trading positions. They might start with 1,000 shares, and if the market moves in the right direction, they would take an additional 1,000 shares or more. In contrast, 1,000-share increments tend to be a norm and a limit for traditional day traders. Position day traders usually have extensive experience in stock investments. They tend to be savvy stock market participants. They also tend to watch the NYSE market closely.

Position traders often take multiple stock positions. Given a large trading account, the position trader could purchase several stocks and monitor their performance simultaneously. Sometimes, position traders create a "basket" of stocks (for example, Internet stocks) and do a *basket trade*. Several day trading software packages have the capability of creating a basket of stocks for quick execution. If the position trader believes that the Internet sector has the potential to go up, the trader might execute a basket order.

With the click of the mouse, the position trader would send a simultaneous order to buy several Internet stocks in 1,000-share increments. From that point on, the position trader would monitor closely the performance of all stocks in the basket. If any stock is not performing as expected (the price is not moving up or decreasing in value), the trader would quickly sell that stock. The trader would continue to monitor the other stocks in that basket. As long as those stocks are performing as expected (the price is increasing), the position trader would keep them. In essence, the position trader would keep the winners and shed the losers.

TRADER PROFILE: POSITION DAY TRADER

Jerry Dye, Age 48, Folsom, California

Jerry is a profitable day trader. He started day trading in July 1998. He came into this field with many years of industry experience as a stockbroker. He was attracted to day trading because it was a new challenge and had the potential for extreme profitability.

He opened a trading account with $150,000, and at first he lost a little money. Jerry learned the day trading business on his own. Given his extensive background in the securities industry, he felt that he did not need to take day trading courses. Jerry's best one-day profit was $56,000. He took several long positions in Internet stocks in a trading day that was "Internet crazy." His worst one-day loss was $15,000. In that case, Jerry failed to recognize and act upon a fundamental turn in the market. He continued to carry several long stock positions well after the overall market had turned and started to decline.

Jerry is a typical position day trader. He makes only a few round-trip trades (approximately three to five) per day. The holding period for his trades (a few hours to a few days) is much longer than the short-term holding period of a typical day trader. He often carries overnight open positions. Jerry justifies this with the fact that he studies a stock extensively before opening a position in that stock. He claims that 95% of his trades are winning trades, with 75% of all trades on the NASDAQ market and 25% on the NYSE. His trading style can be summarized in one word—*patience*. There are trading days when Jerry does not make a single trade. If the market conditions are not right and there are no clear trading signals, Jerry will sit on the sidelines and simply monitor the market.

Jerry's buy signals come mostly from technical analysis tools. He monitors closely the MACD and Bollinger bands indicators, as well as trading volume and Instinet activities. When a stock price penetrates the intra-day price support level, it's his signal to short sell the stock. If Jerry is unable to fill the order within his price parameters, he will stay out of a trade altogether.

Jerry's recommendations to new traders to improve their success rates:

➤ Have patience, patience, patience.

➤ Learn order entry procedures well.

➤ Trade a limited number of stocks.

➤ Be familiar with those stocks.

➤ Do not chase the trades.

➤ Do not trade just for trading's sake (that is, out of boredom, as a hobby).

This presentation on the four groups of day trading styles is an oversimplification of the day trading business. The purpose is only to illustrate different trading styles and to provide information on general day trading standards. Eventually, all day traders develop their own trading styles and philosophies that might incorporate features of any of the four listed day trading styles.

The Psychology of Trading

Confidence breeds success! Or is it that success breeds confidence? What comes first? It is the eternal "chicken versus egg" question. If I must choose between the two, confidence wins. A day trader must be confident to succeed in this business. If a novice day trader starts to trade live with any lingering doubts about the future outcome, the trader is likely to fail. The doubts become self-fulfilling prophecies. It is my opinion that the day trader's beliefs and actions must be congruent. It is crucial that the day trader believe in himself or herself; the belief that one can be a successful trader is essential in reaching that goal.

Visualization

The novice day trader must be able to "visualize" himself or herself as a successful and profitable day trader. The visualization of the day trading process is crucial. The new trader must be able to state clearly what an experienced and successful day trader would do under various trading circumstances. A good day trader visualizes his or her trade before making that trade. He or she understands at what price he or she is willing to buy a stock, how the stock might react while the position is open, and at what circumstances and price he or she is willing to sell.

For instance, if the trading loss were $\frac{1}{4}$ of a point, then the experienced day trader would exit that position immediately at the loss. The novice day trader should be able to visualize himself performing the very same action: exit the trade at the time. When such circumstances arrive, and they will, the novice day trader would know exactly what to do. If the day trader has an open position a few minutes before the market close, the trader would know that a successful day trader would close that open position immediately regardless of the profit and loss status.

The Trading Plan

The novice day trader should have a trading plan that clearly spells out what she will do under different trading scenarios. It is easier to visualize day trading activities with a defined trading plan or "trading map" in place. The trading plan should address the following questions:

1. Why do I want to day trade?

This is an important question. The new day trader should understand his or her underlying motivation for day trading. What is the attraction? Is it the lure of "quick and easy" money or the potential to make a lot of money? Is it the ability to be self-employed, or is there a passion and sincere interest in the stock market? Understanding one's own motivation is an important ingredient to success.

2. What is my time frame for reaching profitability? In other words, when do I become profitable?

The trading plan should state that the novice day trader should expect to lose up to a specific amount at the beginning, and that it may take six months to become profitable. When such losses come at the beginning, and they will, the novice day trader will not panic. The losses are part of the plan. The novice day trader can continue with the plan and move up the learning curve.

3. What do I trade (what stocks and how many shares) in the first month, the second month, and so on?

The trading plan should call for the novice day trader to trade "slow" stocks (the relatively inexpensive NASDAQ stocks that do not move rapidly) in the beginning. If the trading plan requires the novice day trader to trade slow stocks in increments of 100 shares for the first week (and then increase the trading amount each week by an additional 100 shares), the novice day trader should follow that plan.

4. What should my trading style and philosophy be at the beginning? Do I start as a specialist day trader (specializing in a few NASDAQ or

NYSE stocks), or do I adopt a scalper's method (seeking price momentum anywhere on the NASDAQ or NYSE)? What style better fits my personality? How much risk am I willing to tolerate?

5. How do I prepare for the next trading day?

The day trading plan should state how the day trader would prepare for each trading day. Does the day trader plan to read the *Investor's Business Daily* before coming to the day trading shop? Does he or she plan to watch CNBC early every morning to ascertain the public's market sentiment?

6. How do I trade at the opening of the market?

The day trading plan should specify how the trader would react at the market open. Will the day trader sit and watch the first 10 or 20 minutes of trading to ascertain the trend for that day, or will the trader jump into the market at the opening?

7. What do I do when a trade goes against me?

This answer should be the most prominent part of the trading plan. In other words, what is my loss limit for one trade? Do I lose $\frac{1}{4}$ or $\frac{3}{8}$ or $\frac{1}{2}$ or higher before getting out of the trade?

8. What do I do when several trades go against me that day?

In other words, what is the maximum loss I would accept in a given day? If the loss exceeds the maximum, then trader should stop trading for that day.

9. What are my stock buying and selling signals?

The trading plan must be very specific about trading signals. The new day trader must know exactly what signs or signals he or she is waiting to receive from the stock market. For example, is it:

➤ A movement in the Level II screen?

➤ The crossover between the Fast and Slow Exponential Moving Averages?

➤ The price approaching the intra-day support or resistance levels (upper or lower Bollinger bands)?

10. What are my exit points or exit signals?

In addition to being specific and stating when the trader will enter the market (that is, take a long or short position), the plan should also state when to exit the position. In other words, what is the trading signal to close a profitable position? Is it:

➤ A movement in the Level II screen?

➤ The crossover between the Fast and Slow Exponential Moving Averages?

➤ The price approaching the intra-day support or resistance levels (upper or lower Bollinger bands)?

➤ A specific price increase (for example, $\frac{1}{2}$ point)?

11. What do I do at the close of the market?

The trading plan should state what the trader would do at the end of the trading day. Does the day trader plan to review the trades from that day and ascertain what trades were losers and why? How many trades had winning percentages? The key is to create a daily routine to evaluate (analyze) the trading actions and to learn from the trades, and particularly to learn from mistakes. If the trader was trading Dell that day, then print the entire Dell intra-day price chart and locate on the chart the entry and exit points for that day. Are the entry and exit points at the optimum? (The probability is great that they are not.) Learning something new about day trading every day will eventually translate into successful trading in the long run.

In summary, most novice day traders do not plan to fail in their day trading businesses. They simply fail to plan. The new trader would find it easier to visualize the day trading process if he or she would invest time to write a trading plan. The trading plan must be specific. For instance, it should state,

"The following are my buy or sell signals: _____.

The following are my risk management tools:_____.

Finally, I the day trader, will follow my own day trading rules."

Knowledge Needed to Write a Trading Plan

To write an effective day trading plan, one must be able to visualize the trading process. The novice day trader must know the technical side of the day trading business. How does one obtain technical knowledge or expertise of day trading? Reading day trading books is a step in the right direction. In fact, my recommendation would be to read all of the available books on the topic of day trading, of which there are only few. Buying and reading these books would be the most economical way to educate oneself.

In addition, the novice day trader should spend a few weeks paper trading or simulation trading. Most day trading software packages have a "demo" mode. Finally, spend some time in the day trading shop in your town, if there is one, behind a successful trader, if possible, and see for yourself whether the day trading business can be profitable. Knowledge is the key.

Psychological Characteristics of the Successful Trader

In addition to possessing a technical knowledge of day trading, day traders must have a certain psychological makeup. Possessing adequate knowledge of the technical aspects of day trading is important, but it is not an absolute guarantee of success. Many highly knowledgeable traders have lost money day trading. To be a success in this risky endeavor, the day trader must be a disciplined risk taker. Not every aspiring trader has those two key psychological components: discipline and the ability to assume risk.

Day trading activities involve the making and losing of money, and that provokes strong and varied emotions. The range of human emotions present during day trading is significant. At times, the day trader can expect to experience happiness, disappointment, excitement, fear, panic, anxiety, and thrill. Different people are predisposed to deal with such emotions differently.

Traders have well-defined psychological characteristics or traits that permeate their daily trading activities. Let us call these traits a "trading temperament," where *temperament* is defined to be a "constitution of peculiar or distinguishing mental characteristics." So what are the traders' peculiar or distinguishing mental characteristics?

It is my opinion that the two most important psychological characteristics for day traders are

1. Self-discipline and
2. Ability to assume risk.

Self-discipline is the first, the crucial, and the most important characteristic. Day traders must exercise self-discipline at all times. The disciplined day traders know ahead of time what they will do under certain trading circumstances. As mentioned previously on numerous occasions, the day trader must be disciplined enough to accept the fact that his or her trading decision is wrong. Once the day trader recognizes that a particular trade went "bad," the trader must quickly get out of that trade with a minimal loss. This is the core of risk management. This is also easier said than done. Day traders, like most people, are often reluctant to admit they have made an error. They are simply unwilling to take a small loss and move on to other trading opportunities. Instead, undisciplined traders start hoping that their losing stock position will reverse its trend. That is when small losses can turn into large losses.

In addition, the day trader must be disciplined enough to wait patiently for a trading signal to buy or sell a stock. That trading signal can be a technical analysis signal, such as the crossover between the Fast and Slow Moving Average lines, or it could be a movement in the NASDAQ Level II screen. The disciplined day trader will not enter a trade without a clear reason. Otherwise day trading becomes gambling. A disciplined day trader will enter a position only when he or she receives a clear trading signal to buy or sell short.

The ability to assume risk is the second important characteristic of the trading temperament. A day trader must have the courage to take a trade position and assume the associated financial risk. Day traders have to make trading decisions quickly. As mentioned previously, the objective of day trading is to exploit short-term daily price volatility, with the key word in this statement being *short-term*. Trading opportunities will come, but they are short lived. The day trader must be able to recognize a short-term price movement and act upon it. There is little time to complete a time-consuming comprehensive analysis. The day trader must have the psychological courage to "pull the trigger" without the benefit of a comprehensive analysis. Otherwise, if the trader waits too long, the trading opportunity will quickly disappear.

In addition to the two key psychological characteristics listed, successful day traders also tend to exhibit the following characteristics:

➤ Intelligence. Day trading is an extremely competitive business. At any point in time the day trader is trading and competing against professional market makers and other day traders. To survive in this business, day traders must be smart.

➤ Flexibility. Market conditions are fluid and are always in a state of motion. The day trader must be able to change and adapt with the changing trading environment. For instance, day traders should be able to trade both long and short positions with relative ease.

➤ Ability to work hard. Day trading is a business. People who succeed in this business have worked hard to get there, and they have paid their dues.

➤ Willingness to learn. Successful day traders strive to learn something new during each trading day, if not during each trade. They know that there is always room for self-improvement.

➤ Confidence that they will make money in the long run. They are not troubled by a series of bad trades during the day or week. They are confident that their trading discipline, risk management, and perseverance will ultimately translate into success.

➤ Ability to react under stress to trading losses or information overload and subsequently make trading decisions without freezing up or panicking.

To illustrate this point from another angle, I can say that I have never met a successful day trader who was undisciplined, risk averse, lazy, stupid, rigid, indecisive, or unwilling to learn new skills.

Stress Reducers

Trading is a stressful business. The day trader is in and out of the market constantly, continuously processing market information and taking risks. The trader is continuously looking for trading opportunities, and when an opportunity is recognized, must quickly decide whether to enter the trade. Consequently, stress is always present, with some days being more stressful than others. Following is the list of proven and generic stress reducers:

➤ Get at least seven or eight hours of sleep daily.

➤ Exercise for quick relief from stress. Try to maintain a regular exercise routine.

➤ Eat well-balanced meals daily. Avoid skipping meals.

➤ Foster a meaningful emotional life. Make the principle of love a motivating force in your family life.

➤ Foster meaningful social relationships. Talk out your problems with your trusted friends.

➤ Set goals in your life. Having a purpose in life will keep your life happier.

➤ Avoid excessive amounts of change in your life at one time. Change is good. Too much change is not.

➤ Arrange for personal time off, and engage in activities that are relaxing.

➤ Learn to say "No" to additional projects and responsibilities for which you have no time or energy.

Dealing with Trading Stress

Yes, losing money in this business is a distinct possibility. The fear of losing money is at the heart of most day trader's stress. Take away the fear of losing money, and the stress disappears. I have never met anyone who was stressing out over paper trading losses. My recommendation to everyone is to start day trading only with money that you can afford to lose. Do not trade money that you cannot afford to lose.

Also, the day trader should always keep in mind that the one and only item he or she can control is the amount of their loss. Day traders cannot control the amount of profit from each trade, since they cannot influence a stock's price movement. Price is a function of the market supply and demand forces. However, the trader can determine his or her loss. Practicing risk management skills (for example, minimizing trade losses to $\frac{1}{4}$ of a point) rigidly is the most important step in reducing a trader's stress level and promoting the trader's long-term survival.

The other condition that generates anxiety is the general uncertainty that is associated with stock trading. Day trading is not an exact science. There are no guarantees that the price of a stock will continue to go in a certain direction, despite the existence of certain market signals. Every day trader must accept and deal with uncertainty. If you are looking for certainty and guarantees, then day trading is not for you.

In my opinion, day trading is an art that is based on a set of clearly defined trading rules and risk management applications. All day trading decisions should be based on the trading rules as defined in the individual trader's trading plan. Consequently, every trade should be within the limits of the self-imposed risk management parameters. Practicing the risk management steps daily is the best way to manage stress and the only way for the day trader to ensure long-term survival in this business.

Day trading is a competitive business. When the day trader is buying and selling stocks to make money, the day trader is continuously competing against professional NASDAQ market makers, NYSE specialists, and other day traders who are also in business to make money. The results of the trading competition are evident immediately. The trading "score" is always visible on the trader's computer screen. The day trader knows at all times whether he or she is making money or not. Consequently, there are plenty of emotional ups and downs that come with that competition.

A good day trader will try to detach himself from that emotional roller coaster. The trader avoids any emotional attachment to a given stock or position. The buy and sell decisions should be entered unemotionally, if that is possible. A good day trader treats trading as a business. If the successful trader makes a wrong trade decision, then she would simply close that position with a loss, without beating or blaming herself mentally, and move on to the next trading opportunity. If the trader makes a winning trade, he or she simply looks for the next trading opportunity without celebration.

My father used to tell me that there are two important strategies for dealing with stress, and I have heard the same two principles several times from other people. In fact, Richard Carlson wrote a book whose title states these two rules:

1. Do not sweat the small stuff.
2. It is all small stuff.

If the novice day trader is prepared to lose $15,000 trying to learn and start a new business, and if the novice day trader does ultimately lose that $15,000, then losing a predetermined and accepted dollar amount constitutes small stuff.

21

Where Do You Go to Day Trade?

THE FIRST DECISION A NEW DAY TRADER WILL MAKE IS WHETHER TO TRADE on-site on the trading floor of a day trading firm's branch office or remotely from home via an Internet brokerage firm. There are certain advantages to both options. A list with names and Web sites of the larger day trading firms and Internet-based brokerages is provided in appendix 1.

Day Trading Firms

Going to the office to trade seems to be the more professional direction. First, there are fewer distractions when day traders are together on the trading floor. There are no family members to step in with questions or requests. There is also a certain synergy among day traders on the trading floor. The day traders communicate among themselves throughout the day and call out the stocks that are moving at that moment. This is an enormous help. Two pair of eyes can see more than one pair of eyes. A single day trader cannot possibly monitor the entire universe of NAS-DAQ and NYSE stocks. Also, it is in the traders' interest to talk out their relative trade positions. If a trade position is long, the day trader has a vested interest to broadcast that trade, so other people in the shop might join in on the same side of the trade and buy that stock (and increase demand). If it was a winning trade, then all of them profit. If it was a losing trade, then all of them will "share" the pain.

Some professional day trading firms have created their own proprietary "squawk boxes." The firms have hired research assistants who sit in front of computer monitors and sift through the sea of real-time financial data that is provided by Wall Street news service organizations such as Bloomberg. These research assistants continuously review and analyze all the data coming from multiple proprietary news sources. Often the research assistants learn about the news before it is publicly disseminated over CNBC. When they encounter news (for example, company earnings or stock split reports) that can move stock prices, the research assistants broadcast that news immediately to all branch offices. Every office has a speaker in the background that transmits this information. Some traders choose to ignore the squawk box. They focus and specialize on only a few stocks. But for many day traders, who surf the market and actively seek any stock that is moving, the squawk box is an extremely valuable tool.

Professional day trading firms invest money in the best available trading technology. They have to in order to stay in business and compete against the Internet brokers. Day trading firms must maintain that competitive edge by differentiating their day trading services from electronic trading that can be practiced at home via the Internet. In addition to providing direct access to NASDAQ and SelectNet, professional day trading firms must offer at least direct access to Island (ISLD) Electronic Communications Network. Some day trading firms offer direct access to other ECNs, such as Instinet (INCA), Terranova (TNTO), or Bloomberg Tradebook (BTRD).

The professional day trading firms also provide their day traders with a choice of several trading platforms or trading software packages, such as CyberTrader or TradeCast. These are truly sophisticated and completely integrated stock trading packages. A good financial software package will provide more than just Level I and Level II screen information, which is readily available elsewhere. Even the point-and-click order execution interface is a common software feature. The following trading instruments are standard features in most financial software:

➤ "Smart" or "hot" function keys for trade executions that quickly route trade orders in the most efficient manner for the best possible price;

➤ Different types of market alerts, such as alerts for crossed and locked markets;

➤ Information on market makers' movements within the inside and outside BID and ASK quotes;

➤ The trader's "Account Manager" that will keep track of, in real time, the trader's pending and open trade positions, purchasing power, and current profit and loss situation.

Running a day trading branch office requires sophisticated computer and networking technology. Every day trading branch office must have staff on the trading floor who are computer experts. The staff will provide on-site technical support to all day traders in a timely manner. If the network is down, the staff will quickly reboot the servers and reestablish the trading environment. If day traders have questions regarding the software, the tech will have the answers. "Down time," which inevitably occurs sometimes in this electronic trading environment, should be kept at a minimum.

A trader investigating a branch office should take a look at the computer equipment in the office. See what the day traders use for their workstations. Are they using brand-name computer equipment or "clones"? How fast are the computer processors? Each trader should be using at least one 21-inch monitor, if not two linked 21-inch monitors. There is so much data in this business that the monitor screen becomes the trader's "real estate." The larger the monitor screen the more information can be displayed.

Another important advantage to trading on-site is to be in a group of experienced and profitable day traders. This is the best way to learn the business. A novice day trader can learn much from a successful full-time day trader. The successful full-time day trader can become a "mentor" to the novice day traders. Many successful day traders do not mind passing along their day trading knowledge and experience, as long it does not interfere with their individual trading. However, successful day traders are a rare breed. The probability is high that there will be more part-time day traders than full-time day traders on the floor. One day the part-time day traders might "graduate" to full-time day trading. My recommendation to the novice day trader is to look for a firm that has successful full-time day traders in place. Perhaps, there will be some osmosis in the shop, and some of that trading success can rub off on the novice day trader.

Another important advantage to trading on-site in a branch office of a professional day trading firm is that many firms provide a structured training program. The firms usually provide several levels of training. The first level would be an introduction to day trading, and for newcomers, that is the starting point. This book is an introductory text. The second level would be detailed coverage of different and specific day trading topics, such as trade execution, technical analysis, trading strategies, or psychology of trading. The third level of training would be simulation or demo paper trading for a few weeks. The final step would be trading live next to an experienced and successful day trader, who would act as a mentor to the novice day trader.

Ask the branch manager about the firm's training program and the cost of that program. The probability is that the training would not be free of charge. Day trading firms routinely charge for training to cover expenses and also to screen potential traders. If a person is not willing to pay for the training, that person will probably not open an account and trade in that office.

Finally, go to the branch office during trading hours and test the overall atmosphere. Is the atmosphere friendly? Is the office staff friendly and helpful? What kind of support and service do they provide to their traders? Talk to other day traders in the office and ask them if they like trading there. Is the firm competitive in terms of cost? How do they calculate their commission costs? How do they charge for split orders? How do they charge for ECNs and NYSE orders? Finally, if there is more than one day trading firm in town, shop around.

Specialized Trading Software

Day trading depends on the speed and control of the trade order execution. One of the reasons that successful day traders prefer to trade through branch offices of day trading firms rather than through Internet brokers is the ability to execute trades quickly. Most day trading firms utilize advanced trading software packages that create a sophisticated trading environment. Some software vendors provide trading software that have macro keys or "smart" function keys that automate the trade execution orders. This type of sophisticated trading software is usually not available for day traders who are using Internet brokers. Consequently, day traders using these software packages at day trading firms are one step quicker than traders using Internet brokers.

To execute a buy or sell trade, the day trader needs to stop and look at the Level II screen to see who's at the inside quote. If it is an ECN, the day trader cannot use the SOES. If it is a market maker, the day trader needs to determine whether the quantity of shares being offered by the market maker matches the order. The software can do most of that processing in an optimal manner. The day trader can press one function key (such as the F8 key) and the trading execution software can apply a series of execution orders. The software will work out how best to execute the order under the existing exchange rules.

First, the software scans the inside BID or ASK quote and ascertains the best price. If there are any ECNs, such as Island, at the inside quote, the software will send that order to the appropriate ECN directly. That alone might secure up to a $\frac{1}{16}$ better price than going through the SOES. The day trader can specify any preference among the ECNs. For instance, the day trader can preselect in the software configuration settings that all orders go first to Island and then to other ECNs.

Second, the software will see if any ECNs have 1,000 or more shares available so that the day trader can avoid partial fills. Otherwise, the day trader would have to submit orders several times to obtain a 1,000-lot order. The software's Account Manager will confirm how many shares were bought or sold with that ECN. If there are no ECNs at the inside quote, the software will automatically enter a SOES limit order. Again, the software will confirm through the Account Manager how many shares were bought or sold with the particular market maker. If fewer shares were available than the day trader wanted, the software will buy or sell the maximum number of shares available and report to the trader that not all of the requested shares were obtained.

If there are several ECNs and market makers at the inside quote and none have 1,000 shares available, the software will direct orders to the ECNs first, and market makers second. All along, the software will report to the day trader how many shares were bought or sold through each ECN and market maker.

To cancel a function smart key order is also a simple task. The day trader needs to hold down the Shift key while pressing the C key to cancel. If the day trader does not manually send the cancel order, the order will be canceled automatically after a user-defined preset time. At that time, the day trader will receive confirmation messages on the computer screen that the order has been canceled.

The Trading Software Account Manager

The "Account Manager" is a common feature of day trading software packages. It is an invaluable tool for any day trader. The Account Manager keeps track in real time of all trades, open orders, open positions, and the profit and loss of the completed trades and open trades for the day trader. Thanks to this software feature, day traders can know at any point in time what their trading positions are.

The Account Manager shows all of the pending orders that the day trader has entered through the software during that day. In addition, the Account Manager can also allow for canceling of any live or pending orders. The Account Manager will display on the screen the following information: order number, order time, stock symbol, order type, size, price, and market maker or ECN that filled the order.

In short, at the end of the day the day trader will have a document that shows the following information:

➤ The stock that was traded;

➤ The size of the trade;

➤ The time that the stock was bought;

➤ The price that the stock was bought at;

➤ The time that the stock was sold;

➤ The price that the stock was sold at; and

➤ The profit and loss of the completed trade.

Day Trading Records

The major benefit to the day trader of such sophisticated software is that the day trader no longer has to write down his or her trades on a sheet of paper. That information can be imported electronically into a spreadsheet for further analysis of the trading. These electronic trading files can be analyzed to ascertain trading patterns. For example, the day trader can quantify the degree of success or failures on any stock or trading style, so the information can be used to help the day trader become more successful. Such data analysis is possible because the trading data is available and accessible in an electronic format. In addition, these records can be used at the end of the year to complete the trader's annual tax return.

The day trader is ultimately responsible for his or her account. It is my strong recommendation that all day traders keep their trading documents in one binder. The binder will store records of daily trading activities. The NASD requires that all day traders sign a daily trading blotter or trading log. At the end of the trading day, the day trader will receive this record from the branch office manager. The log will list exactly all trades that were made on that day. The day trader should review the records before signing the log, to ensure that there is no misunderstanding regarding what trades were completed that day. Neither the office branch manager nor the trader wants to revisit history a few weeks later on whether the day trader did or did not do a particular trade.

The next morning, the day trader will receive the account activity statement from the clearing firm. Again, it is the trader's responsibility to make sure that the account information is correct. If the information in the account (total equity, margin interest, and so on) does not appear correct, the day trader should approach the office manager and ask for clarification. Mistakes do happen. It is important that the day trader stay on top of his or her account. Active day traders might have one binder for each month. There is a lot of paperwork associated with day trading. Keeping good records will help tremendously when the time comes to file tax returns.

Internet-Based Brokers

Staying home is clearly convenient. The day trader does not need to commute to the day trading office and fight traffic. (However, if the trader lives on the West Coast, then commuting at 6:00 A.M. is not much of an issue.) But there are drawbacks to staying at home. What technical support does the day trader receive? If an account is opened with a mainstream Internet brokerage firm, the level of support will not be significant. Many Internet brokerage firms are not geared toward servicing the accounts of the active day traders who might be entering several dozen orders every day. The day trader's account is one among many thousands of accounts. Most of those accounts are from investors who are only managing their own portfolios. The investors, regardless of how active they might be, are not day traders, and their needs are different.

There are other issues associated with the Internet brokers. How fast is the data feed? Is the data feed delayed or real-time? How fast and reliable is the trade execution? Does the Internet broker route the order to a "Wholesaler" for the order flow payment? Do you get the best price? Do you have access to ECNs? How quickly does the day trader receive trade confirmation? What is the software used by the Internet broker for executing the trades? What are other features in the trading software that is being offered to the day trader? What is the commission cost?

There are many questions. Each Internet broker has different answers. It pays to call and research each Internet brokerage firm. There are plenty of choices among the Internet brokers. Gomez Advisors, Inc. (*www.gomez.com*) currently ranks 69 brokerage firms that offer online stock trading brokerage services. Since the electronic brokerage business has mushroomed in the United States during the past few years, it pays to research your Internet broker.

Many successful day traders started trading initially with an Internet broker and then moved (graduated) to a specialized day trading firm that provides faster execution (due to direct computer access with NASDAQ) and better information (through more sophisticated trading software). Having direct trading access to the ECNs, such as Island and Instinet, becomes an important consideration, because the ECNs allow day traders the ability to play a market maker role. For instance, the day traders can systematically attempt to buy at the BID and sell at the ASK prices by using the Island execution platform. That is simply not possible if one trades with an Internet broker, which has been designed to service stock investors rather than day traders.

Trading Remotely with a Day Trading Firm

Some day traders are able to trade from their homes using remote trading capabilities provided by their local day trading firms. Instead of sitting in the branch office in front of the monitors, the day traders sit at home. The day traders at home are electronically connected to the local branch office, so their workstations at home receive the same information as the traders' workstations in the branch office. At home, the day traders have an electronic router or modem and a dedicated and fast telephone line with a large data bandwidth (an ISDN line or a 56K bps line) that transmits the data. The day traders receive live real-time price quotes from their NASD broker/dealer's quote server and send their execution orders to their NASD broker/dealer's execution server through those ISDN or 56K bps lines. This type of connection is expensive but provides superior speed and reliability.

Furthermore, some day trading firms provide the Virtual Private Network (VPN) as their medium of communication with remote traders. The day trading firms subscribe to the VPN through one of the few national telecommunications firms that provide such service. The VPN provides faster and more reliable communication service. It is a better alternative to Internet-based trading. In essence, the VPN becomes the remote day trader's private lane on the "information superhighway." It is expensive, but it is worth it.

However, not all local day trading firms provide this option. The ISDN line or VPN might not be available everywhere in the country. Also, there is the issue of cost. The ISDN line or VPN costs money to be set up. Some day trading firms do not wish to incur that additional expense. Remote day traders are not as active as the on-site day traders who trade in the office. The level of remote trading activities might not justify the cost of setting up that additional service. The business of remote day trading is also technologically labor-intensive. There are always networking issues. It is not surprising that some day trading firms do not want to provide this option.

Staying home to trade, whether using the services of Internet brokers or remote trading capabilities of a local day trading firm, has its disadvantages. The trader is alone. There is very little personal interaction between the trader and the outside professional world. There may be no one outside of immediate family to speak to and share the daily trading experience. There is no one to turn to and ask a question. Some people have a hard time dealing with that professional isolation. In some cases, the relative isolation could take a certain mental toll.

Full-Time Versus Part-Time Trading

The second trading decision a new day trader will make is whether to trade on a part-time or full-time basis. My advice to new or prospective day traders again is to start slowly. In other words, start day trading on a part-time basis. The new trader can start the business gradually, which is a distinct advantage. Chances are that a new trader would not quit a day job, and there will be less pressure to make money immediately. The trader would have a continuous source of income from his or her regular job. So trading and only breaking even at the beginning would not be a financial disaster. (If the trader was trading on a full-time basis and day trading was the only source of income, then breaking even would be a failure.)

Also, starting on a part-time basis limits overall risk exposure. The day trader can still keep his or her job. In the event that this "career change" does not work out, the day trader has recourse—the old job. Trading on a part-time basis will also test the trader's resolve. The day trader will learn quickly whether he or she has the mental constitution for this line of work. In the event that the financial, mental, and time commitment to day trading is no longer present, the trader can go back to the old job.

Furthermore, trading on a part-time basis requires less capital. There is less pressure to make money immediately. The day trader does not have to trade fast, expensive stocks in increments of 1,000 shares to maximize trading opportunities. The trader can start on a part-time basis with slow stocks, which are often less expensive. In addition, the part-time trader can trade in blocks of 500 shares rather than 1,000 shares. Trading the slow stocks in smaller blocks requires less initial capital, although the profit potential will be smaller as well. But, the pressure to make money immediately is also smaller, since the part-time trader has other full-time employment.

Keeping a full-time job and day trading on a part-time basis can be a very stressful existence. The day trader is sitting on two chairs. Ultimately, both job and trading performance might suffer. Day trading requires focus and concentration. It is difficult to monitor stocks closely and work on another job. Consequently, the full-time job can become a distraction that can have an adverse impact on the trading account equity. Conversely, part-time day trading can lead to poor job performance on the day job.

Securities Investor Protection Corporation

It is extremely important that the day trading firm or Internet-based broker that holds the customers' trading accounts is a member of the Securities Investor Protection Corporation (SIPC). In fact, branch offices of day trading firms make sure that the SIPC label is displayed prominently somewhere on the trading floor. The SIPC is the product of the Securities Investor Protection Act, which was passed by the U.S. Congress to safeguard customers' funds and securities in the event that the NASD broker/dealer becomes insolvent. The SIPC provides insurance coverage to a maximum of $500,000, of which no more than $100,000 may be for cash losses.

Day Trading Suitability Interview

From the day trading firm perspective, the first and most important issue regarding the opening of a day trading account is the customer's suitability for the day trading business. Day trading is not for everyone. It is a risky endeavor. Many individuals have opened day trading accounts with a day trading firm or an Internet broker without fully understanding the skill set required in this business and the associated risks. It is important that the risks are clearly stated up front.

In my opinion, all day trading firms or Internet brokers must disclose up-front and in plain English during the suitability interview the following facts about day trading to their prospective new day traders:

➤ The learning curve for the novice day trader is steep.

➤ It takes time to acquire trading skills.

➤ The new day trader should be prepared to lose money in the first six months.

➤ The amount of these initial losses will vary among day traders; the level of losses depends on the day traders' utilization of risk management skills.

➤ The probability is high that the day trader will lose $15,000 or more before becoming proficient.

➤ The new day traders should not trade money that they cannot afford to lose.

➤ They should not mortgage their homes or ask for credit card advances in order to obtain trading capital or engage in day trading with their retirement funds.

➤ They should also have realistic expectations, since the majority of new day traders who are opening new accounts will not make it in this business.

> ➤ It takes at least three to six months to become a proficient day trader.

> ➤ It is unreasonable to expect to become a proficient day trader quickly and to start making money immediately.

> ➤ Even if one reads this or any other day trading book several times and practices paper trading for months, there are no guarantees that a new day trader will succeed.

I often wonder how many past or present day traders knew about the risks of day trading when they opened their accounts. The risk associated with day trading is usually disclosed somewhat more adequately if the account is opened with a branch office of a day trading firm. At least the new day trader has the opportunity to talk to a live person and ask questions. A new day trader can open a trading account over the Internet without ever talking to a live person.

The first question regarding an individual's suitability to be a day trader involves technical competence. Many new day traders were lured to pursue this career based on initial media coverage that glamorized and romanticized day trading. Few of the individuals had any experience in trading securities or commodities. At best they might have an investment account with a discount brokerage firm. It would not take much time for a branch manager to quickly ascertain such a lack of technical experience. Consequently, these individuals will need to spend time learning new terminology and skills and moving up the learning curve. Before approving the new account, a branch manager would urge prospective day traders to complete all of the firm's training courses (or any other available day trading training).

The second question regarding an individual's suitability involves financial competence. It is important to understand from the beginning that day traders place their money at substantial risk at all times. Thus new day traders must acknowledge that they will use only their "speculative" money for this endeavor. The intent is to trade money that they can afford to lose.

Again, the branch manager would quickly ascertain the financial position of the prospective day trader. The prospective day trader's net worth and liquid net worth status would quickly reveal to the branch manager whether the new day trader could absorb the financial losses. A liquid net worth of $100,000 would indicate that the prospective day trader could afford to lose initially $15,000 or $20,000 before becoming a proficient day trader.

There might be other considerations that would point to an individual's suitability for day trading. There might be questions regarding future expectations. Does the prospective day trader have unrealistic views on day trading? Does the new day trader need to earn money trading immediately in order to support himself or herself? Does the prospective day trader have several dependents in the family? What is the source of the start-up money? Ultimately, the branch manager makes a judgment call. Even if the branch manager approves the new trading account, the day trading firm's NASD rules compliance officer (who is commonly the firm's staff attorney) can overrule that decision.

After the suitability interview with the branch manager, the prospective day trader must sign the required forms and risk-disclosure statements. By signing those forms, the new day trader acknowledges that all the risk always resides with the day trader. The day trading firm will not assume or accept any risk or liability. The day trader is responsible for any action regarding the trading account. The associated market risk that comes with the buying and selling of securities is common sense—it always goes with the day trader. In addition, the day trader will also always assume the accompanied technology risk (for example, computer breakdowns).

But consider this hypothetical situation: The day trader who has an open overnight position comes to the branch office in the morning and finds the door locked. The branch manager overslept. The open position turned into a large loss within a few minutes of opening of the market. Who is responsible for the loss? The answer is again the day trader! It is not fair, but that is life. The day trading firm is never responsible for trading losses.

Clearing Trades

Most, if not all day trading firms, are not self-clearing brokerage firms. The day trading firms are relatively small brokerage firms without the necessary financial and staffing resources to process, record, and administer several thousand trades every day in a hundred, and sometimes a thousand, different customer accounts. Consequently, day trading firms must use or hire some other NASD broker or dealer firm to clear or process their trades. The clearing firms are specialized Wall Street firms that have the financial resources, such as the fidelity bonding requirements, and the staffing and computer data management expertise to process efficiently many thousands of trades every day. There are only a few securities clearing firms (for example, Southwest Securities, Penson Securities) that can handle the day trader's trading requirements. Traditional investors are satisfied if the trade settlement date is three days after the trade date. That is unacceptable for the day trader. The clearing firm will settle all trades on that very same day and e-mail the settlement statement to the branch office during the off hours. At the beginning of the next trading day, the traders receive from the branch manger an account activity statement from the previous day.

All of the money goes through the clearing firm as well. When a new day trader opens a trading account with a day trading firm, the day trader issues a check in the name of the clearing firm. The clearing firm keeps track of all trades done by all traders in that day trading firm. The clearing firm calculates the profit or loss from each trade and deducts the commission cost. When the trader closes the account, the clearing firm will cut the check or transfer the money to another account. At the end of the month, the clearing firm also sends a check to the day trading firm for the portion of the traders' commission.

22

Day Traders' Margin Accounts

Aᴌᴌ ᴅᴀʏ ᴛʀᴀᴅᴇʀs ᴏᴘᴇɴ ᴍᴀʀɢɪɴ ᴀᴄᴄᴏᴜɴᴛs ғᴏʀ ᴛʜᴇɪʀ ᴅᴀʏ ᴛʀᴀᴅɪɴɢ transactions. They receive from the clearing firm daily margin account activity statements. It is important that the day traders be able to read and understand this statement. Following is a brief explanation of margin account terminology.

The Federal Reserve Board, under Regulation T (Reg. T) of the Securities and Exchange Commission Act of 1934, regulates the extension of credit by NASD broker/dealers to traders and investors. The Regulation T is expressed as a percentage of the total purchase price. The current Reg. T margin requirement is 50% for long and short securities transactions. Only "marginable" securities, which include all stocks on the NYSE and NASDAQ national market system, may be purchased on margin.

When the NASD broker or dealer extends a credit to a day trader who wants to trade securities, the trading transactions must be executed in a margin account. Opening a margin account requires that the day trader sign a margin agreement, which specifies the following:

➤ The day trader agrees to pledge the securities in the margin account to the NASD broker/dealer as collateral for the loan.

➤ The day trader grants permission to the NASD broker/dealer to repledge (that is, "rehypothecate") the same securities at the bank as collateral for the loan. The bank will issue a loan to the NASD broker/dealer at a specific interest rate, which is called in the industry the "brokers' call rate."

> ➤ The day trader also grants permission to the NASD broker/dealer to lend the same security to other broker's customers who sold short that particular security.

The entire hypothecation process has four distinct steps:

1. The day trader pledges or hypothecates securities to the NASD broker/dealer.
2. The NASD broker/dealer rehypothecates the same securities that were used as collateral for the loan to the bank.
3. The bank lends to the NASD broker/dealer money at the broker's call rate.
4. The NASD broker/dealer lends to the day trader at the margin interest rate, which is a bit higher than the broker's call rate.

The Long Margin Account

Figure 22.1 shows what happens when a day trader purchases a security on margin. The long market value will fluctuate with the price of the security throughout the day. Suppose that the day trader has purchased 1,000

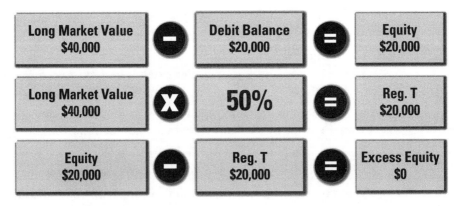

Figure 22.1 *Long Margin Account*

shares of a stock that is priced at that time at $40. The long market value is $40,000. The debit balance represents the amount that was borrowed by the day trader and is owed to the NASD broker/dealer firm. In this example, given the 50% Reg. T requirement, the maximum amount that the trader can borrow is $20,000. That is the base amount that will be used to calculate the interest charges paid by the customer. The annual interest rate charged is usually in the range of 8% to 9%. The equity is the customer's deposited money. The customer will deposit $20,000 in the margin account. That initially is the customer's equity. The equity can be also calculated by subtracting the amount owed from the current market value of the stock position. Figure 22.1 illustrates this point.

If the security appreciates in value, the long market value will increase. Since the borrowed amount remains the same (the debit balance remains at $20,000), the trader's equity increases as well. When the equity in the account exceeds the Reg. T requirement of 50%, the day trader has excess equity in the account. Figure 22.2 elaborates further on this point.

Suppose that the stock price increases from $40 to $60. The long market value is now $60,000. Since the borrowed amount or the debit balance remains the same at $20,000, the trader's equity increases to $40,000. The Reg. T 50% requirement on the $60,000 current market

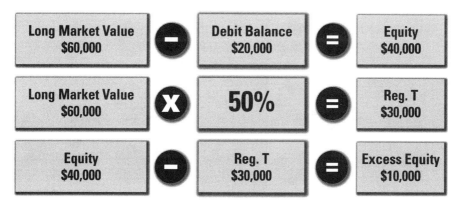

Figure 22.2 *Long Margin Account with Stock Price Appreciation*

value is $30,000. That means that the day trader has excess equity in the account of $10,000.

The excess equity in a margin account is referred to in the industry as the Special Memorandum Account (SMA). In this example, the trader can use the $10,000 SMA to purchase additional securities or to withdraw cash. In fact, the trader can purchase $20,000 worth of securities with the $10,000 SMA. The trader has higher buying power because the excess equity or SMA can be used to buy additional securities. The quickest way to calculate buying power is to divide the SMA by the Reg. T requirement. The formula for the buying power is the following:

$$\text{Buying Power} = \frac{\text{SMA}}{\text{Reg. T}}$$

While the higher price results in excess equity, a decline in stock value might cause a long margin account to become "restricted." A margin account becomes a restricted account if the equity falls below the Reg. T 50% requirement. Figure 22.3 illustrates this point.

Now, let us suppose that the stock price has decreased from the initial price of $40 to $30. The long market value is now $30,000. Since the initial borrowed amount or the debit balance remained the same at $20,000, the trader's equity decreased to $10,000. The Reg. T 50%

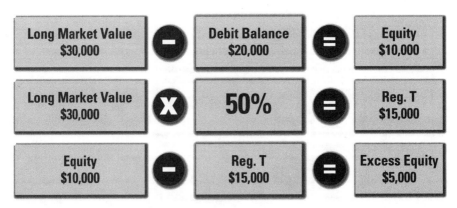

Figure 22.3 *Restricted Margin Account*

requirement on the $30,000 current market value is $15,000. That means that the day trader now has negative excess equity in the account of minus $5,000. The account is now restricted.

If a margin account is restricted, the day trader can continue making additional purchases by meeting the Reg. T requirement on a particular additional purchase. It is not mandatory to deposit additional money to bring the entire account up to the Reg. T requirement. With a restricted margin account, 100% of any sale proceeds will be used to reduce the debit balance in the margin account. If the price drops dramatically, the day trader will receive a margin maintenance call from the broker. The NASD requires that all customers maintain at least 25% equity of the current market value in their accounts. Figure 22.4 illustrates this point.

Now, let us suppose that the stock price decreased dramatically from the initial price of $40 to $25. The long market value is now $25,000. Since the initial borrowed amount or the debit balance remains the same at $20,000, the trader's equity has decreased to $5,000. The NASD and NYSE minimum maintenance requirement is 25%; that 25% requirement on a $25,000 current market value is $6,250. That means that the day trader's equity in the account is below the minimum maintenance requirement. The day trader will receive a maintenance call from the broker. The broker will require that the day trader deposit $1,250 into the account.

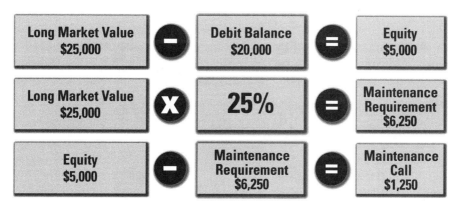

Figure 22.4 *Margin Maintenance Requirement*

The Short Margin Account

When a day trader sells short a security in his or her margin account, the day trader has established a "credit balance" in the margin account. Figure 22.5 shows what happens when the day trader sells short a security on margin. First, the short sale value will fluctuate with the price of the security. Suppose that the day trader has sold short 1,000 shares of a stock that is priced at $40. The short sale value is $40,000.

The credit balance represents the total short sale proceeds and the Reg. T margin requirement on the short sale value. In this example, given the 50% Reg. T requirement, the maximum amount that the trader can borrow for the short sale is $20,000. That is also the base amount that will be used to calculate the interest charges paid by the customer. The equity is the customer's deposited money. The customer had to deposit $20,000 in the short margin account. Equity can be calculated by subtracting the credit balance from the current short market value of the security that was initially sold.

The day trader anticipates that the security will decrease in value, so the trader has opened a short position. If the price were to decrease, the short market value would decrease. Since the borrowed amount remains the same (the credit balance remained the same at $60,000), the trader's equity has increased. When the equity in the account exceeds the Reg. T

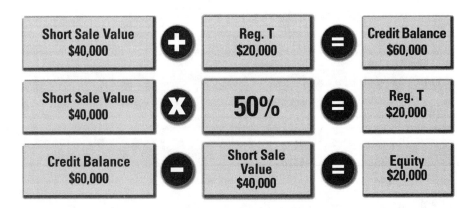

Figure 22.5 *Short Margin Account*

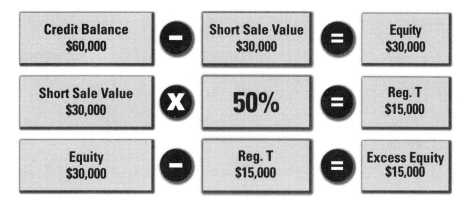

Figure 22.6 *Short Margin Account with Stock Price Depreciation*

requirement of 50%, the day trader has excess equity in the short margin account. Figure 22.6 elaborates on this point.

For example, suppose that the stock price decreased from $40 to $30. The short market value is now $30,000. Since the borrowed amount or the credit balance remained the same at $60,000, the trader's equity increased from $20,000 to $30,000. The Reg. T 50% requirement on the $30,000 current short market value is $15,000. That means that the day trader has excess equity in the account of $15,000. In this example, the trader can use the $15,000 excess equity to purchase or short sell additional securities or to withdraw cash. In fact, the trader can purchase $30,000 worth of securities with the $15,000 excess equity.

The NASD and NYSE minimum maintenance requirement for stocks in a short margin account and selling for more than $5 per share is 30%. The brokerage firm will regard the long and short margin accounts as one margin account. The combined equity for the long and short margin accounts is displayed in Figure 22.7.

Figure 22.7 *Combined Equity for Long and Short Margin Accounts*

It is important that day traders can read and interpret their daily margin activity statements. If a day trader has an overnight position, they must be able to understand how the total equity and interest charges are being calculated. After all, the total equity, buying power, and margin interest charged to the traders is the traders' money.

Intra-Day Margin Call

If the day traders always close their open positions before the close of the market, they do not need to worry about the margin interest charges or maintenance calls. (Some clearing firms, however, do charge margin interest for intra-day trading, even if all positions are closed at the close of market. The day trader should definitely ask about margin interest charges when opening an account.) However, the day traders should worry about intra-day *margin calls*. It is very common for a day trader sometime during the trading day to exceed his or her buying power. Day traders transact so many trades during the day that it is quite possible to lose track of one's daily purchasing power. Even if the day trading software has an "Account Manager" feature, which dynamically updates the trader's buying power, it is still easy to exceed one's buying power. Also, it must be acknowledged that day traders commonly try to maximize their leverage. In doing so, they sometimes push the "envelope" too far and exceed their purchasing power.

For example, if the day trader deposited $20,000 into his or her account, then given the Reg. T requirement, the trader's buying power is $40,000. Suppose that the day trader makes only one trade that day. The trader purchased and sold 1,000 shares of a stock that was priced at the point of the purchase and sale at $44. After the closing sale, the day trader is flat. He did not even make any money on this trade. (In fact, the trader lost money if the cost of the trade transactions is taken into account, but let us ignore that.) Nevertheless, the day trader purchased $44,000 worth of the stock even though the trader had only $40,000 in buying power.

The day trader will receive an intra-day margin call for $2,000 from the clearing firm. The clearing firm will ask that the day trader deposit into the account an additional $2,000 within the next five trading days. That is because the trader purchased stocks with credit the trader did not have. The trader needs to bring the account purchasing power to

$44,000. Even though the day trader is "flat" (having no long positions) in the stock, the trader would still need to come up with the extra cash. Given the 50% Reg. T credit requirement, a $2,000 deposit would increase the purchasing power to $4,000, and the total purchasing power would be $44,000.

A $2,000 intra-day margin call should not be difficult to meet. But suppose that the intra-day margin call is for $20,000 rather than $2,000. If the trader has net worth liquidity, then the $20,000 intra-day margin call would not be an issue. However, if the trader does not have $20,000 and the intra-day margin call is not met in the next five trading days, the clearing firm will most likely close that account. Then, if the day trader wants to continue trading in that branch, the trader would have to open another account under a different tax identification number. This is not that simple. The day trader would need to establish a legal entity (that is, a General Partnership or Limited Liability Company) and ask the IRS for a new tax identification number. This takes time and effort.

It is easier to meet the intra-day margin call and deposit $20,000 within the next five trading days. Day trader A can ask one of his fellow traders in the office, such as trader B, for an intra-day margin call loan of $20,000 for a 24-hour period. This procedure is relatively simple and risk-free. Both traders A and B have accounts with the same clearing firm. Day trader A is flat. In other words, that particular stock position is already closed. There is no market risk for trader B.

The two traders need to sign and fax to the clearing firm's margin desk the one-page document with their instructions. The trading colleague (trader B) who is providing the loan would simply ask the clearing firm to "journal in" $20,000 from his account to trader A's account to meet that intra-day margin call. At the same time, the signed document will request that on the next day the clearing firm "journal out" $20,100 back into trader B's account from trader A's account. Note that a $100 fee is attached to the original $20,000 loan balance.

Since both day traders A and B have signed this faxed document, the clearing firm will honor this request. The journal entry would have satisfied the intra-day margin call for day trader A, and trader B would have received $100 compensation for this risk-free service. However, day trader B will have $20,000 less cash or $40,000 less purchasing power for that trading day (24 hours). If trader B has an account with a large trading capital, the lower purchasing power should not be an issue.

This loan procedure becomes an easy and risk-free way to pick up an additional $100 for one day. Again, however, such a transaction is between two private individuals. A day trading firm will not facilitate this intra-day margin call loan, although the firm would be the indirect beneficiary of this common practice. Both traders would continue to trade with the firm and thus continue to generate the commission income.

23

Day Traders and Taxes

IT IS AXIOMATIC THAT DEATH AND TAXES ARE UNAVOIDABLE. THIS BOOK would be incomplete without a chapter on the topic of trader's tax issues. Here we attempt to briefly cover this complex issue. This chapter is not designed to be an authoritative source on traders' tax issues, since the author is not a tax attorney or tax accountant. There are only a few books that deal specifically with the tax issues facing stock investors and traders. I strongly encourage readers to do their own research on this topic. One good reference is Ted Tesser's *The Trader's Tax Survival Guide*.

Tax Rates

Since this is not a tax book, the author will cover only the basic tax concepts. The starting point is to reiterate that "cash basis accounting" is the foundation of the day trader's tax return. Cash basis accounting is a method of reporting income when it is received and expenses when they are incurred. All income is subject to progressive or graduated federal tax. In other words, as the individual income increases, the average and marginal tax rate increase as well. There are five marginal tax rates or tax brackets in the United States; they vary from 15% to 39.6%. Table 23.1 shows the 1998 tax rate schedule for taxpayers who are filing returns as single, or married and filing jointly.

Table 23.1 *1998 Tax Rate Schedule*

Single Filing Status			Married Filing Jointly Status	
Taxable Income Over	Taxable Income Under	Marginal Tax Rate	Taxable Income Over	Taxable Income Under
$ 0	$ 25,350	15%	$ 0	$ 42,350
$ 25,350	$ 61,400	28%	$ 42,350	$102,300
$ 61,400	$128,100	31%	$102,300	$155,950
$128,100	$278,450	36%	$155,950	$278,450
$278,450		39.6%	$278,450	

Table 23.1 states that if your filing status is single, you pay a 15% tax rate on the first $25,350 and a 28% tax rate on income higher than $25,350 and lower than $61,400. In addition to paying taxes to the federal government, individuals also pay income taxes to the state in which they live. However, there are a few states, such as Florida and Nevada, which do not have a state income tax.

Income

The next step is to define income. The federal tax law defines "income" as any acquisition of wealth that excludes gifts and inheritances. In other words, income may be defined as any gain derived from capital and labor. In fact, the Internal Revenue Service (IRS) defines the following fourteen specific categories of income:

1. Compensation for services,
2. Income from business,
3. Gains from dealings in property,
4. Interest,
5. Rents,
6. Royalties,
7. Dividends,

8. Annuities,
9. Income from life insurance policies,
10. Pensions,
11. Partnership income,
12. Income from ownership interest in an estate or trust,
13. Income from discharge of debt, and
14. Alimony payments.

Day traders and stock investors need to know what is specifically excluded from the definition of income:

1. The return of capital or return of an original investment, such as the cost of stocks; and
2. Unrealized stock gain or appreciation, which means that the investor is not liable for stock appreciation until the stock is sold.

The U.S. Tax Reform Act of 1986 also differentiates between three different types of income:

1. Earned income,
2. Investment income, and
3. Passive income.

The different types of income are taxed at the same rate as regular income, with the exception of long-term capital gains. This income differentiation becomes important when determining which losses can be deducted on tax returns. The IRS tax code has always had earned income and investment income categories. But, in 1986 the U.S. Congress created for the first time a new type of income—passive income. Passive income comes from passive activities. A "passive activity" is an activity in which the taxpayer is not directly and materially involved. This definition covers all rental income and the income from limited partnerships where limited partners do not participate in management decisions.

"Earned income" is compensation received for providing goods or services. "Investment income" is portfolio income that includes interest, dividends, royalties, annuities, as well as gains or losses from the disposition of an investment. Earned and investment incomes are considered ordinary incomes, and are thus taxed at the individual tax rate.

Capital Gains and Losses

The other important tax issue is the concept of capital gains and losses. Capital gain (or loss) is defined as a gain (or loss) that comes from the sale of capital assets. The IRS has defined a "capital asset" to be any business or non-business property. The exceptions are inventories, accounts receivable, and properties that are held for sale in the normal course of trading. Securities are considered to be capital assets. If a capital asset, such as stock, is sold for less than its cost, the IRS considers this to be a capital loss. If the capital asset is sold for more than its cost, the IRS considers this to be a capital gain.

Capital losses may be used to offset capital gains. Furthermore, within certain IRS limits, capital losses may be used to offset ordinary income. The IRS also differentiates whether capital gains are short-term or long-term. The holding period starts on the day the buy order was executed or the trade date. Conversely, the holding period ends on the day the sell order was executed. All capital gains or losses are considered short-term if the holding period is less than one year. Conversely, capital gains or losses are considered long-term if the holding period is more than one year.

Another tax concept is the issue of the stock cost *basis*. The cost basis of a security is the total price paid for the stock including the commission cost. The cost basis will be adjusted periodically for any stock dividends or stock *splits*. A stock split occurs when a company decides to divide its share in two, three, four, or more. In the event of 2:1 stock split, the stockholders would get twice as many shares, but each will be worth half as much. Since nothing else about the company has changed, shareholders aren't better or worse off. All capital gains or losses are realized or recognized in the tax year of the trade date on which the security has been sold.

The final step is to determine the net impact of the capital gains and losses. Given the stock cost basis, the holding period, and the final stock selling price (that includes the cost of the commission, which would be deducted from the proceeds), the trader or investor can determine the level of short-term and long-term capital gains and losses. The trader would net the short-term losses against the short-term gains, and the long-term losses against the long-term gains.

If the trader or investor had a poor year and the net result is both short-term and long-term losses, the tax treatment is the following: The net short-term and long-term losses can be combined and deducted against ordinary income up to a $3,000 maximum. If the net losses exceed $3,000, the unused portion can be carried forward and used to offset ordinary income for the next tax year. The losses can be carried forward indefinitely.

As you can see, there is a double standard. There is no limit on capital gain that is subject to federal taxation. If you made money, the federal government wants a percentage cut of that entire gain. On the other hand, there is a $3,000 limit on capital losses that can be used to offset ordinary income.

If the trader or investor had a mixed performance that year and the net result is a short-term gain and long-term loss, the long-term loss can be used to offset the short-term gain. If the net is positive, the net gain is added to the ordinary income and taxed at the ordinary tax rate. That tax rate will depend on that individual's federal income tax bracket (the progressive tax schedule).

If the trader or investor had an overall positive performance and the net result is both short-term and long-term gains, the positive short-term net gain is added to ordinary income and is taxed at the ordinary tax rate. That tax rate again will depend on the individual's federal income tax bracket. The positive long-term net gain is taxed at the ordinary tax rate up to a maximum of 28%, even if the taxpayer's other ordinary income is taxed at the higher rate.

Expenses

The first half of the tax equation is income; the second half of the tax equation is expenses. The IRS looks keenly at what expenses can be deducted from income. The IRS test on whether expenses are allowed has four questions:

1. Is the expense necessary to produce that income?
2. Is the expense ordinary and common in conducting that type of business activity?

3. Is the expense reasonable with regard to the level of the generated income?

4. Is the expense allowed or legal under the existing federal tax code?

The answers to the questions of whether or not the expenses incurred in day trading are necessary, ordinary, and reasonable are clearly subjective. Since each tax return is unique, the answers will vary from one trader to another. This means that day traders have the ability or potential to interpret what constitutes necessary, ordinary, and reasonable expenses. A word of caution—there are many self-employed individuals who are clashing with the IRS over business expenses that they thought are necessary, ordinary, and reasonable expenses. The question of the legality of certain expenses is much more precise and clear-cut. The IRS code might state that certain expenses are not allowed regardless of how necessary, ordinary, and reasonable they might be to day trading activities.

The best tax preparation strategy is to be prepared to document and explain to the IRS why certain trading expenses are claimed to be necessary, ordinary, and reasonable. The day trader who might someday be audited must be prepared to back up (with supporting documents) and substantiate their trading expense claims.

Ted Tesser's tax book for traders lists several trading expenses that are commonly accepted by the IRS. These deductible trading expenses are the following:

➤ Computer and software expenses if trading from the home;

➤ Real-time data feed cost;

➤ Brokerage fees;

➤ Margin interest expense;

➤ Cost of books, seminars, and other educational tools on trading;

➤ Subscriptions to professional magazines, papers, and publications;

➤ Tax advice;

➤ Trading advice;

➤ Legal fees;

➤ Accounting fees;

➤ Safe deposit box fees for the storage of trading documents; and

➤ Portion of your home expenses that qualify as home office deductions if trading from the home.

The IRS code differentiates among three classes of "investors": investor, trader, and market maker.

Market Maker Tax Classification

The market maker definition for tax purposes is clear. The market maker is the NASD broker or dealer who is a merchant of securities. The NASD broker/dealer might be an individual, a partnership, or a corporation. The market maker has an established place of business and regularly buys and sells securities in the ordinary course of business. Securities are the market maker's inventory; they are not capital assets.

All of the income made by the market maker is automatically considered to be ordinary income. There are no short-term capital gains or losses. The market maker can claim an unlimited amount of losses. Since the market maker is a business, a self-employment tax must be paid. All expenses, such as interest charges, are treated as business-related expenses.

Investor Tax Classification

The IRS defines an investor to be an individual who buys and sells securities for his or her own account. All expenses incurred in investment activities are considered to be investment expenses, and not business expenses. Since the expenses are investment expenses, they are deducted as miscellaneous itemized deductions on Schedule A of the investor's tax return. Investment expenses are subject to a 2% limitation. All income is treated as an investment income, and not ordinary income. Finally, the maximum net loss that can be used to offset ordinary income is $3,000.

Trader Tax Classification

One of the main points in this book is that day trading is a business. The trader must treat it seriously as a business if he or she has any hope of being successful. The business of day trading requires individual time commitment, dedication, and hard work. It is not surprising that the IRS treats equities trading as a business as well. The IRS treats the day trader as a hybrid between the investor and the market maker. Consequently, there are certain tax advantages available to day traders that are not available to investors.

Day traders buy and sell securities for their own accounts, just like investors. Unlike the investor, the day trader's level of trading activity is dramatically higher. Subsequently, the IRS will look at the frequency of the trades, the length of the holding period, and the source of profit. A typical day trader makes several dozen trades every day while holding the stock for a few minutes or a few hours, and profits from the daily short-term price fluctuations. On the other hand, the investor holds the securities for a longer period of time (sometimes more than one year), performs fewer securities transactions, and earns profit from dividends as well as capital gains. It is not surprising that the IRS considers day trading to be a business.

All day trading expenses are considered to be business-related expenses and are 100% deductible on Schedule C of the individual's tax return. However, day trading income is considered to be short-term capital gains, and thus must be reported on Schedule D. There is a $3,000 limit on the amount of short-term losses that can be applied on Schedule D to offset ordinary income for that year. There is no self-employment tax, because the income is considered to be a short-term capital gain and not ordinary income.

Day traders must use two different forms to report their income and expenses from day trading activities. They will report the day trading income as investment income (short-term capital gains) on Schedule D, and trading expenses as ordinary business expenses on Schedule C. In terms of tax liability, one can argue that day traders are better off than market makers. Both the market makers and day traders can claim trading expenses. However, the market makers are subject to self-employment tax, and day traders are not. This is one of the few times that market makers do not have an advantage over day traders.

Table 23.2 summarizes the IRS tax treatment for the three classifications.

Table 23.2 *IRS Tax Classification Summary*

Tax Issue	Market Makers	Traders	Investors
Trading profits treated as:	Earned income	Short-term capital gains or losses within investment income and reported on Schedule D	Short-term capital gains or losses within investment income and reported on Schedule D
Loss limits applied against earned income	No limits	$3,000 limit per year with carry forward to next year	$3,000 limit per year with carry forward to next year
Subject to self-employment tax	Yes	No	No
Trading expenses treated as:	Business expenses	Business-related expenses with 100% deductible and reported on Schedule C	Investment-related expenses itemized and reported on Schedule A

IRS Tax Audits

It is always good practice to expect the best and be prepared for the worst. There is always a possibility that the IRS will audit a day trader. This section covers that worst case scenario—the IRS tax audit.

All of us have an interest in minimizing our tax liabilities. None of us want to pay more to the government than we have to. In fact, most Americans believe, rationally or irrationally, that we already pay too much in taxes anyway. However, minimizing taxes does not mean cheating on your tax returns. That is clearly illegal. It also does not mean finding tax loopholes in the IRS code and exploiting them. Minimizing taxes legally means obtaining knowledge of the IRS code (as applied to your individual tax circumstances) and using current allowable deductions and exemptions to the fullest advantage. Tax attorneys and accountants call this "tax planning."

Often investors and traders push the envelope of IRS code interpretation on their tax returns, and consequently their returns are selected for an IRS audit. It is always important to keep good records of your trading transactions and expenses. In the event that the IRS audits your return, these records can substantiate your deductions and expense claims.

It is also preferred that these records be in an electronic format. Since day traders conduct thousands of trades in a single year, it can be difficult to provide a quick summary of all trades. Trading software often has the capability to export or copy the daily trade activity records onto a disk that can be imported at a later date into any spreadsheet program.

The Probability of Being Audited

The good news is that the odds are in your favor that you will not get audited. The IRS simply has a colossal task. Every year the IRS collects over $1.5 trillion to fund the U.S. government. It processes over 200 million tax returns from more than 110 million U.S. tax-payers. It issues over 80 million refunds and distributes over 1 billion forms and publications. In addition, the IRS has the responsibility to enforce the tax laws of this country and to ensure that the tax-paying public pays the proper amount of tax. As you can see, the IRS is overwhelmed. Consequently, only a small portion of the 110 million taxpayers will ever be subject to an IRS audit. The IRS audits approximately only 3 million tax returns annually.

The news is even better. The first target of the IRS audit is the known criminal. (Let us hope that this does not apply to you.) The next targets are certain highly paid professionals. The IRS customarily targets doctors, dentists, lawyers, and CPAs because of their relative high-income levels and their propensity for practicing creative accounting. The next groups of targeted individuals are salespeople, airline pilots, flight attendants, and business executives, because they tend to have unusually high expense deductions relative to their income, and these expenses are poorly documented. If you are not in any of these listed professions, your chances of being audited are often less than 1%.

The process of selecting individual tax returns for an audit is highly computerized. The IRS computer program selects tax returns that do not comply with the IRS code or that have certain discrepancies between the reported incomes as being reported by the taxpayer and other businesses that issue the W-2 or 1099 forms. Make sure that all income is being reported. The IRS computer matching process will spit out the individual tax returns that show discrepancies between what has been reported by the individual taxpayer and by other business entities that are required to report W-2 or 1099 forms.

It is also important that tax returns are clean and fully completed. All questions must be answered completely. Avoid including large sums of money under the "miscellaneous income" or "miscellaneous expenses" sections. It is always better to be specific. Avoid making sloppy or careless adding mistakes. There are several computerized tax preparation software packages on the market that will ensure that your completed tax return is clean, complete, and mathematically correct.

Avoid using certain deductions that customarily trigger the IRS audits. The home office deduction is one item that commonly raises IRS scrutiny. Avoid using rounded-off expense deductions, since they point to guessing. It is always a good idea to work with a professional and capable tax accountant. If the IRS suspects that a tax accountant is too aggressive or unscrupulous, it can trigger IRS audits for the accountant's entire client base.

Unfortunately, a small number of IRS audits are randomly selected. The IRS uses this type of random selection to ascertain the overall taxpayers' compliance with the tax laws. In addition, each IRS district office has a different percentage of returns audited. Some districts are more aggressive (or efficient) and perform substantially more audits, while some districts are more relaxed. The bottom line here is that the probability is great that you will *not* be audited.

24

Summary

N ATURA NON FACIT SALTUM. THIS IS LATIN FOR "NATURE DOES NOT make leaps." A century ago, the famous economist Alfred Marshall started his *Principles of Economics* textbook with that statement. His point was that any change is always small and gradual. I would like to close this book with the same reminder. Success in the day trading business does not come fast, easily, or with any degree of certainty.

It will take many months and many good and bad trades to get there. And the majority of new day traders will never get there. So start slowly. Start day trading slowly with "slow" stocks that do not move dramatically and trade in increments of 100 shares. Then gradually move up. Increase the number of shares each week by 100. After a few weeks of live trading experience, consider trading more volatile stocks.

It takes time to become a proficient day trader. Experienced traders estimate that it takes three to six months of live trading before one matures into an accomplished day trader. Add to that the time required to acquire the basic day trading skill set. Before making a single trade, a new day trader invests many hours reading and researching about day trading. In addition, the new day trader will allocate several weeks to paper trading before becoming comfortable with trading software and its execution system.

It is also extremely unrealistic to expect that anyone will start making money immediately. In fact, expect to lose money at the beginning. The learning curve is steep, but it does not need to be expensive. Losses at the beginning are inevitable. It will take several thousand dollars of losing trades before one graduates into a profitable day trading business. Losses can be $15,000 or higher before a novice day trader turns the corner. The level of losses depends on the trader's discipline and risk management skills. My advice is to have minimal expectations at the beginning.

It is also important that a new day trader trade only the money that he or she can afford to lose. If you cannot afford to absorb the loss, then please do not even start the business of day trading. As a day trader, one continuously makes trading decisions on whether the price of a stock will move in a certain direction. Critics of day trading state that this activity constitutes speculation. If speculating means buying and selling stocks in expectation of profiting from market fluctuations, then all day traders are short-term speculators. Any speculative endeavor assumes a substantial risk of losing money. If you cannot assume that risk, then do not trade.

Starting a day trading venture is very much comparable to starting a new business. After investing the time to learn the basic skills and investing the start-up capital to open a trading account, the new day trader is finally in business. Each trading decision is a business decision that translates immediately into a profit or loss. Is it realistic to expect that every new business will take off immediately? Is it realistic to expect that everyone who has started a new business will succeed?

If the business of day trading were that simple, lucrative, and low risk, then everyone would be day trading. Why would anyone bother to work and commute to a 9-to-5 job? Why not simply sit in front of a computer monitor at a day trading branch office or at home via an Internet connection and make a living trading stocks? If this new business of day trading were that promising, there would be a line of people in front of every day trading firm's branch office eager to get in the business. Well, there are no such waiting lines. This business looks deceptively easy to start; yet it is very difficult to master and profit from.

I have always wondered why so many people have failed in the day trading business. Sometimes I believe that the day trading success fits the infamous "80–20 rule." Eighty percent of the profit goes to 20% of day traders. Conversely, 80% of the day traders fight over the remaining 20% of the profits. Why is it that so many traders have lost money day trading?

The answer to this question lies in the core of this deceptively simple trading practice. The nature of day trading is to exploit short-term price volatility and earn small incremental profits by trading in increments of 1,000 shares. The rewards and risks of this business rest in the fact that 1,000 shares are always at risk. Trading a large block of shares is a double-edged sword. The day trader can quickly earn $125 profit if the price goes in a favorable direction by $\frac{1}{8}$ of a point; conversely, the day trader can quickly lose the same amount if the price goes in an unfavorable direction.

This is where the trader's discipline comes in. The key is to minimize the losses and maximize the upside potential. If $\frac{1}{8}$ is the day trader's loss limit, then he or she should not lose more than $125 on that trade. However, many new day traders do not have the discipline necessary to control their losses. They allow a small loss to turn into a large loss. They wait too long, so that an initial $\frac{1}{8}$ loss turns into $\frac{1}{4}$ or $\frac{3}{8}$ or an even larger loss.

Another common and costly mistake is that many day traders force their trades. They enter a trade position without receiving a clear buy or sell signal. The day trader does not need to anticipate the price momentum. There is no obligation to be proactive and forecast or time the market's next peak or valley. All day traders need to do is to be reactive (and not proactive) and recognize an existing or observable price momentum.

Treat day trading as a real business. If trading is treated as a hobby, it will evolve into a very expensive hobby. So, be focused and keep a daily log of your trades. Review your trades and learn from your mistakes. Appendix 4 is a simple "True or False" quiz that will test the reader's general understanding of basic day trading principles. Take the quiz and see if you know this business.

Success in day trading comes with acquired knowledge of trading, invested time and effort, and continuous and disciplined practice of risk management skills. Since there are few "home runs" in this kind of trading, the trading success appears in small and incremental profits with numerous successful trades. *Natura non facit saltum.*

Glossary

absolute liquidity The total number of shares being traded on an exchange in a day.

absolute price volatility The total dollars change in the price of the stock.

accumulation An addition to a trader's original market position; the first of three distinct phases in a major trend in which investors are buying.

advance-decline Each day's number of declining issues is subtracted from the number of advancing issues. The net difference is added to a running sum if the difference is positive, or subtracted from the running sum if the difference is negative.

arbitrage The simultaneous purchase and sale of two different and closely related securities to take advantage of a disparity in their prices.

ASK The price at which a holder of a security is willing to sell (as opposed to the BID price, which is what someone is willing to pay). In general, the asked price is the price you pay when you buy and is lower than the bid. In over-the-counter trading, securities dealers or market makers profit from the spread between these two so much that they are often willing to pay discount brokers for "order flow." These payments help make it possible for discount brokers to charge customers rock-bottom, flat-rate commissions per trade. The question is whether discount brokers are choosing the highest "order flow" payers rather than market makers who can get the best price on a trade.

ASK size   The number of shares associated with the current ASK price or the number of shares the seller(s) is(are) offering for sale at the ask price.

average daily volume   The number of shares traded in a given number of days, divided by that number of days. This is useful for judging how liquid a stock is (thinly traded issues are riskier) and whether any one day's volume marks a sharp departure from the norm. The latter usually indicates some news or change of circumstances that could be relevant to shareholders.

bar chart   A chart that displays a security's open, high, low, and close prices using one vertical line for each time period whether it is a day, week, month, or so forth. Bar charts are the most popular type of security chart. On the left side of the bar is a "tick" that indicates the opening price. The tick that appears on the right side of the bar is the closing price. The vertical length of the bar shows the price range.

basket trades   Large transactions made up of a number of different stocks.

bear or **bearish market**   When stocks trend downward for a long period of time, it's a "bear" market. The term was based on the way the animal attacks. When a bear attacks, it strikes downward with its paws.

Beta (coefficient)   A measure of the market/nondiversifiable risk associated with any given security in the market. A ratio of an individual's stock historical returns to the historical returns of the stock market. If a stock increased in value by 12% while the market increased by 10%, the stock's Beta would be 1.2.

BID   The price at which someone is willing to buy a security. This is what you get when you sell (as opposed to the asked price, which is what you hoped to get). In over-the-counter trading, securities dealers profit from the spread between bid and asked prices.

bidding   The act of buying securities at the posted BID price.

BID size   The number of shares associated with the current BID price or the number of shares the buyer(s) is(are) offering to buy at the posted BID price.

Bollinger band John Bollinger created trading bands (upper and lower boundary lines) plotted at standard deviation levels above and below a Moving Average. Because standard deviation measures volatility, the bands widen during volatile markets and contract during calmer periods.

breakout If a stock has traded in a narrow range for some time (in other words, built a base) and then advances above the resistance level, this is said to be an upside breakout. Breakouts are suspect if they do not occur on high volume (compared to average daily volume). Some traders use a buy stop, which calls for purchase when a stock rises above a certain price.

bull/bear ratio A market sentiment indicator based on a weekly poll of investment advisors as to whether they are bullish, bearish, or neutral on the stock market. The bull/bear ratio is published by Investor's Intelligence of New Rochelle, New York. Extreme optimism on the part of the public and even professionals almost always coincides with market tops. Extreme pessimism almost always coincides with market bottoms. Historically, readings above 60% have indicated extreme optimism (which is bearish for the market) and readings below 40% have indicated extreme pessimism (which is bullish for the market).

bull or **bullish market** When stock prices have risen steadily over several months, experts call it a "bull" market. The term was selected based on the way the animal attacks. When a bull rushes forward, he holds his head low and then gores upward with his horns.

buy on margin The practice of buying stock with money borrowed from a broker. The loan is collateralized by the security you've purchased, which is held in a margin account. The broker will charge you interest, but the rate is usually attractive compared with other forms of debt, since it is secured by an easily marketable stock. Still, you need to make enough on the stock to pay commissions and cover interest. Trading on margin can improve investment returns, but it's risky. If you buy a stock on margin and it goes down, you'll need to pony up more cash to maintain your collateral, or watch your broker sell out your position. "Margin calls" of this kind were a major feature of the 1929 meltdown. The federal government imposes strict limits on margin trading of stocks.

call option   A contract that gives the buyer of the option the right but not the obligation to take delivery of the underlying security at a specific price within a certain time.

candlestick chart   A chart that displays the open, high, low, and close prices of a security for each time period and illustrates the relationship between these prices. The chart elements look like a candlestick with wicks at both ends. The actual candle portion is called the "real body" and is determined by the day's open and close prices. The wicks, called "shadows," show the price range for the day. When the close is higher than the open, the body is colored red (if color is available) or left white. When the close is lower than the open, the body is filled in or colored black.

change   The dollar difference between the preceding day's closing price and the most recent price. (Prices are delayed by at least 20 minutes.)

close   The final trading price for a security at the end of the most recent trading day.

closed trades   Positions that have been liquidated.

commission   A fee brokers charge for executing a transaction. The amount is usually based on the number of shares or the total dollar amount of the trade.

common stock   An ownership stake in a company. Holders of common stock shares are last in line in terms of their claim to dividends and assets.

confirmation   Indication that at least two indexes, in the case of Dow theory, the industrials and the transportation, corroborate a market trend or a turning point.

correction   A sharp, short drop in stock prices, after which the market resumes an upward climb. Of course, when the correction is happening, it's hard to distinguish it from the beginnings of a bear market. Any price reaction within the market leading to an adjustment by as much as $1/3$ to $2/3$ of the previous gain.

current offer   The price at which the owner of a security offers to sell it at the posted ASK price.

daily range   Intra-day price volatility or the difference between the high and low price during one trading day.

daily volume (13-week average)   The average number of shares of a company's stock traded daily over the previous 13-week period. Daily volume is one indicator of how liquid a security is. A low daily volume could imply low interest in a stock, a limited float (number of shares outstanding), and/or a highly volatile share price, since even relatively small trades will have an exaggerated effect. Low-volume stocks, also known as thinly traded, generally are seen as riskier than more heavily traded shares. Pay special attention to changes in volume; a sudden increase may mean news about the company has just been issued or is foreseen by those in the know.

day order   A trade order to buy or sell a security during the market hours in a trading day.

day trader   A person who buys and sells stocks rapidly during the day in order to exploit the stocks' intra-day price volatility.

day's high   The highest price of the security during the current day's trading. By checking this in relation to the low, you can get an idea of how much the stock is fluctuating.

day's low   The lowest price of the security during the current day's trading. By comparing to the high, you can get an idea of how much the stock is fluctuating.

derivatives   Financial contracts the value of which depends on the value of the underlying instrument commodity, bond, equity, currency, or a combination.

distribution   Any set of related values described by an average (that is, mean), which identifies its midpoint, a measure of spread (that is, standard distribution), and a measure of its shape (that is, skew or kurtosis); also, the act of selling stocks or when the traders or investors use the current rally to liquidate old positions in the face of good news. It is opposite of accumulation.

divergence   Two or more averages or indices fail to show confirming trends.

diversification   An investing strategy that seeks to minimize risk by diversifying among many types of investments. Diversification and risk are directly related to each other. The more you diversify your portfolio, the less risk you have.

dividend   The distribution of corporate earnings to shareholders.

Dow Jones Industrial Average   The Dow Jones is probably the most widely watched indicator of American stock market movements. The index is more than 100 years old; it is well known; and by including only 30 stocks, it is manageable. These stocks tend to be those of the largest, most established firms and represent a range of industries. Unfortunately, there are only 30 of them, and they are not always an ideal proxy for the thousands of stocks that make up the market as a whole. Broader indexes such as the Standard & Poor's 500 (for large companies), the Russell 2000 (for smaller companies), and the Wilshire 5000 (for an especially broad measure) have gained popularity.

down-tick   Indicates that the current BID price is lower than the previous BID.

drawdown   The reduction in account equity as a result of a bad trade or series of bad trades.

dynamic data updates   Ability to automatically update an application from within another application.

earnings   Profit, or net income, in this case the sum of the trailing four quarters' net income from continuing operations and discontinued operations.

earnings per share (EPS)   Net income divided by common shares outstanding. A company that earns $1 million for the year and has a million shares outstanding has an EPS of $1. This EPS figure, which represents how much of earnings each share is entitled to, is important as the basis for various calculations an investor might make in assessing a stock's price.

earnings surprise   The difference between what analysts expected a company to earn and what was actually earned. Earnings estimates have gained importance in recent years, and companies that don't measure up often find their shares hammered. (The difference can also be expressed as a percentage.)

earn the spread   The act of buying a stock at the BID price and selling a stock at the ASK price and thus earning the difference between the BID and ASK prices.

Electronic Communication Networks (ECNs)   These networks allow market makers and any traders to post and display their BID and ASK prices on a national system, so that others can fill these orders.

Most often the ECN buy or sell orders would become the best buy and sell prices for the security. All ECNs are proprietary systems. They must be registered with the NASDAQ and NASD in order to participate in the marketplace. As of the end of 1998, there were eight ECNs on the NASDAQ system: Instinet Corporation (INCA), Island ECN (ISLD), Archipelago (ARCA), Bloomberg Tradebook (BTRD), Spear Leeds & Kellogg (REDI), Attain (ATTN), BRASS Utility (BRUT), and Strike Technologies (STRK).

equilibrium market   A price region that represents a balance between demand and supply.

exchange   The organization that provides for the trading of a listed security. The biggest, most established companies generally trade on the New York Stock Exchange (NYSE), but many giants in technology and other newer companies trade on NASDAQ.

Exponential Moving Average (EMA)   The EMA for day D is calculated as: where PR is the price on day D and α (alpha) is a smoothing constant. Alpha may be estimated as $2/(n + 1)$, where n is the simple Moving Average length.

exponential smoothing   A mathematical-statistical method of forecasting that assumes future price action is a weighted average of past periods; a mathematics series in which greater weight is given to more recent price action. An example of exponential smoothing is the Exponential Moving Average line.

extreme   The highest or lowest price during any time period, a price extreme; in the CBOT Market Profile, the highest/lowest prices the market tests during a trading day.

fade   Traders' term for an act of selling a stock at rising price or buying a stock at falling price.

fast market   A declaration that market conditions in the trading pit are so temporarily disorderly with prices moving rapidly that floor brokers are not held responsible for the execution of orders.

52-week High   The highest price for a security or fund during the past 52 weeks or one year.

52-week Low   The lowest price for a security or fund during the past 52 weeks or one year.

fill An executed order; sometimes the term refers to the price at which an order is executed.

fill order A trade order that must be filled immediately on the floor or immediately canceled.

filter A device or program that separates data, signal, or information in accordance with specified criteria. Moving Average line is considered to be a filter.

floor brokers Employees of brokerage firms working on exchange trading floors.

fundamental analysis The analytical method by which only the sales, earnings, and value of a given tradable's assets may be considered. The analysis holds that stock market activity may be predicted by looking at the relative company performance data as well as the management of the company in question.

futures Futures are contracts to make or accept delivery of a given commodity on a given date at a prearranged price. Futures are traded on all sorts of things, including corn, pork bellies, and Treasury securities. Hardly anyone actually delivers (or accepts) all the bacon implied by a futures contract on pork bellies, though. Investors simply settle up with money and that's that. Futures are a legal way to bet on the direction of a commodity's price, or (in the case of Treasury securities) on the direction of interest rates. Using leverage, you can make a killing in futures; margin rules are much more relaxed than for stocks, and you can control a vast quantity of corn, for instance, with a very small up-front investment. Of course, this helps make futures extraordinarily risky.

gap A day in which the daily range is completely above or below the previous day's daily range.

head and shoulders For technicians or chartists, a chart pattern indicating a peak, a decline, a second even higher peak, a decline, a rebound to the level of the first peak, and yet another decline. A head and shoulders pattern is supposed to be bad news, indicating the stock is headed downward.

historical data A series of past daily, weekly, or monthly market prices (open, high, low, close, and volume).

index A composite of securities that serves as a barometer for the overall market or some segment of it. The best known of these are the

Dow Jones Industrial Average and the Standard & Poor's 500, both of which reflect the performance of large American companies. Other indexes include the Russell 2000, which is an index of smaller stocks. Many indexes are much more specific.

initial public offering (IPO) The first stock sold by a company in going public. IPOs are a feature of runaway bull markets, since there is proven demand for stock and it makes sense to sell shares when they are likely to bring the highest prices. The hottest IPOs can make their purchasers a quick profit by soaring soon after trading begins.

in play A stock that is the focus of a public bidding contest, as in a takeover.

insider trading Buying and selling by a company's own officers and directors for their personal accounts. When investors buy or sell based on material nonpublic information, they are engaged in illegal insider trading.

Instinet Instinet was established in 1969 to serve large institutional investors. Instinet offers to the participating institutions the ability to trade NASDAQ and NYSE stocks among themselves 20 hours a day. Instinet is a private market with often better prices.

institutional ownership The percent of a company's shares owned by banks, mutual funds, pension funds, insurance companies, and other institutions, all of them characterized by a propensity to buy and sell in bulk. Big institutional trades are having an increasing impact on the securities markets, as the institutional share of savings increases.

interest-sensitive stock A stock whose price is very much affected by rising or falling interest rates. Auto makers, home builders, mortgage lenders, financial institutions, and others find that when rates soar, their business dries up. But some stocks can show rate sensitivity because these are stocks that pay hefty dividends. When rates fall, this dividend looks even better. But when rates rise, this dividend is less appealing compared to Treasury securities and other riskless investments.

Island (ISLD) Island was established in 1996, and it is the fastest growing ECN. It is an increasingly more popular trading platform among day traders because Island is fast, reliable, and relatively inexpensive.

lag The number of data points that a filter, such as a moving average, follows or trails the input price data.

last price   The current trading price of one unit of a particular security.

last trade size   The most recent number of shares traded of the security.

leverage   The use of debt to increase returns. Investors also use leverage when buying stocks on margin. But leverage is associated with risk. An investor who buys stock on margin may run into trouble if the stock falls, leaving the loan insufficiently collateralized.

limit order   An order to buy or sell when a price is fixed. When traders or investors instruct a broker to buy shares at or below a certain price, or sell shares at or above a certain price, you've entered a limit order. Limit orders reduce the risk that an order will be filled at a price the traders or investors don't like. Since most stocks move around a little on any given day, a trader can often get an extra $\frac{1}{8}$ of a point in the trader's favor just by entering a limit order and being patient. The down side is that by waiting for that particular stock price, the stock you want may get away from you, or the stock you want to unload just keeps falling in price.

line chart   A chart that displays only the closing price for a security for each time period. A line connects closing values from each period. Often used for plotting mutual funds, which typically only have a daily close value. Over time, these points present a telling performance history for the security.

liquidity   Ability to quickly convert or sell an asset, such as a stock, into cash.

long   Establishing ownership of the responsibilities of a buyer of a tradable; holding securities in anticipation of a price increase in that security.

margin account   In stock trading, an account in which purchase of stock may be financed with borrowed money. This amount varies daily and is settled in cash. In essence, a brokerage account that lets an investor or trader buy securities on credit or borrow against securities held in the account. Interest is charged on such borrowing, but usually at attractive rates compared with other forms of debt. Trading on margin can enhance investment returns considerably, but like all leveraged activities, can also backfire. The federal government limits the extent to which margin can be used in equities trading.

margin call   A call for additional capital to bolster the equity in an investor's or trader's margin account. If the trader or investor can not provide additional cash or securities, the broker will sell the shares.

market maker   A broker or bank continually prepared to make a two-way price to purchase or sell for a security or currency.

market on close   An order specification that requires the broker to get the best price available on the close of trading, usually during the last five minutes of trading.

market order   Instructions to the broker to immediately sell to the best available bid or to buy from the best available offer.

market risk   The uncertainty of returns attributable to fluctuation of the entire market.

market sentiment   Crowd psychology, typically a measurement of bullish or bearish attitudes among investors and traders.

market timing   Using analytical tools to devise entry and exit methods. A technique used by traders or investors who believe they can predict when the market will change course. If the traders or investors can time the market correctly, then he or she could make a huge profit.

market value   Company value determined by investors, obtained by multiplying the current price of company stock by the common shares outstanding.

mean   When the sum of the values is divided by the number of observations.

momentum   A time series representing change of today's price from some fixed number of days back in history.

momentum indicator (MOM)   A market indicator utilizing price and volume statistics for predicting the strength or weakness of a current market and any overbought or oversold conditions, and to note turning points within the market.

money flow   A technical indicator that keeps a running total of the money flowing into and out of a security. Money flow is calculated daily by multiplying the number of shares traded by the change in closing price. If prices close higher, the money flow is a positive number. If prices close lower, the money flow is a negative number. A running total is kept by adding or subtracting the current result from the previous total.

most-active list   The stocks with the highest trading volume on a given day.

Moving Average   A mathematical procedure to smooth or eliminate the fluctuations in data and to assist in determining when to buy and sell. Moving Averages emphasize the direction of a trend, confirm trend reversals, and smooth out price and volume fluctuations or "noise" that can confuse interpretation of the market; the sum of a value plus a selected number of previous values divided by the total number of values.

Moving Average Convergence/Divergence (MACD)   The crossing of two exponentially smoothed Moving Averages that are plotted above and below a zero line. The crossover, movement through the zero line, and divergences generate buy and sell signals.

Moving Average crossover   The point where the various Moving Average lines intersect each other or the price line on a Moving Average price bar chart. Technicians use crossovers to signal price-based buy and sell opportunities.

moving window   A snapshot of a portion of a time series at an instant in time. The window is moved along the time series at a constant rate. For instance, three-minute Moving Average line takes into account continuously the observation of the last three minutes.

narrow range day   A trading day with a smaller price range relative to the previous day's price range. In other words, the stock prices were stable during that day.

National Association of Securities Dealers (NASD)   An industry organization that regulates the behavior of member securities dealers. It owns and operates NASDAQ, the automated quotation system for over-the-counter trading. The NASD derives its authority from the federal government, and every securities dealer in the country is required by law to be a member.

National Association of Securities Dealers Automated Quotation System (NASDAQ)   NASDAQ is the electronic stock exchange run by the National Association of Securities Dealers for over-the-counter trading. Established in 1971, it is America's fastest growing stock market and is a leader in trading technology shares. It has more listed companies than the New York Stock Exchange, and handles more than half the stock trading that occurs in the country.

negative divergence   Two or more averages, indices, or indicators fail to show confirming trends.

noise   Price and volume fluctuations that can confuse interpretation of market direction.

non-trend day   A narrow range day lacking any discernible movement in either direction.

normal distribution   For the purposes of statistical testing, simulated net returns are assumed to be drawn from a particular distribution. If net returns are drawn from a normal distribution, low and high returns are equally likely, and the most likely net return in a quarter is the average net return.

New York Stock Exchange   America's biggest and oldest securities exchange. It is the exchange with the most stringent requirements for being listed, and it is where most of the nation's largest and best-established companies are listed. Although computers are used, the NYSE remains old-fashioned in that buyers and sellers (representing investors all over the globe) shout orders at one another face to face. In fact, the NYSE's "auction" system, in which buyers and sellers meet in the open market, generally produces fair market pricing. To maintain an orderly market, "specialists" on the trading floor manage buying and selling of assigned stocks and have the responsibility of buying when no one else will.

odd lot   An order to buy or sell fewer than 100 shares of stock.

offering   An act of trying to sell a stock at the posted ASK price.

On-Balance Volume (OBV)   Plotted as a line representing the cumulative total of volume. Volume from a day's trading with a higher close compared with the previous day is assigned a positive value, while volume on a lower close from the previous day is assigned a negative value. Traders look for a confirmation of a trend in OBV with the market or a divergence between the two as an indication of a potential reversal.

open   The price paid in a security's first transaction of the current trading day.

opening range   The range of prices that occur during the first 30 seconds to 5 minutes of trading, depending on the preference of the individual analyst.

open trades   Current trades that are still held active in the customer's account.

opportunity cost   Income foregone by the commitment of resources to another use.

oscillator   Technical indicator used to identify overbought and oversold price regions; an indicator that trends data, such as price.

overbought market   Market prices that have risen too steeply and too fast.

overbought or **oversold indicator**   An indicator that attempts to define when prices have moved too far and too fast in either direction and thus are vulnerable to a reaction.

oversold market   Market prices that have declined too steeply and too fast.

preferred stock   Stock that acts a lot like a bond but confers an ownership stake in the company. Preferred shares typically pay a fixed dividend and give their holder a claim to earnings and assets prior to that bestowed by common stock. In general, the higher the preferred yield, the greater the risk. Preferred stock often comes with a conversion clause permitting it to be traded in for common shares.

previous close   The price of the security at the end of the previous day's trading session.

price   The current market price of a security or the amount paid to buy one unit of a security.

price/earnings ratio   Stock price divided by annual earnings per share. Also known as the P/E multiple. P/E is the single most widely used factor in assessing whether a stock is pricey or cheap. In general, fast-growing technology companies have high P/Es, since the stock price is taking account of anticipated growth as well as current earnings.

program trading   Trades based on signals from computer programs, usually entered directly from the trader's computer into the market's computer system.

put/call ratio   Volume of put options divided by the volume in call options. A high ratio (put volume much higher than call volume) is considered by technical analysts as a sign of bearish sentiment indicating the market is headed south.

put option   A contract to sell a specified amount of a stock or commodity at an agreed time at the stated exercise price.

pyramid To increase holdings by using the most buying power available in a margin account with paper and real profits.

range The difference between the high and low price during a given period.

ratio The relation that one quantity bears to another of the same kind, with respect to magnitude or numerical value.

reaction A short-term decline in price.

relative strength A comparison of the price performance of a stock to a market index such as Standard & Poor's 500 stock index.

resistance A price level at which rising prices have stopped rising and either moved sideways or reversed direction; usually seen as a price chart pattern.

retracement A price movement in the opposite direction of the previous trend.

risk The chance that something bad (that is, a loss) will happen. Risk in the context of trading and investing simply refers to the variability of returns.

risk tolerance The amount of psychological pain the trader or investor is willing to suffer from the investments.

round trip Buying and selling the same stock or opening and closing the trade position, especially in a relatively brief period.

running market A market wherein prices are changing rapidly in one direction with very few or no price changes in the opposite direction.

screening stocks A practice, abetted by computers, whereby investors or traders search for all stocks meeting a given set of criterion. For instance, traders can screen for all NASDAQ companies with market capitalization above $500 million, daily trading volume of 500,000 shares, and Beta value greater than 1.5.

Securities and Exchange Commission (SEC) The federal agency charged with regulating the securities markets.

SelectNet SelectNet was introduced in 1990 and was designed so that market makers could communicate and execute trades electronically among themselves. SelectNet orders are broadcast to NASDAQ market makers only. SelectNet has provided the day trader with a tool to electronically submit orders directly to the market makers at a better price than the posted best BID and ASK prices. SelectNet is not a mandatory system for the market makers. Market makers have the option to accept or to ignore that offer; a SelectNet order is filled only if the market maker chooses to execute that order.

selling short   Selling a security and then borrowing the security for delivery with the intent of replacing the security at a lower price.

settlement   The price at which all outstanding positions in a stock or commodity are marked to market; typically, the closing price.

short covering   The process of buying back stock that has already been sold short.

short interest   Shares that have been sold short but not yet repurchased; shares sold short divided by average daily volume. This "days to cover" ratio represents the number of days of average trading needed to cover short positions in a given stock. This ratio is especially worth investigating if you are considering a short sale. When too many shares of a given stock have been sold short and days to cover stretches past 8 or 10 days, covering your position could prove difficult.

short interest ratio   A ratio that indicates the number of trading days required to repurchase all of the shares that have been sold short. A short interest ratio of 2.50 would tell us that based on the current volume of trading, it will take two and a half days' volume to cover all shorts.

signal   In the context of stock or commodity time series historical data, usually daily or weekly prices.

signal line   In Moving Average jargon, the first Moving Average, such as the Fast Moving Average line of 3-minute data, is smoothed by a second Moving Average, such as the Slow Moving Average line of 9-minute data. The second Moving Average is the signal line.

Simple Moving Average   The arithmetic mean or average of a series of prices over a period of time. The longer the period of time studied (that is, the larger the denominator of the average), the less impact an individual data point has on the average.

slippage   The difference between estimated transaction costs and actual transaction costs.

smoothing   A mathematical technique that removes excess data variability while maintaining a correct appraisal of the underlying trend.

specialist A trader on the market floor assigned to fill bids or orders in a specific stock out of his or her own account when the order has no competing bid or order, to ensure a fair and orderly market.

spike A sharp rise in price in a single day or two; may be as great as 15% to 30%, indicating the time for an immediate sale.

split A stock split occurs when a company decides to divide its shares in 2, 3, 4, or more. Thus a stock worth $100 might be the subject of a 2 for 1 split, resulting in a share price of $50. Holders in this case get twice as many shares, but each is worth half as much than before, and since nothing else about the company has changed, shareholders aren't better or worse off. Stock splits traditionally are seen as a good sign; companies split their shares when the price of each share is considered high enough to discourage ownership.

spread A trade in which two related contracts/stocks/bonds/options are traded to exploit the relative differences in price change between the two.

Standard & Poor's 500 A widely followed benchmark of stock market performance, the S&P 500 includes 400 industrial firms, 40 financial stocks, 40 utilities, and 20 transportation stocks. All the firms are large. The S&P 500 is also the basis of a good deal of index investing. Inclusion in the index usually causes a stock to rise.

standard deviation The positive square root of the expected value of the square of the difference between a random variable and its mean; a measure of the fluctuation in a stock's monthly return over the preceding year.

stochastic Literally means "random."

stochastics oscillator An overbought/oversold indicator that compares today's price to a preset window of high and low prices. These data are transformed into a range between zero and 100 and then smoothed.

stockbroker An individual registered with the National Association of Securities Dealers (NASD) who is authorized to buy and sell securities for his or her customers.

stock index futures A futures contract traded that uses a market index, such as the S&P 500 Index, as the underlying instrument. The delivery mechanism is usually cash settlement.

stock symbol　A unique, market-approved code that identifies a particular security on an exchange. The symbol generally reflects the name of the security. It is also known as the "ticker symbol."

stop loss　The risk management technique in which the trade is liquidated to halt any further decline in value.

stops　Buy stops are orders that are placed at a predetermined price over the current price of the market. The order becomes a "Buy at the market" order if the market is at or above to the price of the stop order. Sell stops are orders that are placed with a predetermined price below the current price. Sell-stop orders become "Sell at the market" orders if the market trades at or below the price of the stop order.

street name　The name under which a brokerage firm holds the securities of its customers. Most brokerage companies hold their customers' securities in the firm's street name rather than in the name of each individual customer. By using its street name rather than your own, your brokerage firm can process trades faster because you don't have to run down to the office to deliver or pick up stock certificates every time you make a trade.

support　A historical price level at which falling prices have stopped falling and either moved sideways or reversed direction; usually seen as a price chart pattern.

target price　The price that an investor or a trader hopes a given security will reach within a certain period of time.

technical analysis　A form of market analysis that studies demand and supply for securities and commodities based on trading volume and price studies. Using charts and modeling techniques, technicians attempt to identify price trends in a market.

technology sector　A category that includes computer hardware, software, electronics, electrical equipment, and wireless communications companies.

tick　The last reported stock transaction and is reported in increments of $\frac{1}{8}$, or $\frac{1}{16}$ or $\frac{1}{32}$.

ticker tape or **screen**　A real-time report that states the last price and the unique, market-approved code that identifies a particular security on an exchange.

tick indicator   The number of stocks whose last trade was an up-tick or a down-tick.

time series   A collection of observations made sequentially in time and indexed by time. All stock price data is the time series data.

trading bands   Lines plotted in and around the price structure to form an envelope or a band, answering whether prices are high or low on a relative basis and forewarning whether to buy or sell by using indicators to confirm price action. Bollinger bands are an example of trading bands.

trading range   The difference between the high and low prices traded during a period of time.

trailing stop   A stop-loss order that follows the prevailing price trend.

trend   The general drift, tendency, or bent of a set of statistical data as related to time.

trend following   Moving in the direction of the prevailing price movement.

trending market   Price moves in a single direction.

trendless   Price movement that vacillates to the degree that a clear trend cannot be identified.

trendline   A line drawn that connects either a series of highs or lows in a trend. The trendline can represent either support, as in an up-trend-line, or resistance, as in a down-trend-line. Consolidations are marked by horizontal trendlines.

triple witching hour   The last hour of trading on the third Friday of March, June, September, and December, when investors rush to unwind their positions in index options and futures, all of which are expiring on the same day. Triple witching hour has produced some major price swings as investors buy and sell both the derivatives and the underlying securities.

turning point   The approximate time at which there is a change in trend.

up-tick   Indicates that the current BID price is higher than the previous BID.

value stock   A value stock is one that is undervalued by the current stock market. Value stocks can be identified on the most basic level simply by examining the key ratios.

volatility   A measure of a stock's tendency to move up and down in price, based on its daily price history over the latest twelve months.

volume   The total units of a security traded on the most recent trading day. An unusually high volume means that important news has just come out, or will come out soon. Rising volume coupled with a rising share price is considered a bullish indicator for a stock, while the opposite is considered a bearish indicator. Technical analysts also track a "volume price trend" to relate volume and price. Technical analysts believe that the biggest price gains are associated with the heaviest volume trading.

whiplash or **whipsaw**   Alternating buy and sell signals that result in losses; an investment or trade where the price goes in the opposite direction from that which was anticipated right after the transaction is made. A trade is made based on a buy signal generated by a technical indicator and then shortly thereafter, the price moves in the opposite direction giving a sell signal. It results frequently with a trading loss. Whipsaws can also substantially increase the trading commission cost.

Resources with Internet Sites

Media, Exchanges, Information Firms, Magazines, and Government Organizations

Media	Internet Information Firms	Magazines, Government
www.bloomberg.com	www.bigcharts.com	www.aaii.org
www.centrex.com	www.briefing.com	www.better-investing.org
www.cnbc.com	www.businesswire.com	www.forbes.com
www.cnnfn.com	www.dailystocks.com	www.fortune.com
www.dowjones.com	www.dismal.com	www.iionline.com
www.foxmarketwire.com	www.dynamictraders.com	www.inc.com
www.infobeat.com	www.einvestor.com	www.money.com
www.instinet.com	www.financialweb.com	www.nasd.com
www.investor.msn.com	www.flash.net/~hesler/	www.sec.gov
www.isld.com	www.fool.com	www.smartmoney.com
www.marketwatch.com	www.home.ptd.net/~wcs/	www.worth.com
www.msnbc.com	www.investorguide.com	www.wsdinc.com
www.nasdaq.com	www.investorlinks.com	
www.nasdaqnews.com	www.investorword.com	
www.nyse.com	www.murphymorris.com	

continues

continued

Media	Internet Information Firms	Magazines, Government
www.quote.yahoo.com	www.news.com	
www.wsj.com	www.newspage.com	
	www.pristine.com	
	www.quote.com	
	www.rightline.net	
	www.siliconinvestor.com	
	www.stockhouse.com	
	www.thestreet.com	
	www.tradealert.com	
	www.tradingtech.com	
	www.wallstreetcity.com	

Real Time DataFeed

Company Name	Web Site
BMI	www.bmiquotes.com
Signal (Data Broadcasting Company)	www.dbc.com
Quote.com	www.quote.com
DTN Spectrum	www.dtn.com
Telescan	www.telescan.com
Bridge	www.bridge.com
CQG	www.cqg.com
FutureSource	www.futuresource.com
InterQuote	www.interquote.com
S&P ComStock	www.spcomstock.com
PC Quote	www.pcquote.com
Bloomberg LP	www.bloomberg.com
A-T Financial	www.atfi.com

Trading Software Platforms

Product or Company Name	Web Site
Bloomberg	www.bloomberg.com
CyberTrader	www.cybercorp.com
TradeCast	www.tcast.com
Omega Research Trade Station	www.omegaresearch.com
Reuters Quotron	www.reuters.com
Bridge	www.bridge.com
S&P ComStock	www.spcomstock.com
PC Quote	www.pcquote.com
ADP Financial Information	www.fis.adp.com
Track Data	www.tdc.com
BMI	www.bmiquotes.com
CQG	www.cqg.com
FutureSource	www.futuresource.com
DTN Spectrum	www.dtn.com
Aspen Graphics	www.aspenres.com
FirstAlert	www.chartist.com
A-T Financial	www.atfi.com
AIQ Trading Expert	www.aiq.com
Real Tick III	www.taltrade.com
Metastock	www.equis.com
Trendsetter Personal Analyst	www.trendsoft.com
Mesa Software	www.mesasoftware.com
Telechart 2000	www.tc2000.com
Window on Wall Street	www.windowonwallstreet.com

Day Trading Firms

Company Name	Web Site
Momentum Securities	www.soes.com
Cornerstone Securities	www.protrader.com
On-Line Investment Services	www.onli.com
All-Tech Investment Group	www.attain.com
Andover Trading	www.andovertrading.com
Summit Trading	www.summittrading.com
Landmark Securities	www.landmarksecurities.com
Bright Trading	www.stocktrading.com
Broadway Trading	www.broadwaytrading.com
Harbor Securities	www.soes-trade.com
Castle Online	www.castleonline.com
Tiger Investment Group	www.tigerinvestment.com
DirecTrade	www.d-trade.com
Self Trading	www.selftrading.com
Yamner & Co.	www.yamner.com
Van Buren Securities	www.vbsecurities.com
Remote Trading International	www.remotetraders.com
Investors Street	www.investors-street.com
Daylight Trading	www.daylighttrading.com
Navillus Securities	www.navillus.com

Internet Brokers

Company Name	Web Site
E*Trade	www.etrade.com
National Discount Broker	www.ndb.com
Schwab	www.schwab.com
DLJdirect	www.dljdirect.com
Discover Brokerage	www.discoverbrokerage.com
AB Watley	www.abwatley.com
Datek	www.datek.com
Suretrade	www.suretrade.com
Quick & Reilly	www.quick-reilly.com
Fidelity	www.fmr.com
My Discount Broker	www.mydiscountbroker.com
Bidwell	www.bidwell.com
Firstrade	www.firstrade.com
Waterhouse	www.waterhouse.com
Banc One	www.oneinvest.com
RJ Forbes	www.forbesnet.com
Wall Street Electronica	www.wallstreete.com
Scottrade	www.scottrade.com
Wang	www.wangvest.com
Mr. Stock	www.mrstock.com

A P P E N D I X

2

NASDAQ and NYSE Stocks with High Price Volatility and Volume

Note that table is organized by Beta coefficient, from high to low.

Symbol	Company Name	Beta	Avg. Daily Volume
CNKT	ConnectInc.com	7.4	713,700
AIPN	American International Petroleum Corporation	6.4	646,300
CDNW	CDnow, Inc.	5.0	766,700
ONSL	ONSALE, Inc.	4.5	1,370,000
BAMM	Books-A-Million, Inc.	4.5	1,100,100
XCIT	Excite, Inc.	4.1	5,084,700
DCLK	DoubleClick Inc.	3.9	994,200
RNWK	RealNetworks, Inc.	3.7	631,500
SRCM	Source Media, Inc.	3.6	586,900
LCOS	Lycos, Inc.	3.4	4,913,300
EGRP	E*TRADE Group, Inc.	3.3	3,850,200
YHOO	Yahoo! Inc.	3.3	15,269,800
PWAV	Powerwave Technologies, Inc.	3.3	592,000
AMZN	Amazon.com, Inc.	3.2	11,971,700
NTKI	N2K Inc.	3.2	712,700
AFCI	Advanced Fibre Communications, Inc.	3.2	2,619,600

Symbol	Company Name	Beta	Avg. Daily Volume
OMKT	Open Market, Inc.	3.1	1,074,500
PRMS	Premisys Communications, Inc.	3.1	705,200
CKFR	CheckFree Holdings Corporation	3.0	690,800
ATHM	At Home Corporation	3.0	1,745,300
MSPG	MindSpring Enterprises, Inc.	3.0	1,683,000
FLEX	Flextronics International Ltd.	3.0	628,900
LRCX	Lam Research Corporation	3.0	1,068,900
CLST	CellStar Corporation	2.9	1,217,700
WAVO	WavePhore, Inc.	2.9	953,100
GTSG	Global TeleSystems Group, Inc.	2.9	714,300
DMIC	Digital Microwave Corporation	2.8	744,400
ATML	Atmel Corporation	2.8	1,476,200
ASML	ASM Lithography Holding N.V.	2.8	1,047,200
EGGS	Egghead.com, Inc.	2.8	2,781,000
MALL	Creative Computers, Inc.	2.8	622,800
CMGI	CMGI, Inc.	2.7	2,666,400
IMON	ImaginOn, Inc.	2.7	776,000
USWB	USWeb/CKS	2.7	1,288,600
VIAS	VIASOFT, Inc.	2.7	559,800
GSTRF	Globalstar Telecommunications Limited	2.7	842,400
KMAG	Komag, Incorporated	2.7	994,000
ITWO	i2 Technologies, Inc.	2.7	867,100
LHSPF	Lernout & Hauspie Speech Products N.V.	2.6	698,400
SCI	SCI Systems, Inc.	2.6	704,000
NVLS	Novellus Systems, Inc.	2.6	1,505,200
DIMD	Diamond Multimedia Systems, Inc.	2.6	819,000
AMAT	Applied Materials, Inc.	2.6	7,681,900
ABTX	AgriBioTech, Inc.	2.6	1,248,500
NAVR	Navarre Corporation	2.6	1,472,800

Symbol	Company Name	Beta	Avg. Daily Volume
TLK	Perusahaan Perseroan (Persero) PT Telekomunikasi Indonesia	2.6	877,400
KLIC	Kulicke and Soffa Industries, Inc.	2.6	510,200
MRVC	MRV Communications, Inc.	2.6	588,700
IFMX	Informix Corporation	2.5	2,781,200
FEET	Just For Feet, Inc.	2.5	524,800
SDTI	Security Dynamics Technologies, Inc.	2.5	1,183,200
AOL	America Online, Inc.	2.5	25,261,100
TER	Teradyne, Inc.	2.4	1,088,900
ASND	Ascend Communications, Inc.	2.4	6,516,600
CREAF	Creative Technology Ltd.	2.4	720,800
PRGN	Peregrine Systems, Inc.	2.4	557,200
ICGX	ICG Communications, Inc.	2.4	902,200
LEH	Lehman Brothers Holdings Inc.	2.4	1,233,700
PTVL	Preview Travel, Inc.	2.4	628,200
SAVLY	Saville Systems PLC	2.4	1,012,500
HTCH	Hutchinson Technology Incorporated	2.4	655,000
CYCH	CyberCash, Inc.	2.4	625,300
KLAC	KLA-Tencor Corporation	2.3	2,069,700
BNYN	Banyan Systems Incorporated	2.3	668,800
ICN	ICN Pharmaceuticals, Inc.	2.3	636,800
NSCP	Netscape Communications Corporation	2.3	5,285,000
OXHP	Oxford Health Plans, Inc.	2.3	1,673,200
PCMS	P-Com, Inc.	2.3	1,161,600
QNTM	Quantum Corporation	2.3	3,230,700
DBCC	Data Broadcasting Corporation	2.2	1,676,900
PSIX	PSINet Inc.	2.2	1,346,800
CHKP	Check Point Software Technologies Ltd.	2.2	972,700
IOM	Iomega Corporation	2.2	3,918,600

Symbol	Company Name	Beta	Avg. Daily Volume
SEEK	Infoseek Corporation	2.2	3,662,500
MWD	Morgan Stanley Dean Witter & Co.	2.2	2,234,300
ADCT	ADC Telecommunications, Inc.	2.1	1,596,600
ADI	Analog Devices, Inc.	2.1	1,359,200
RDRT	Read-Rite Corporation	2.1	1,165,800
SCH	Charles Schwab Corporation	2.1	1,688,500
CS	Cabletron Systems, Inc.	2.1	1,254,800
GMGC	General Magic, Inc.	2.1	1,244,000
NXTL	Nextel Communications, Inc.	2.1	3,407,300
KRB	MBNA Corporation	2.1	2,281,500
UIS	Unisys Corporation	2.1	1,506,000
FLC	R&B Falcon Corporation	2.1	1,864,000
MU	Micron Technology, Inc.	2.0	4,559,300
NETA	Network Associates, Inc.	2.0	2,627,100
ALTR	Altera Corporation	2.0	2,418,400
TXN	Texas Instruments Incorporated	2.0	2,861,000
SEG	Seagate Technology, Inc.	1.9	2,664,400
CIEN	CIENA Corporation	1.9	5,749,500
TLAB	Tellabs, Inc.	1.9	4,332,100
MER	Merrill Lynch & Co., Inc.	1.9	3,363,400
COMS	3Com Corporation	1.8	8,155,600
PMTC	Parametric Technology Corporation	1.8	3,965,600
LU	Lucent Technologies Inc.	1.7	7,271,400
CD	Cendant Corporation	1.7	7,540,000
DELL	Dell Computer Corporation	1.7	59,022,500
C	Citigroup Inc.	1.7	8,386,000
NOVL	Novell, Inc.	1.7	4,711,200

APPENDIX

3

Key NASDAQ Market Makers

ABSA	Alex Brown & Sons, Inc.
AGIS	Aegis Capital Corp.
BEST	Bear Stearns & Co., Inc.
BTSC	BT Securities
CANT	Cantor Fitzgerald & Co., Inc.
CHGO	Chicago Corp.
CJDB	CJ Lawrence Deutsche Bank
COST	Coastal Securities
COWN	Cowen & Co.
DAIN	Dain Bosworth, Inc.
DEAN	Dean Witter
DWP	Donaldson Lufkin & Jenrette
DOMS	Domestic Securities
EXPO	Exponential Capital Markets
FACT	First Albany Corp.
FAHN	Fahnestock & Co.
FBCO	First Boston Corp.
FPKI	Fox-Pitt, Kelton, Inc.
GRUN	Gruntal & Co., Inc.
GSCO	Goldman Sachs & Co.

GVRC	Gvr Co.
HMQT	Hambrecht & Quist, Inc.
HRZG	Herzog, Heine, Geduld, Inc.
JEFF	Jefferies Co., Inc.
JPMS	J. P. Morgan
KEMP	Kemper Securities, Inc.
LEHM	Lehman Brothers
MADF	Bernard Madoff
MASH	Mayer & Schweitzer, Inc. (Charles Schwab)
MHMY	M. H. Meyerson & Co., Inc.
MLCO	Merrill Lynch
MONT	Montgomery Securities
MSCO	Morgan Stanley & Co., Inc.
MSWE	Midwest Stock Exchange
NAWE	Nash Weiss & Co.
NEED	Neddham & Co.
NMRA	Nomura Securities Intl. Inc.
OLDE	Olde Discount Corp.
OPCO	Oppenheimer & Co.
PERT	Pershing Trading Co.
PIPR	Piper Jaffray
PRUS	Prudential Securities Inc.
PUNK	Punk Siegel & Knoell, Inc.
PWJC	Paine Webber, Inc.
RAGN	Ragen McKenzie, Inc.
RPSC	Rauscher Pierce Refsnes, Inc.
RBSF	Robertson Stephens & Co., Lp
SALB	Salomon Brothers
SBNY	Sands Brothers & Co., Ltd
SBSH	Smith Barney Shearson, Inc.
SELZ	Furman Selz, Inc.

SHWD	Sherwood Securities Corp.
SNDV	Soundview Financial Group, Inc.
SWST	Southwest Securities, Inc.
TSCO	Troster Singer Corp. (Spear Leads)
TUCK	Tucker Anthony, Inc.
TVAN	Teevan & Co., Inc.
UBSS	UBS Securities
VOLP	Volpe Weity & Co.
WARB	S. G. Warburg & Co., Inc.
WBLR	William Blair & Co.
WEAT	Wheat First Securities, Inc.
WEDB	Wedbrush Morgan Securities
WEED	Weeden & Co., Lp
WERT	Wertheim Schroder & Co., Inc.
WSEI	Wall Street Equities, Inc.
WSLS	Wessels, Arnold & Henderson

4

Day Trading Quiz

Some time ago, the author of this book taught undergraduate and graduate level university courses and presented to students many quizzes and exams. Giving quizzes is a bad habit. So here we go. This simple "True or False" quiz will test the reader's general understanding of basic electronic day trading principles. Simply note next to each statement whether the statement is true or false. The correct answers are on a page following this quiz.

1. Counterclockwise movement on the Level II screen as more market makers are leaving the inside ASK and joining the inside BID means that the stock price is going up.

2. A series of red or down-tick BID and ASK prices showing on the Market Ticker window for a particular stock means that prices are going down.

3. An "ax" or key market maker joining the inside BID on the Level II screen means that stock is going down.

4. Trades going off at the ASK price on the Time and Sales window indicate that the public is buying.

5. An "ax" or key market maker simultaneously leaving the inside BID and joining the inside ASK means that the stock is going up.

6. When the Fast Exponential Moving Average line has crossed over and above the Slow Exponential Moving Average line, this would be a buy signal.

7. The MACD line is positive and is increasing at an increasing rate; this indicates that the Fast EMA is increasing at a faster rate than the Slow EMA line, and the bulls in the stock market are getting stronger.

8. When the price reaches the lower Bollinger band, that constitutes the intra-day price support level at that point in time.

9. When the momentum (MOM) indicator is positive and is increasing at an increasing rate, this means that there is price increase momentum at this point in time.

10. If both the price and the On-Balance Volume (OBV) indicator are moving up, there is a distinct possibility of price reversal.

11. An indicator of an overbought market would be a fast stochastic (%K) line that has reached 75 or goes above 75.

12. The first and foremost risk management measure for most day traders is to go flat at the end of the trading day.

13. Another common risk management measure for most day traders is to pyramid or double or triple the shares position to recover previous losses.

14. When day traders wish to buy or sell securities at a specific price, they enter SOES market orders.

15. As a general rule, day traders customarily use the buy limit order rather than the buy market order.

16. The maximum SOES order size for a security is either 1,000, 500, or 200 shares, depending on the price and trading volume of that NASDAQ security.

17. SelectNet is an execution order service owned and operated by NASDAQ, and its execution is mandatory for market makers.

18. The day trader can bid to buy or offer to sell orders through Select-Net that are greater than the SOES tier size limit.

19. Bidding is passive buying when the day trader is trying to purchase securities at a better or lower price than the inside ASK price.

20. Offering is passive selling when the day trader is trying to sell securities at a better or higher price than the inside BID price.

21. An SOES buy limit order is aggressive purchasing, because the day trader is sending an order to purchase a stock at the posted or advertised inside ASK price.

22. An SOES sell limit order is aggressive selling, because the day trader is sending an order to sell a stock at the posted or advertised inside BID price.

23. An ECN or Electronic Communications Network is a proprietary electronic execution system that widely disseminates to the public all trade orders entered by day traders, market makers, or specialists.

24. The Island ECN execution system will display the day trader's Island order on the Level II screen only if the day trader entered the highest BID or the lowest ASK.

25. The day trader cannot bid to buy a stock through Island ECN at a higher BID price than the posted inside BID.

26. The day trader cannot offer to sell a stock at a lower ASK price than the posted inside ASK.

27. The Island book allows the day trader to see the price and size of every Island buy and sell order for a particular stock.

28. The day traders can use Island order execution and short sell a stock on a down-tick by offering to sell the stock 1/16 higher than the current inside BID price.

29. When the NASDAQ ASK price is identical to the Instinet BID price, this would constitute locked-up markets and a buy signal.

30. When the Instinet BID and ASK prices are substantially higher than the NASDAQ BID and ASK prices, and the Instinet BID is greater than the NASDAQ ASK, this constitutes a very strong buy signal.

31. The larger the spread in the crossed-up or down markets between the Instinet and NASDAQ, the weaker the trading signal.

32. The NYSE specialist is the only "market maker" available for that security.

33. The specialist will never take on the role of the principal in order to counter temporary imbalances in the supply and demand of a security.

34. The SIPC provides insurance coverage to the NASD broker/dealer customers' accounts to a maximum of $500,0000, of which no more than $100,000 may be for cash losses.

35. The Federal Reserve Board under Regulation T of the Securities and Exchange Commission Act of 1934 regulates the extension of credit by the NASD broker/dealers to traders and investors; the current Reg. T margin requirement is 50% for long and short securities transactions.

36. When the equity in a margin account exceeds the Reg. T requirement of 50%, the trader has excess equity in the account, which can be used to purchase additional securities.

37. The quickest way to calculate a trader's buying power is to divide the SMA or excess equity by the Reg. T requirement.

38. If day traders always close their open positions before the close of the market, they do not need to worry about margin interest charges or maintenance calls, but they need to worry about the intra-day margin calls.

39. The novice day trader should have a trading plan that spells out clearly and exactly what he or she will do under different trading scenarios.

40. The level of losses depends on the day trader's discipline and risk management skills, and the losses can be as high as $15,000 dollars or higher before a novice day trader can turn the corner.

Answers

1. True (Chapter 7)
2. True (Chapter 7)
3. False (Chapter 7)
4. True (Chapter 7)
5. False (Chapter 7)
6. True (Chapter 8)
7. True (Chapter 8)
8. True (Chapter 9)
9. True (Chapter 9)
10. False (Chapter 9)
11. True (Chapter 9)
12. True (Chapter 12)
13. False (Chapter 12)
14. False (Chapter 13)
15. True (Chapter 13)
16. True (Chapter 13)
17. False (Chapter 13)
18. True (Chapter 13)
19. True (Chapter 13)
20. True (Chapter 13)
21. True (Chapter 13)
22. True (Chapter 13)
23. True (Chapter 14)
24. True (Chapter 14)
25. False (Chapter 14)
26. False (Chapter 14)
27. True (Chapter 14)
28. True (Chapter 14)
29. True (Chapter 15)
30. True (Chapter 15)
31. False (Chapter 15)
32. True (Chapter 16)
33. False (Chapter 16)
34. True (Chapter 17)
35. True (Chapter 17)
36. True (Chapter 17)
37. True (Chapter 17)
38. True (Chapter 17)
39. True (Chapter 18)
40. True (Chapter 19)

Trading Fractions

0.031	1/32	0.281	9/32	0.531	17/32	0.781	25/32
0.063	1/16	0.313	5/16	0.563	9/16	0.813	13/16
0.094	3/32	0.344	11/32	0.594	19/32	0.844	27/32
0.125	**1/8**	0.375	**3/8**	0.625	**5/8**	0.875	**7/8**
0.156	5/32	0.406	13/32	0.656	21/32	0.906	29/32
0.188	3/16	0.438	7/16	0.688	11/16	0.938	15/16
0.219	7/32	0.469	15/32	0.719	23/32	0.969	31/32
0.250	**1/4**	0.500	**1/2**	0.750	**3/4**	1.000	**1**

Factor: 0.031 x 1,000 shares = $31

6

Learn the Basics of Day Trading—Hands On

Day trading demonstration is located at *www.prima-daytrading.com.*

This appendix provides readers with a brief and general introduction to trading tools and software. Prima Publishing has arranged with CyBer-Corp, Inc., creators of CyBerTrader day trading software, to display a modified version of the CyBerTrader 1.7 software demonstration at *www.prima-daytrading.com.* This Web site is not a place to trade stocks, but to learn about the dynamics of day trading and the CyBerTrader software. Please note that stock information at *www.prima-daytrading.com* is prerecorded and is not live.

By accessing the CyBerTrader software, you agree to the following terms:

Day trading and other forms of online investing involve substantial financial risk. You can potentially lose significant sums of money, and therefore you should not invest funds in day trading or online investing that you cannot afford to lose. All persons should receive proper training and education before engaging in such activities.

The CyBerTrader software provided on this site is for demonstration purposes only. While Prima believes the software to provide a useful introduction to day trading, its appearance on this site should not be considered an endorsement by Prima of its use for day trading. All uses of CyBerTrader software shall be in accordance with the terms and conditions specified in that software. Please read those terms and conditions before proceeding.

Any use of the software or services of CyBerCorp is at the user's sole risk, and Prima cannot accept any responsibility for any loses, liabilities, expenses, or costs incurred by users in connection within. PRIMA, THE AUTHOR, AND CYBERCORP GIVE NO EXPRESS OR IMPLIED WARRANTIES (INCLUDING BUT NOT LIMITED TO WARRANTIES OF MERCHANTABILITY OR FITNESS FOR A PARTICULAR USE) WITH RESPECT TO THIS SOFTWARE.

If you plan to use CyBerTrader 1.7, you must read the complete CyBerTrader manual before using it in the "demo" mode and particularly before going "live." If you need additional facts on the software, then contact:

CyBerCorp, Inc.
1601 Rio Grande, Suite 405, Austin, TX 78701
Phone: 512-320-5444
Fax: 512-320-1561
Web address: http://www.cyber-corp.com

Tools of the Trade

The following CyBerTrader tools are summarized in this appendix:

- ➤ Statistics Panel;
- ➤ Stock Box;
- ➤ Point and Click Execution Control Panel;
- ➤ Account Management;
- ➤ Position Management and Position Management Alerts;
- ➤ Dynamic Ticker;
- ➤ Charts;
- ➤ Top Ten;
- ➤ NASDAQ and NYSE Highs and Lows; and
- ➤ Market View.

Visit *www.prima-daytrading.com* for more information.

Statistics Panel

The Statistics Panel displays your daily trading statistics. During the trading day, the statistics panel serves as a quick reference to your day's profits or losses; it gives you an instant reading of how much of your account is tied up in open trades and whether you're nearing your margin.

The top line of the CyBerTrader title bar shows the following:

➤ Current Time;

➤ Current Date;

➤ Ticket Average: Shows the total dollar amount of profits or losses for closed transactions divided by the number of tickets, before commissions and expenses;

➤ Tickets: Shows number of completed transactions (including partial fills);

➤ Closed P&L: Calculates and shows today's closed P&L based on completed trades;

➤ Open Positions: Shows number of current open positions;

➤ Open P&L: Calculates and shows current open P&L marked to market in real time;

➤ Dollars Used: Shows total amount of cash currently invested (value of holdings); and

➤ Look Up Symbol: Finds an NASD or NYSE symbol by typing in the company name.

Stock Box or Market Maker Level II Screen Box

The Stock Box is one of the most important and sophisticated tools for the trader. Not only does it display in real time all Level I and II data, but it can also be customized with various execution features. From the Stock Box you can send and cancel orders. More than one Stock Box can be opened at a time to monitor various stocks or open positions concurrently.

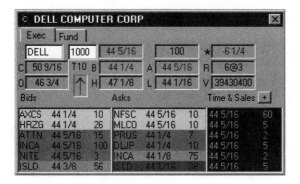

The previous figure displays the following:

➤ Stock symbol;

➤ Price from yesterday's close;

➤ Price at the open;

➤ Tick direction;

➤ Level II: Market maker/ECN/exchange, price, share amount, time;

➤ Current share size to buy/sell;

➤ Tier limit view: SOES tier limit on a stock (T10 = 1,000, T5 = 500) above the tick arrow on Level I.

➤ Last trade;

➤ Share size of last trade;

➤ Change on the day;

➤ Ratio: Ratio of market makers and ECNs at the BID to the ASK (can be changed to share amount, as well);

➤ Volume;

➤ High for the day;

➤ Low for the day;

➤ Time and Sales: Displays all trades and trade sizes in real time for your chosen stock;

➤ Current BID; and

➤ Current ASK.

The spread for the stock you are monitoring sits on the top line of the Level II screen in the Stock Box. Level II information gives you the depth of the BID or ASK fields for a stock, to give you an idea of the way a stock is moving. Usually, the thicker a price field, the stronger the momentum on the stock. For most trades, you will buy from the ASK (right-hand column) and sell to the BID (left-hand column)—be sure to monitor the movement between these two columns and trade into strength.

Time and Sales   A useful tool to monitor liquidity in the Level II Stock Box is the Time and Sales window. Time and Sales information can be used to monitor how many shares are being bought and sold according to where the market makers and other day traders are posting their BIDs and ASKs on the Level II screen. Time and Sales prints can be color coded to show whether trades are on the BID and ASK, or inside or outside the spread.

ECN Book   The ECN Book looks like a Level II Stock Box but serves a different purpose. It displays the depth of the Island "book," showing all BIDs and offers at every price level, as well as the quantity of shares available on Island. This tool allows you to monitor what other traders are doing on a particular ECN (such as Island) and gives you a better sense of the stock's momentum. The ECN Book displays the inside BID and ASK, the price and total number of shares available at that particular price level. You can link the ECN Book to a Stock Box so that both are updated at the same time for a particular stock.

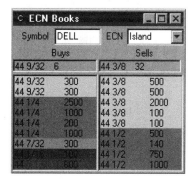

Executing Trades

Most executions are done from the Stock Box, using a number of keystrokes for different types of executions. Order size, trade route, limit price, and so on all can be determined on the keyboard without your ever having to take your eyes off the screen. However, a bad keystroke can introduce any one of a number of errors into your trade. Day traders should become very proficient with keyboard commands by practicing in a demo mode before trying to trade live.

Point and Click Execution Control Panel

The Execution Control Panel is designed for traders who do not like using the keyboard and function keys to execute orders. This tool lets you execute with your mouse, pointing and clicking on a series of buttons on the screen. Day traders must still exercise a high degree of care when using the point and click execution panel: Be sure you have entered correctly the stock, type of order, size of order, and price you want before executing.

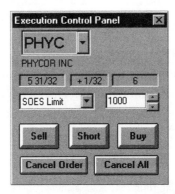

Here are the various elements of the Execution Control Panel from the previous figure.

1. Name of the stock;
2. Current BID price;
3. Order route (a drop-down menu lists all the types of orders available);
4. Type of order;
5. Spread between the current BID and ASK;
6. Current ASK price;
7. Order share size; and
8. The Cancel Order button will cancel the current order for the stock in the Execution Panel.

Order Confirmation Messages   The Messages Box displays the status of your executions. Here are some of the most common messages you might see:

➤ ORDER CONFIRMED: Confirmation message upon entry of an order;

➤ OPEN LONG/SHORT: An order was executed confirming an open position;

➤ CLOSED LONG/SHORT: An order was executed on a stock in a previously open position, thus closing out a position;

➤ UR_OUT: A general message displayed when an order cannot be executed as sent or a cancel request has been executed. The order is no longer live;

➤ MARKET OPEN;

➤ MARKET CLOSED;

➤ 1 MINUTE UNTIL MARKET CLOSE;

➤ UPTICK RULE; NO LONG POSITION: Trader might have tried to short the stock and instead of pressing the Short key, pressed the Sell key;

➤ NO SOES MM: No market maker available. A Smart order that has gone from searching for an ECN to a market maker cannot revert to searching for an ECN in the case that one might reappear;

➤ CANNOT SEND ORDER: EXCEEDS MARGIN: Buying power has been exceeded;

➤ MUST WAIT 'X' SECONDS TO CANCEL ORDER;

➤ MUST OFFER SHORT: If the trader is trying to sell on an up-tick and he or she is not long in the stock;

➤ UP-TICK RULE—NO LONG POSITION: On ISLAND, TNTO AND SNET ORDERS, order must always be $\frac{1}{16}$ above inside BID, regardless of up-tick or down;

➤ SMART ORDERS: Appears if the trader is trying to short a stock on a down-tick;

➤ MUST SHORT SELL OFFER $\frac{1}{16}$TH ABOVE THE INSIDE BID: Appears if sending an order to sell through Island when actually trying to short (Offer key); will also appear when trying to short through SelectNet using the Offer key instead;

➤ MUST SHORT SELL: If trying to short a stock on an up-tick, trader presses the Sell button instead of the Short key;

➤ UP-TICK RULE—NO LONG POSITION: If trying to short a stock, but instead of pressing the Short key the trader presses the Sell key;

➤ MUST BE LONG IN THE POSITION: Appears if the trader tries to sell a stock (when actually trying to short it);

➤ NOT EXECUTABLE: If the trader's SOES order doesn't get filled and an ECN comes in the inside BID/ASK, *and* when a limit order (of any kind) is sent and the price level moves prior to the order being filled;

➤ SIZE GREATER THAN ALLOWED SM LEVEL: Stock that has a tier limit (look at the quote levels for size limits);

➤ CAN'T SEND ORDER—MUST WAIT FOR PENDING ORDERS: A second order has been resent for a stock while the first one is still open or live;

➤ ORDER TO CANCEL CANNOT BE FOUND: Order has either already been canceled (and the message has not been returned) or order has been filled;

➤ WARNING: ONLY ➤ SHARES OF ➤ HAVE BEEN SENT. REMAINING ➤ MUST BE SHORTED: When an order to sell has been sent to close a long position, but the sell order was for more shares than the current number of shares held long;

➤ REJ INVALID SNET ORDER: Could appear for many reasons, most commonly if the market maker or ECN is typed in incorrectly or if the price is set at a price level much higher or lower than the inside BID or ASK;

➤ ALREADY CANCELED: Order has already been canceled—confirmation of cancellation has not been returned;

➤ SPEAK TO YOUR BROKER IF YOU WISH TO SHORT THIS STOCK!: If a stock is not on the short list.

Open Trades   This window gives you a quick view of all your open trades, showing the stock you've traded, the price and volume, and a graphic representation of whether your trade is winning or losing.

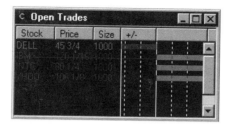

Account Management

The Account Manager automatically tracks all of your trades, open orders, positions, and P&L. The Account Manager consists of six separate "pages" and automatically switches among the different pages to make sure you are looking at the most relevant information at the right time.

Account Manager pages are the following:

1. Orders page;
2. Exec page (Execution page);
3. Trades page;
4. Opens page;
5. Holds page; and
6. Stats page (Statistics page).

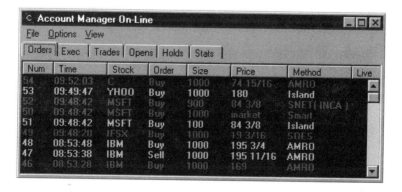

The Orders page shows all of the orders that you have entered that day. It also allows for canceling of any live order (live orders are highlighted). The Account Manager order box shows the following:

➤ Order number;

➤ Order time;

➤ Stock symbol;

➤ Order type;

➤ Size; and

➤ Price.

The Exec page in the Account Manager shows you all the orders that were executed during that day. The format is similar to the Orders page and shows the following:

➤ Order number;

➤ Execution time;

➤ Stock symbol;

➤ Type of transaction;

➤ Executed size;

➤ Executed price; and

➤ Market maker, exchange, or ECN that filled the order.

The Trade page in the Account Manager shows an electronic trade sheet listing all your trades, with P&L. The trader sheet automatically catalogs each trade you've made; traders need not write down each trade on a blotter or trader sheet for records. The trade sheet shows the following:

➤ The stock that was traded;

➤ The size of the trade;

➤ The time that the stock was bought;

➤ The price at which the stock was bought;

➤ The time that the stock was sold;

➤ The price at which the stock was sold; and

➤ The P&L of the completed trade.

The Opens Trade page window displays your current open positions. The trades are color coded, green for long positions and red for short positions. The profit and loss is also color coded, green for profit and red for loss.

The Holds page will display any long-term positions you held during the day.

In the Statistics page, you can view vital information about your account, including your margin, money used, buying power, hedges, and holds.

The Account Manager provides a reliable system for tracking your trading history, displaying your open trades, and calculating your P&L, which allows you to keep your eyes vigilantly on the screen and your hands at the ready on the keyboard.

Position Manager and Position Manager Alerts

The Position Manager displays in real time the status of every one of your current positions. These are color coded to indicate whether the market makers are moving in favor or against your current position.

The red and green highlights are relative to the trader's position in the stock being monitored:

➤ Green highlights: Market makers are moving in a favorable direction relative to your current position.

➤ Red highlights: Market makers are moving in an adverse direction relative to your current position.

The bar graph below the Position Manager is a "graphic ticker" that converts market data into a graphic representation of market movement.

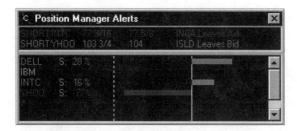

This tool offers a simple illustration of your open trades, allowing you to determine at a glance the general direction your stocks are heading. When any trade has been executed, the stock is automatically loaded into the Position Manager, and is excluded when the position is closed.

Dynamic Ticker

The Dynamic Ticker gives you an instant picture of what the market makers are doing in the stocks you're monitoring for the day. Are they buying? Selling? Leaving or entering the BID or ASK? This information is important when you are trying to gauge the direction and activity of a stock. The real-time bar graphs in the Dynamic Ticker convert the market maker activity into a mean representation of how the stock is moving.

Downside Movement

➤ Joins ASK: The market maker decreases their ASK price to the inside ASK.

➤ Leaves BID: The market maker increases their BID price from the inside BID price.

➤ Refreshes ASK: The market maker sells at the ASK and chooses to keep their price at the inside ASK (these are displayed in white).

➤ New Low ASK: A market maker quotes a lower ASK than the rest of the market makers.

➤ Drops BID: The last market maker at the inside BID decreases their price, thereby lowering the price of the inside BID.

➤ BID to ASK: The market maker leaves the BID and simultaneously joins the ASK.

Upside Movement

➤ Leaves ASK: The market maker changes their price upward from the inside ASK price.

➤ Joins BID: The market maker changes their price to the inside BID.

➤ New High BID: A market maker quotes a higher BID than the rest of the market makers.

➤ Refreshes BID: The market maker buys at the BID and chooses to keep their price at the inside BID (these are displayed in white).

➤ Lifts ASK: The last market maker at the inside ASK increases their price, thereby raising the price of the inside ASK.

➤ ASK to BID: The market maker leaves the ASK and simultaneously joins the BID.

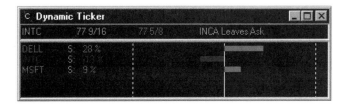

Charts

CyBerCharts are valuable and versatile tools that give in real time instantaneous stock price charting information that can be modified with a number of analysis tools. There are numerous intervals for which stocks can be displayed on a chart:

➤ Tick: Shows the best BIDs and ASKs at the time of every trade;

➤ Intra-day: Can be tailored to show minute intervals over a market day;

➤ Daily: Can be set for any number of days;

➤ Weekly: Shows a 52-week display of the stock's history.

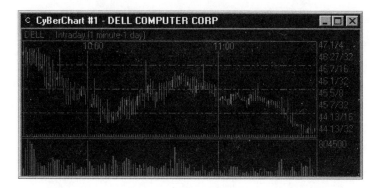

Most day traders use intra-day charts to monitor the small price changes for their stocks, but the longer daily and weekly charts are important for studying the stock's history and for estimating where the stock will be in a week, a day, or even an hour. Charts may be drawn as lines, bars, or candlesticks, depending on your preference. Here, an intra-day candlestick chart is displayed in one-minute intervals.

Technical Analysis Studies   Advanced charting features allow you to overlay certain indicators on your chart according to your trading style and your methods of technical analysis. For example, you can chart the S&P 500 Futures Index over your stock to compare trendlines, or you can add a share volume indicator.

Here are some of the indexes and overlays you might want to use on your charts:

- ➤ DJIA;
- ➤ S&P 500;
- ➤ NASDAQ;
- ➤ Simple Moving Average;
- ➤ Exponential Moving Average;
- ➤ Rate of change;
- ➤ Relative strength index;
- ➤ %K;
- ➤ %D;
- ➤ %D slow;
- ➤ Bollinger bands;

➤ Moving Average Convergence/Divergence;

➤ Signal line;

➤ On-Balance Volume;

➤ Momentum;

➤ Money flow; and

➤ Money flow percent.

Charts are valuable monitoring tools, but by no means should they take the place of your Level II screen. A movement up or down on a chart is sometimes just noise in the market. Using your Level II screen in conjunction with your charts and overlays will give you a better idea of a stock's true momentum.

The Hammer The Hammer Box displays in real time the number of times a particular market maker has been at the inside BID and ASK of the stocks you are monitoring. This allows the trader to see which market maker is the "hammer" in a selected stock—that is, that market maker who may be trading the highest volume for the stock or dumping or accumulating a large number of shares by masking their orders in small batches.

Determining the hammer for a particular stock is a good way to gauge which direction the stock may move. Some traders shadow the hammer as a trading strategy, buying when the hammer buys and selling when the hammer sells. Before Level II information was available to individual traders, it was nearly impossible to mirror—much less find—the hammer.

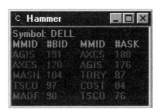

Top Ten

Top Volume, Gainers, and Decliners shows "Top 10" stocks in terms of volume and biggest dollar advance and decline. The Top Ten displays the symbol, total points (up or down from yesterday's close), and total volume in each window. You can monitor the top ten stocks from both NASDAQ and NYSE.

Top Ten information is important for understanding at a glance the day's most active stocks. The list of top ten stocks is rarely static; some stocks appear based on earnings reports from the previous day, others are just popular stocks among the market makers. Look for movement of stocks in the Top Ten to indicate a possible trend in that stock's sector.

Top Volume 02:04:31			Top Gainers 02:04:01			Top Declined 02:04:07		
DELL	+ 1/8	17938200	QCOM	+16 3/16	10870700	UNEM	-7 3/16	7345100
MSFT	-1 7/16	15615100	TBFC	+11 1/2	772900	EXDS	-7	11 39860
NXTL	+3 1/4	12339300	NTBK	+7 1/2	743400	VERT	-6 1/2	303708
QCOM	+16 3/8	10876400	NSOL	+7 5/16	4149700	DCLK	-5 3/4	1090300
BICO	0	10611700	HIFN	+5 7/8	1578600	YHOO	-5 3/16	4080000
INTC	+1 1/16	9954200	ATHM	+5 9/16	3151000	AALI	-5 1/16	1010680
AMZN	-1/2	9851800	CNCX	+5 1/8	607700	CMGI	-4 7/16	11 81800
ORCL	+1 1/16	7602000	XCIT	+4 3/4	1903500	UCLI	-3 3/4	1900000
COMS	-5/16	6336900	VIGN	+4 3/8	528400	GNET	-3 5/8	320000
CUACF	0	-5000	LWIN	+4 3/8	2218500	HCOW	-3 1/2	379900

Top Volume 02:04:13			Top Gainers 02:04:19			Top Declined 02:04:25		
AOL	-3/4	12697800	LXK	+6 7/8	916500	SNE	-3 3/4	236800
CPQ	+ 3/8	8743400	CBZ	+5 13/16	258600	ICO	-3 11/16	1630600
WLA	-2 13/32	8327100	VIA	+4 1/16	227200	CLX	-3 5/8	244400
MOT	+3 15/16	6293800	MOT	+3 13/16	6304000	BTH	-2 1/2	1490000
T	+1 3/16	6018900	CAH	+3 3/4	1279400	WLA	-2 13/32	8335500
KEP	-3/16	5693300	MNX	+3 1/4	295500	GT	-2 1/4	618300
C	+1 1/16	5054600	SCH	+3 3/16	1951200	TIN	-2 1/16	160000
MU	+1 1/16	4625200	IBM	+3 1/8	3000300	DEX	-2 1/16	444100
LU	+ 1/2	4287900	KSU	+3	816700	U	-1 7/8	344200
FLC	+1	4236500	PNU	+2 15/16	3039100	IPG	-1 3/4	371000

NASDAQ and NYSE Highs and Lows

The NASDAQ and NYSE High and Lows window displays all stocks within the eliminator limits that are breaking daily highs and lows, plus 52-week breaks and proximity alerts. Prints can be color coded to signify whether they are approaching or low.

A quick way to check a stock's momentum is by watching whether it breaks through its daily or 52-week high or low. Many times, a stock that breaks through its high will continue to rise, and the break is a good buy signal. Conversely, a stock that breaks through its low sometimes will continue to fall, and the break is a good sell signal. Other times a stock will oscillate between its high and low without ever breaking through. When it approaches the high, this is generally a good sell or short signal; when it approaches its low, this is generally a good buy order. Remember, these are loose rules of thumb. Any trade should be based on a number of strong signals, according to your trading style.

 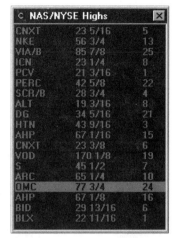

Market View

The Market View allows you to select and view a broad range of market data for your stocks, all in one window. You can compile a long list of data for your stocks, such as last trade, today's open, yesterday's close, change from the close, BID, ASK, volume at the BID and ASK, volume, spread, and so on. The trader simply picks which stocks or indexes and which criteria to track.

Market View can display up to 16 columns of data fields:

- ➤ Symbol: Stock symbol or index;
- ➤ Index/Last Trade Price: If an index is one of the symbols, this field will display the last price;
- ➤ Last: Last trade price;
- ➤ Open$: Price at which the stock opened for the day;
- ➤ Close$: Price at which the stock closed the day before;
- ➤ Close*: Total change the stock has gained or declined since yesterday's close;
- ➤ Prev*: Total change for the stock between the last and second to last trade;

> ➤ BID: Current BID price;

> ➤ ASK: Current ASK price;

> ➤ BIDQ: The highest number of shares available from a particular market maker/ECN within the inside BID;

> ➤ ASKQ: The highest number of shares available from a particular market maker/ECN within the inside ASK;

> ➤ High: High for the day;

> ➤ Low: Low for the day;

> ➤ Volume: Volume for the day;

> ➤ Tick: Displays direction of the last tick; and

> ➤ Spread: Displays the current spread between the BID and the ASK.

ID	Last	Open$	Close$	Close*	Prev*	Bid	Ask	
INTC	77 5/8	76 13/16	76 7/8		1/16	77 9/16	77 5/8	
IBM	118 7/8	120 3/4	120 3/4			118 7/8	118 15/16	
DELL	44 5/16	46 3/4	46 3/4		1/16	44 1/4	44 5/16	
CPQ	23 9/16	24	24 15/16		1/16	23 1/2	23 9/16	
/SPZ8	944.50	954.00	979.00					

Index Client

The Index Client displays indexes' symbol, last price, change on the day, and last price direction arrow. Stock symbols may be added, as well. You can monitor the general trends of the major indexes like the DJIA and the S&P 500 Futures for forecasting your trade signals.

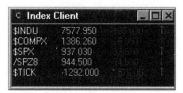

Island Orders

These windows focus on and report executions taking place on the Island ECN. The Executed Island Orders displays any Island orders that are being executed within the Island book. These are color coded: sold orders are red and buys are green. The window displays the stock, the number of shares, and the price at which it executed. The Open Island Orders displays all unfilled orders that are going through the Island book.

Island is an important avenue of exchange for day traders, because orders can be matched on the ECN without ever going through a market maker or the NASDAQ. Consequently, many Island orders are not posted to the Level II screen and can go virtually undetected. It is helpful to know what orders for your stocks are going through Island, especially because this information gives you a primary view of what your fellow day traders are doing.

On to the Next Step

The tools described in this appendix are just examples of the type and number of tools available to day traders, but they are the kind of tools a typical beginning trader might use at first. There are many other specialized tools available to use, depending on what software you use and what trading style you adopt.

When you become more proficient in your trading and more familiar with the information in each window, you will develop your own day trading tool box. The possibilities are endless, but I recommend that you experiment with different set-ups and the options within each tool to find what's right for you. Good luck!

not permitted to use the Marks without the prior written consent of CYBERCORP or such third party that may own the Marks.

For further information on Intellectual Property matters contact CYBERCORP: CyBerCorp, Inc, Suite 405, 1601 Rio Grande, Austin, TX 78701.

Copyright; Limited License

The information on this web site is protected by copyright: Copyright © CyBerCorp, Inc 1997–1998. All rights reserved. Except as specifically permitted herein, no portion of the information on this web site may be reproduced in any form or by any means without the prior written permission from Prima Publishing or CyBerCorp.

DISCLAIMER—PLEASE READ BEFORE ACCESSING CYBERTRADER SOFTWARE

By Accessing the CyBerTrader software you agree to the following terms:

Day trading and other forms of online investing involve substantial financial risk. You can potentially lose substantial sums of money and therefore you should not invest funds in day trading or online investing that you cannot afford to lose. All persons should receive proper training and education before engaging in such activities.

The CyBerTrader software provided on this site is for demonstration purposes only. While Prima believes the software provides a useful introduction to day trading, it's appearance on this site should not be considered an endorsement by Prima of its use for day trading. All uses of the CyBerTrader software shall be in accordance with the terms and conditions specified in that software. Please read those terms and conditions before proceeding.

Any use of software or services of CyBerCorp is at the user's sole risk and Prima cannot accept any responsibility for any losses, liabilities, expenses, or costs incurred by users in connection therewith. PRIMA, THE AUTHOR, AND CYBERCORP GIVE NO EXPRESS OR IMPLIED WARRANTIES (INCLUDING BUT NOT LIMITED TO WARRANTIES OF MERCHANTABILITY OR FITNESS FOR A PARTICULAR USE) WITH RESPECT TO THE SOFTWARE ON THIS SITE.

Index